CLARK PUBLIC LIBRARY

3 9502 00121 7025

823.5   Daniel Defoe.
Dan

D0966318

CLARK PUBLIC LIBRARY
303 WESTFIELD AVENUE
CLARK, NJ 07066
732-388-5999

Bloom's Modern Critical Views

Modern Critical Views

DANIEL DEFOE

Edited and with an introduction by

Harold Bloom
Sterling Professor of the Humanities
Yale University

CHELSEA HOUSE PUBLISHERS
Philadelphia

823.5
Da n
12-14-04

Jacket illustration by Robert C. Morris

*Daniel Defoe, novelist and pamphleteer, is seen
against the background of an encyclopedia of natural
history, illustrative of his Robinson Crusoe's world.*
—H.B.

© 1987 by Chelsea House Publishers, a subsidiary of
Haights Cross Communications

Introduction © 1987 by Harold Bloom

All rights reserved. No part of this publication may be
reproduced or transmitted in any form or by any means
without the written permission of the publisher.

Printed and bound in the United States of America

10 9 8 7 6 5

∞ The paper used in this publication meets the minimum
requirements of the American National Standard for
Permanence of Paper for Printed Library Materials,
Z39.48-1984.

Library of Congress Cataloging-in-Publication Data
Daniel Defoe.
    (Modern critical views)
    Bibliography: p.
    Includes index.
    Summary: A collection of thirteen critical essays on Defoe
and his works arranged in chronological order of publication.
    1. Defoe, Daniel, 1661–1731—Criticism and
interpretation. [1. Defoe, Daniel, 1661–1731—Criticism and
interpretation. 2. English literature—History and criticism]
I. Bloom, Harold.   II. Series.
PR3407.D35   1987   823'.5   87-6346
ISBN 1-55546-284-7

Clark Public Library - Clark, N. J.

Contents

Editor's Note

This book gathers together a representative selection of the best criticism that has been devoted to the writings of Daniel Defoe during the last three decades. The critical essays are reprinted here in the chronological order of their original publication. I am grateful to Christina Büchmann for her erudition and judgment as a researcher.

My introduction sketches some displacements of the Puritan spirit in the figures of Robinson Crusoe and Moll Flanders. E. M. W. Tillyard commences the chronological sequence of criticism with his overview of *Robinson Crusoe* as a middle-class "epic," with some of the formal limitations so strange a genre might suggest. In a moving account of both *Crusoe* and *Moll Flanders*, Martin Price centers upon Puritan conflicts and self-divisions in each work. Relating Defoe's novels to his nonfictional writings, James Sutherland emphasizes the common element as being an interest in precisely how the individual copes with her or his circumstances. *A Journal of the Plague Year*, crucial among the nonfictional books, is seen by Manuel Schonhorn as a tribute to the energy of the common people of London.

Homer O. Brown, questing after the self in Defoe's novels, praises him for making "the novel an apt genre for a society of isolated and mutually suspicious individuals." In a reading of *Robinson Crusoe*, H. Daniel Peck traces the work's "moral geography," its implicit sense that Crusoe could achieve real satisfaction only upon his island. Leo Braudy finds in all of the novels Defoe's quest for an "introspection without society," thus giving autobiography and the novel a new fusion.

Defoe's style is seen by George Starr as an interpretive mode in its own right, after which Arnold Weinstein and David Durant respectively analyze two formidable women, Moll and Roxana. John J. Burke, Jr., concentrates upon how to interpret Defoe's narrator-observers, while Mary Butler returns us to what is most problematical in *Robinson Crusoe*, the narrator's wavering voice. In a final essay, we are given a second reading of *Roxana* by James Maddox, who sees Defoe's last heroine as a failed Moll Flanders unable to emulate Moll in achieving a new power-relationship to the family and to society.

Introduction

I

Of his prayers and the like we take no account, since they are a source of pleasure to him, and he looks upon them as so much recreation.
—KARL MARX on *Robinson Crusoe*

I got so tired of the very colors!
One day I dyed a baby goat bright red
with my red berries, just to see
something a little different.
And then his mother wouldn't recognize him.
—ELIZABETH BISHOP, "Crusoe in England"

Had Karl Marx written *Robinson Crusoe*, it would have had even more moral vigor, but at the expense of the image of freedom it still provides for us. Had Elizabeth Bishop composed it, Defoe's narrative would have been enhanced as image and as impulse, but at the expense of its Puritan plainness, its persuasive search for some evidences of redemption. Certainly one of Defoe's novelistic virtues is precisely what Ian Watt and Martin Price have emphasized it to be: the puzzles of daily moral choice are omnipresent. Robinson Crusoe and Moll Flanders are human—all-too-human—and suffer what Calvin and Freud alike regarded as the economics of the spirit.

Defoe comes so early in the development of the modern novel as a literary form that there is always a temptation to historicize rather than to read him. But historicisms old and new are poor substitutes for reading, and I do not find it useful to place *Robinson Crusoe* and *Moll Flanders* in their contemporary context when I reread them, as I have just done. Ian Watt usefully remarked that "Defoe's heroes . . . keep us more fully informed of their present stocks of money and commodities than any other characters in fiction." I suspect that this had more to do with Defoe than with his age,

1

and that Defoe would have been no less obsessed with economic motives if he had written in the era of Queen Victoria. He was a hard man who had led a hard life: raised as a Dissenter in the London of the Great Plague and the Great Fire; enduring Newgate prison and the pillory in bankrupt middle age; working as a secret agent and a scandalous journalist until imprisoned again for debt and treason. Defoe died old and so may be accounted as a survivor, but he had endured a good share of reality, and his novels reflect that endurance.

Dr. Johnson once said that only three books ought to have been still longer than they were: *Don Quixote*, *The Pilgrim's Progress*, and *Robinson Crusoe*. Defoe has authentic affinities with Bunyan, but there is nothing quixotic about Robinson Crusoe or Moll Flanders. All of Defoe's protagonists are pragmatic and prudent, because they have to be; there is no play in the world as they know it.

II

I did not read *Robinson Crusoe* as a child, and so missed an experience that continues to be all but universal; it remains a book that cannot fail with children. Yet, as Dickens observed, it is also "the only instance of an universally popular book that could make no one laugh and could make no one cry." Crusoe's singular tone, his self-baffled affect, does not bother children, who appear to empathize with a near-perfect solipsist who nevertheless exhibits energy and inventiveness throughout a quarter-century of solitude. Perhaps Crusoe's survival argues implicitly against every child's fear of dependency and prophesies the longed-for individuality that is still to come. Or perhaps every child's loneliness is answered in Crusoe's remarkable strength at sustaining solitude.

Though the identification of Defoe with Crusoe is never wholly overt, the reader senses its prevalence throughout the narrative. Defoe seems to me the least ironic of writers, and yet Crusoe's story is informed by an overwhelming irony. A restless wanderer, driven to travel and adventure by forces that he (and the reader) cannot comprehend, Crusoe is confined to an isolation that ought to madden him by turning him towards an unbearable inwardness. Yet his sanity prevails, despite his apparent imprisonment. Defoe had borne much; Newgate and the pillory were nightmare experiences. Crusoe bears more, yet Defoe will not describe his hero's suffering as being psychic. As Virginia Woolf noted, Defoe "takes the opposite way from the psychologist's—he describes the effect of emotion on the body, not on the mind." Nowhere is this stronger than in Crusoe's agony as he views a shipwreck:

> Such certainly was the Case of these Men, of whom I could not so much as see room to suppose any of them were sav'd; nothing could make it rational, so much as to wish, or expect that they did not all perish there; except the Possibility only of their being taken up by another Ship in Company, and this was but meer Possibility indeed; for I saw not the least Signal or Appearance of any such Thing.
>
> I cannot explain by any possible Energy of Words what a strange longing or hankering of Desires I felt in my Soul upon this Sight; breaking out sometimes thus; O that there had been but one or two; nay, or but one Soul sav'd out of this Ship, to have escap'd to me, that I might but have had one Companion, one Fellow-Creature to have spoken to me, and to have convers'd with! In all the Time of my solitary Life, I never felt so earnest, so strong a Desire after the Society of my Fellow-Creatures, or so deep a Regret at the want of it.
>
> There are some secret moving Springs in the Affections, which when they are set a going by some Object in view; or be it some Object, though not in view, yet rendred present to the Mind by the Power of Imagination, that Motion carries out the Soul by its Impetuosity to such violent eager embracings of the Object, that the Absence of it is insupportable.
>
> Such were these earnest Wishings, That but one Man had been sav'd! *O that it had been but One!* I believe I repeated the Words, *O that it had been but One!* a thousand Times; and the Desires were so mov'd by it, that when I spoke the Words, my Hands would clinch together, and my Fingers press the Palms of my Hands, that if I had had any soft Thing in my Hand, it would have crusht it involuntarily; and my Teeth in my Head wou'd strike together, and set against one another so strong, that for some time I cou'd not part them again.

These are the reactions of a compulsive craftsman who has found his freedom but cannot bear its full sublimity. Crusoe, himself the least sublime of personages, is embedded throughout in a sublime situation best epitomized by the ghastly cannibal feasts he spies upon and from which he rescues his man Friday. Against his superior technology and Puritan resolve, the cannibals offer almost no resistance, so that the rapid conversion of the cannibal Friday to Protestant theology and diet is not unconvincing. What may baffle the average rereader is Crusoe's comparative dearth of Protestant inwardness. It is not that Marx was accurate and that Crusoe becomes Protestant only upon the Sabbath, but rather that Defoe's God is himself a technocrat and an individualist, not much given to the nicer emotions. Defoe's God can be visualized as a giant tradesman, coping with the universe as Crusoe makes do on his island, but with teeming millions of adoring Fridays where Crusoe enjoys the devotion of just one.

III

With *Robinson Crusoe*, aesthetic judgment seems redundant; the book's status as popular myth is too permanent, and so the critic must ground arms. *Moll Flanders* is another matter and provokes a remarkably wide range of critical response, from the late poet-critic Allen Tate, who once told me it was a great novel of Tolstoyan intensity, to equally qualified readers who deny that it is a novel at all. The overpraisers include James Joyce, who spoke of "the unforgettable harlot Moll Flanders," and William Faulkner, who coupled *Moby-Dick* and *Moll Flanders* as works he would like to have written (together with one of Milne's Pooh books!). Rereading *Moll Flanders* leaves me a touch baffled as I thought it had been better, it being one of those books that are much more vivid in parts than as a unit so that the memory holds on to episodes and to impressions, investing them with an aura that much of the narrative does not possess. The status of the narrative is curiously wavering; one is not always certain one is reading a novel rather than a colorful tract of the Puritan persuasion. Moll is a formidable person who sustains our interest and our good will. But the story she tells seems alternately formed and formless, and frequently confuses the rival authorities of fiction and supposed fact.

Martin Price notes how little thematic unity Defoe imposes upon the stuff of existence that constitutes *Moll Flanders*. As a man who had suffered Newgate, Defoe gives us only one key indication of his novel's vision; Moll was born in Newgate and will do anything to avoid ending there. The quest for cash is simply her equivalent of Crusoe's literal quest to survive physically upon his island, except that Moll is more imaginative than the strangely compulsive Crusoe. He does only what he must, she does more, and we begin to see that her obsession has in it an actual taste for adventures. This taste surprises her, but then, as Price observes, she is always "surprised by herself and with herself." She learns by what she does, and almost everything she does is marked by gusto. Her vehemence is her most winning quality, but most of her qualities are attractive. Male readers are charmed by her, particularly male readers who both exalt and debase women, among whom Joyce and Faulkner remain the most prominent.

Puritan force, the drive for the soul's exuberant self-recognition, is as much exemplified by Moll as by Bunyan's protagonist. I suspect that was why William Hazlitt, the greatest literary critic to emerge from the tradition of Protestant Dissent, had so violent a negative reaction to *Moll Flanders*, which otherwise I would have expected him to admire. But, on some level, he evidently felt that she was a great discredit to Puritan sensibility. Charles Lamb greatly esteemed her and understood how authentic the Puritan dialectic was in her, pointing to "the intervening flashes of religious visitation upon the rude and uninstructed soul" and judging this to "come near to the tenderness of Bunyan." Infuriated, Hazlitt responded, "Mr. Lamb admires *Moll Flanders*; would he marry Moll Flanders?" to which the only response a loyal Hazlittian could make is, "Would that Hazlitt had married a Moll Flanders, and been happy for once in a relationship with a woman." All proportion abandoned Hazlitt when he wrote about *Moll Flanders:*

> We . . . may, nevertheless, add, for the satisfaction of the in-
> quisitive reader, that *Moll Flanders* is utterly vile and detestable:
> Mrs. Flanders was evidently born in sin. The best parts are the
> account of her childhood, which is pretty and affecting; the fluc-
> tuation of her feelings between remorse and hardened impenitence
> in Newgate; and the incident of her leading off the horse from
> the inn-door, though she had no place to put it in after she had
> stolen it. This was carrying the love of thieving to an *ideal* pitch
> and making it perfectly disinterested and mechanical.

Hazlitt did not understand Moll because he could not bear to see the Puritan impulse displaced into "carrying the love of thieving to an *ideal* pitch." Brilliant as the horse-stealing is, it is surpassed by Moll's famous second theft, the episode of the child's necklace:

> I went out now by Day-light, and wandred about I knew not
> whither, and in search of I knew not what, when the Devil put
> a Snare in my way of a dreadful Nature indeed, and such a one
> as I have never had before or since; going thro' *Aldersgate-street*
> there was a pretty little Child had been at a Dancing School, and
> was going home, all alone, and my Prompter, like a true Devil,
> set me upon this innocent Creature; I talk'd to it, and it prattl'd

to me again, and I took it by the Hand and led it a long till I came to a pav'd Alley that goes into *Bartholomew Close*, and I led it in there; the Child said that was not its way home; I said, yes, my Dear it is, I'll show you the way home; the Child had a little Necklace on of Gold Beads, and I had my Eye upon that, and in the dark of the Alley I stoop'd, pretending to mend the Child's Clog that was loose, and took off her Necklace and the Child never felt it, and so led the Child on again: Here, I say, the Devil put me upon killing the child in the dark Alley, that it might not Cry; but the very thought frighted me so that I was ready to drop down, but I turn'd the Child about and bade it go back again, for that was not its way home; the Child said so she would, and I went thro' into *Bartholomew Close*, and then turn'd round to another Passage that goes into *Long-lane*, so away into *Charterhouse-Yard* and out into *St. John's-street*, then crossing into *Smithfield*, went down *Chick-lane* and into *Field-lane* to *Holbourn-bridge*, when mixing with the Crowd of People usually passing there, it was not possible to have been found out; and thus I enterpriz'd my second Sally into the World.

The thoughts of this Booty put out all the thoughts of the first, and the Reflections I had made wore quickly off; Poverty, as I have said, harden'd my Heart, and my own Necessities made me regardless of any thing: The last Affair left no great Concern upon me, for as I did the poor Child no harm, I only said to my self, I had given the Parents a just Reproof for their Negligence in leaving the poor little Lamb to come home by it self, and it would teach them to take more Care of it another time.

This String of Beads was worth about Twelve or Fourteen Pounds; I suppose it might have been formerly the Mother's, for it was too big for the Child's wear, but that, perhaps, the Vanity of the Mother to have her Child look Fine at the Dancing School, had made her let the Child wear it; and no doubt the Child had a Maid sent to take care of it, but she, like a careless Jade, was taken up perhaps with some Fellow that had met her by the way, and so the poor Baby wandred till it fell into my Hands.

However, I did the Child no harm; I did not so much as fright it, for I had a great many tender Thoughts about me yet, and did nothing but what, as I may say, meer Necessity drove me to.

The remarkable moment, which horrifies us and must have scandalized Hazlitt, is when Moll says, "the Devil put me upon killing the Child in the dark Alley, that it might not Cry; but the very thought frighted me so that I was ready to drop down." We do not believe that Moll will slay the child, but she frightens us because of her capacity for surprising herself. We are reminded that we do not understand Moll, *because Defoe does not understand her*. That is his novel's most peculiar strength and its most peculiar weakness. Gide's Lafcadio, contemplating his own crime, murmurs that it is not about events that he is curious, but only about himself. That is in the spirit of Defoe's Moll. The Protestant sensibility stands back from itself, and watches the spirits of good and of evil contend for it, with the detachment of a certain estrangement, a certain wonder at the immense energies that God has placed in one's soul.

E. M. W. TILLYARD

Defoe

INTRODUCTORY

"Mr Jennings, do you happen to be acquainted with Robinson Crusoe*?"*

I answered that I had read Robinson Crusoe *when I was a child.*
"Not since then?" inquired Betteredge.
"Not since then."
"He has not read Robinson Crusoe *since he was a child," said Betteredge, speaking to himself—not to me. "Let's try how* Robinson Crusoe *strikes him now!"*

—WILKIE COLLINS, *The Moonstone*

Defoe wrote the *Life and Strange Surprizing Adventures of Robinson Crusoe* within the quinquennium (1715–20) when Pope's *Iliad* was being published. Pope's *Iliad* is the first of the two great Augustan works that prolonged in England the tradition of the formal neoclassic epic. On the other hand, *Robinson Crusoe* (the first part) heads the small list of those English novels which, owing little or nothing to that tradition, embody, to a larger or smaller degree, the qualities that mark the epic as an autonomous literary kind. Anyone with a taste for historical processes may like to put Pope's *Iliad* alongside *Robinson Crusoe* and thus create the spectacle of old age and youth, the doomed and the promising, retrospect and prospect, subsisting vigorously at the same moment.

From *The Epic Strain in the English Novel.* © 1958 by E. M. W. Tillyard. Chatto & Windus, 1958.

The two works also demonstrate neatly the unhappy division that had afflicted England since the Civil War. Pope's *Iliad* spoke only for the upper part of English society, and especially for the men of high affairs in the age of Queen Anne. Writing on that translation in my *English Epic*, I noted how remote were the shepherds in a famous passage there from the society Pope addressed himself to. The passage describes a clear night and the shepherds' joy at the good weather; and Pope ends with

> The conscious Swains, rejoicing in the Sight,
> Eye the blue Vault, and bless the useful Light.

Homer's shepherd simply rejoiced, and in his gratuitous addition of the other actions Pope removes himself from, even patronises, his swains. They are not just fellow human beings but useful inferiors in a society that exists for the sake of its upper end. And I pointed in contrast to Shakespeare's "Looke, th'unfolding Starre calles up the Shepheard" and Milton's

> The Star that bids the Shepherd fold
> Now the top of Heav'n doth hold,

where the shepherds are a part of total society as they had ceased to be in the age of Pope. And what holds for Pope's shepherds in particular holds in general for all classes other than the top, and especially for the lower middle-class Non-conformity. It was to this class that Defoe belonged; and, as Pope was powerless to span total English society from below, so was Defoe from the other end.

Thus, so much had happened and society had so split and complicated itself since the age of Elizabeth and the early Stuarts that an all-embracing epic was not to be expected in the ages of Queen Anne and George I.

In writing on the Puritans and Bunyan I pointed out that in its expanding and militant phase puritanism found no worthy mouthpiece. Milton never wrote that Arthuriad which might, among other things, have celebrated the completion of the glorious religious revolution that began in the age of Henry VIII. By the time Bunyan was mature, the movement had failed politically and, though still alive, was oppressed. Moreover, Bunyan's experience did not extend over much of the social scale. Nevertheless, he spoke for many people and in the *Holy War* produced the nearest thing to an epic of seventeenth-century puritanism. After Bunyan (the *Holy War* was published in 1682), and with the revolution of 1688, puritanism began to lose its religious fanaticism. It also extended its grip on the nation's commerce, so that in 1705, through his political allegory, the *Consolidator*, Defoe was able to hint that the Dissenters, having most of the country's trade in their hands, needed only to unite and agree on a common fiscal policy to be able to dictate to the government. But "trade" was no simple matter and suited more than one kind of temperament. It could lead to thrift, sobriety, and the stable domestic life, or it could lead to enterprise, travel, hard competition, and even violence. The puritanism of the early eighteenth century comprised both these sides of trade and sanctified them through a religion which, though no longer fanatical, still favoured its holders with the notion that they were the elect and blessed by peculiar interventions of Providence on their behalf.

Now though it was the Puritans, or rather we should now say the Dissenters, who were central to the habits of mind I have just described, those habits marked the whole of English society in its lower reaches; they were wide as well as strong. And as such they were capable of giving any writer who expressed them powerfully a choric quality; they were potential epic material.

How were they to be expressed powerfully? Not in the traditional epic manner, which, though it once dealt with total humanity through every social rank, did so from the aristocratic side. Homer viewed his chieftains from their own position, not from that of the private soldier, and Virgil and Tasso and Spenser followed him. It is true that Du Bartas, the French Protestant, gave his little classicising epic *Judith* (on the story of Judith and Holofernes) a middle-class setting, and that Sylvester made that setting even more homely in his translation, *Bethulians Rescue*. It is true, too, that in some details Milton repudiated martial pomp, exalted the sober Puritan virtues, and even hinted at an approval of the practical inventiveness of a Robinson Crusoe. But Milton's mind is essentially exalted and aristocratic. Though he cannot praise a fugitive and cloistered virtue and however ready he may be to sally forth and meet his adversary, he is not at home primarily in the market-place or work-shop. He belongs essentially to the Court, the private oratory, and the study. Nor was the prose epic of the classical Heliodoran variety more helpful. Its two chief examples, Sidney's *Arcadia* and Fénelon's *Télémaque*, were, if anything, more uncompromisingly aristocratic than their poetic kin. Nothing short of an unexploited medium had the chance of giving epic expression to the new middle-class energy and achievements.

In seeking to show that in the first part of *Robinson Crusoe* Defoe thus succeeded, I do not at all imply that he knew what he was doing. If he excelled himself in this one book, it was because his subject caught him and shaped him, not because he deliberately planned a masterpiece of a certain kind. As a writer Defoe was pure opportunist, the remotest possible from the seventeeth-century writer of epic who, acutely aware of the theory of the epic and of classical precedent, solemnly attempted the patriotic task of realising the epic idea in a great, conventional work in his native language.

When I say "an unexploited medium" I mean of course relatively, for

Robinson Crusoe has a kind of ancestry. Right behind it are the narratives of
Bunyan: a statement reinforced by the likelihood that Defoe heard Bunyan's
voice as well as read his books, for Bunyan preached at Newington Green
during Defoe's schooling at the dissenting academy there and "the greater
part of the boys trooped off to hear him." Anyhow, Bunyan's *Mr Badman*,
a life story of a notorious man, was in a popular tradition that led to Defoe's
romances generally, while the allegories of the *Pilgrim's Progress* and the *Holy
War* may have been the unconscious inspiration of things in *Robinson Crusoe*
that are not found in Defoe's other tales. What differentiates *Crusoe* is the
impression it conveys of symbolic meaning. Crusoe is a *typical* figure as Moll
Flanders and Roxana are not, and is nearer to Bunyan's Christian than to
them. The island, too, is not merely realistic but symbolises a human state
of isolation. It thus has a lingering kinship (and probably through Bunyan)
with the old allegories of man as a fortress, a city, or an island. When his
subject seized Defoe, he sought unconscious help not from the simple tales
of adventurers and criminals but from the richer examples of the prose
narrative.

   How was it that Defoe was equipped to represent a powerful body of
opinion? First, he combined in himself the two strains of enterprise and
domestic virtue that marked the middle-class ethos of the time. There is no
need to comment on his enterprise. His own varied life and the fertility of
his invention in, for instance, his *Essay on Projects* are well-known, as well
as sufficient, testimony. No doubt of his qualification to speak confidently
of the adventurous side of trade. His belief in the creative possibilities of
the middle way of life at home is less a matter of common knowledge, but
it is equally important. When Crusoe Senior at the beginning of *Robinson
Crusoe* uses his eloquence to persuade his son of the virtues of the middle
station of life, he makes the tactical mistake of dwelling mainly on the ills
attending the two social extremes. He was a retired merchant in the decline
of life, and it is dramatically appropriate that he should argue from his own
point of view instead of thinking what would appeal to a young man and of
enlarging on the many outlets for action that the middle way of life afforded.
Had Defoe allowed Crusoe Senior a higher intelligence and a vivider imagination, he would have alienated our sympathies too violently from his hero.
As it is, we cannot really expect Robinson to be persuaded by his father's
argument. But if Defoe showed dramatic tact in making Crusoe Senior
employ mainly negative pleas in favour of the middle way of life, he did not
himself think the life of domestic trade dull. On the contrary, he thought it
full of scope and stir, while his ideal of the retired tradesman as set forth in
the *Complete English Tradesman* little resembles Crusoe Senior's, who liked

men to go "silently and smoothly through the world, and comfortably out of it." Defoe's retired tradesman had been wise in his trading days and had thriven and grown rich. He had served a kind of apprenticeship in the world's business and had acquired a high authority. "Such a man has more opportunity for doing good than almost any other person I can name." He is a natural magistrate in his home town, he is a general peacemaker, he is a kind of economic consultant able to help merchants in their difficulties and disputes far better than lawyers, who are of little use in commerce. This is a picture that shows Defoe sharply aware of the large prospects of power open to the home merchant and of the ambition of the middle classes to have their share of influence in the destinies of their country. Brought up in Puritan sobriety, aware of the enterprise of trade, he was qualified to interpret a great body and thrust of middle-class feeling.

Whether Defoe shared the religious emotions and beliefs of his fellow Protestants has been disputed. There is a good deal of piety in his works; but was it sincere? I need not enter this dispute, for, whether he was personally sincere or no, he knew and understood the type of piety in question very thoroughly and had an imaginative sympathy with it sufficient for the purposes of his art. This is no light matter, for it especially concerns *Robinson Crusoe*, whose piety is woven into the whole texture of the book. If Defoe merely assumed piety for the sake of popularity, if it was not an organic part of himself, the quality of the whole book must suffer. But, bred as he was in the very cradle of English dissent, how could Defoe have avoided getting the gist of it into his system? His father was of the congregation of the Rev. Samuel Annesley, Vicar of St Giles's Cripplegate, who left the Anglican Church on refusing to subscribe to the Act of Uniformity in 1662, and he followed his minister into Nonconformity. Samuel Annesley died late in 1696; and in the next year Defoe celebrated his death with a poem in couplets, the "Character of the late Dr Samuel Annesley, by way of Elegy." There was no need for Defoe to do this; and whether or not they testify to Defoe's personal piety, his couplets are patently sincere in their tribute to the piety and the good works of the dead man. Not only was Defoe brought up under the ministry of one distinguished dissenting divine, but he attended the academy governed by another, the Rev. Charles Morton. When Robinson Crusoe keeps on noting the special interventions of Providence on his behalf, his behaviour is something with which his creator had been familiar over a long lapse of years.

To sum up and repeat: what Defoe *thought* of the Puritan religion is secondary; what matters, and what assures his artistic sincerity, is that he had it in his bones.

On the side of experience, then, Defoe was well equipped to represent a vigorous and widespread mass of opinion. And I can go on to the further matter: to what use he put this advantage in his greatest novel.

ROBINSON CRUSOE

Introductory

In spite of its former great popularity, I doubt if *Robinson Crusoe* was usually read aright. Robinson's lonely struggle with physical conditions on the island caught men's imaginations so powerfully that they failed to do justice to anything else and especially to the events which Defoe planned with such care in order to lead up to the culminating shipwreck. Thus the book was made simpler than it actually is and was degraded from adult to adolescent reading. Today, superseded as the classic book for boys, it has lost its ill-grounded vogue. Of course, it has its readers, and of these a bigger proportion than for many years before may read it in the right way. Even so, it is read too little and prized too low.

To Defoe's other novels, *Moll Flanders, Colonel Jacque*, and *Roxana*, modern readers do better justice than did their elders, but tend to make them Defoe's norm. By so doing they fail to see that as a work of art *Robinson Crusoe* is in a different and a higher category. It is constructed with a closeness that the other novels (rightly enough in view of their nature) do not attempt, and it touches greater depths of the mind.

It is hard to believe that Defoe was anything but an opportunist in his initial motions towards a piece of writing. He wrote immensely and as occasion presented or demanded. Excited by stories of seafarers surviving alone on uninhabited islands, he thought the theme might reach the hearts of others and that he might profit by writing it up. But his excitement went deeper than ever before or after (and probably deeper than he knew) and drove him to fasten on to his theme with unique intensity. In his other novels he could have added or removed incidents with no detriment to the whole: in *Robinson Crusoe* this is not so; even the removal of things which at first sight could be spared easily would in fact damage the total proportions. The notorious example of such a thing occurs near the end: the elaborate incident of Crusoe and his fellow travellers from Lisbon being attacked by wolves in the Pyrenees. Now, in the middle, just before the great battle with the wolves, as darkness falls, Defoe lets us know through a sudden reference back to the book's beginning that he has his total impression in mind:

> The howling of wolves run much in my head; and indeed, except
> the noise I once heard on the shore of Africa, of which I have
> said something already, I never heard anything that filled me
> with so much horror.

Crusoe heard these other dreadful animal noises when he was escaping from
his Moorish captor in the boat with the shoulder-of-mutton sail. But then
as later, when the wolves attacked, he was a free man, and he had a companion, the Moorish boy, Xury. Alone on the island, Robinson had no wild
beasts to contend with: the arena was cleared for the struggle with himself.
Freed from the island, he reverts to his old liability to the bestial foe. The
Pyrenean wolves join with the African lions in framing Robinson's island
life, and they cannot be spared. They serve, too, to prevent Robinson's final
return to the safety and the comforts of England from being too abrupt.

The Theme

If, then, an episode, usually thought superfluous, turns out to be in-
dispensable, we should be the readier to expect the closest interlocking
elsewhere.

To counteract the old habit of reading *Robinson Crusoe* merely for the
sake of certain happenings on the island and to show that it is a richer and
closer-knit work of art than Defoe's other narratives, I shall have to describe
its plotting in some detail. In so doing I shall have in mind not only this
closeness of construction but the richness of reference the plot contains, the
amount of tradition which, consciously or unconsciously, it embodies. I shall
in fact have my eye on the epic quality of variety as well as that of control.

You can describe the plot of *Robinson Crusoe* in several ways; and this
possible multiplicity is one reason why the book holds us so strongly. You
can begin by describing it as a version of the story of the Prodigal Son,
references to which, either implied or stated, occur often in the opening
pages. Robinson is the Prodigal who leaves his father's house against advice,
who ruins himself not by riotous living but by a roaming disposition, who
is left solitary and apparently desolate, who repents, and returns to his father
(now in the form of God), and for whom God as it were kills the fatted calf,
blessing him with abundance on the island and restoring him to favour and
lordship. The climax of this succession comes before the dreadful sight of
the footprint in the sand ruins Robinson's peace and enlarges the action's
scope. It is marked by his exclamations:

> How mercifully can our great Creator treat his creatures, even
> in those conditions in which they seemed to be overwhelmed in

destruction! How can he sweeten the bitterest providences and give us cause to praise him for dungeons and prisons! What a table was here spread for me in the wilderness, where I saw nothing at first but to perish for hunger! It would have made a stoic smile to have seen me and my little family sit down to dinner. There was my majesty, the prince and lord of the whole island; I had the lives of all my subjects at my absolute command. . . . Then to see how like a king I dined, too, all alone, attended by my servants.

Or you can describe the book in terms not unlike the progression from Do-well through Do-bet to Do-best in *Piers Plowman:* the progression from the practical life to the life of contemplation in its turn fitting man for an existence where action and contemplation are combined. Crusoe, at first making a wreck of his life, rehabilitates himself on the island, beginning with his success in making the best practical job of his condition, then brought, through his solitude and his perils, face to face with God, and finally returning to society and meeting its problems in a way he could not do in his first state.

Or, most justly of all, you can describe the book in more abstract theological terms. Crusoe is Everyman, abounding in original sin, falling into specific folly and crime, incriminated more and more through repeated opportunities granted him by God for amendment, yet one of the elect whom God has mysteriously reserved to be saved through chastisement.

These accounts of the theme of *Robinson Crusoe* should have brought out what is a great source of the book's strength: its large, if unconscious, debt to an old tradition. Just as the Puritan preachers were the heirs of the medieval preachers, so Defoe inherits a didactic or allegorical scheme rooted in the Middle Ages and modified by Puritan theology. And it is through applying these inherited things to the current mode of the realistic tale of unaristocratic life that Defoe creates so adorable an impression of freshness and rejuvenation. He combines the emotional appeals both of being the good old firm and of being under entirely new management.

The Development of the Theme

I said above that most readers of *Robinson Crusoe* were so centred in the island and what happened there that they paid little heed to the rest. I had therefore better point out what is abundantly plain to any unprejudiced reader: that Defoe both leads up to the shipwreck on the island with solemn leisure and abundant motivation and throughout the book refers back to those preliminary events with an insistence and an accuracy that show he had the whole book in solution in his head throughout composition. The opening pages, describing Robinson's "propension of nature to rove" and his father's persuasions against indulging it, ending with the prophecy that, if he does, God will not bless him and that he will "have leisure hereafter to reflect upon having neglected his counsel when there might be none to assist in my recovery," state the theme. Robinson makes matters worse than they might have been by succumbing at once to the chance of a free passage from Hull to London and by failing to say a word to his parents about it or to ask God's blessing. Thus it was that "in an ill hour, on the first of September, 1651, I went aboard a ship bound for London."

Defoe was too much of an artist and too vividly aware that God was slow to wrath to proceed at once to retribution. On the contrary, God both warns Crusoe and gives him repeated chances to mend his ways before confining him to his island prison. First, there is the storm off the Humber, in the terror of which his conscience reproaches him for "the breach of my duty to God and my father." But he cheers up and hardens his conscience when the weather mends. Then comes the great storm, the loss of the ship, and the safe landing of the crew near Yarmouth. And Defoe makes Crusoe say:

> Had I now had the sense to have gone back to Hull, and have gone home, I had been happy, and my father, an emblem of our blessed Saviour's parable, had even killed the fatted calf for me.

Further, the captain of the boat warned Robinson that he was a predestinate Jonah and had no business to go to sea anymore after God's visible warning. Unpersuaded, Crusoe goes to London by land. Again, God does not proceed at once to ruin him. He is fortunate in falling in with honest acquaintance in London and makes a successful voyage to Guinea and back, which brings him £300. Here was another good chance of reverting to the middle way of life at home. But Crusoe chooses a second voyage to the Guinea coast and undergoes his first chastisement in being captured by Moorish pirates and made the slave of a Moor of Sali on the coast of Morocco. But it is not an extreme chastisement. He is well treated and has company. Ultimately he escapes in a small boat with a Moorish boy and after sampling the terrors of beasts on the African coast is picked up by a Portuguese boat and taken to Brazil. As in London before, so on the Portuguese boat and in Brazil Crusoe falls in with honest acquaintance. He prospers as a planter. And yet he fails to learn the lessons both of his captivity and of his subsequent prosperity in the middle way of life. He decides he must get rich quicker and, needing more labour, joins with others in an illicit voyage to capture slaves: illicit, because the slave trade was a royal monopoly. This wanton abandonment of a settled life for a forbidden venture at last provokes God's anger, and Crusoe is thrown up, after shipwreck, on the desert island. Defoe links the preliminary adventures together by making Crusoe begin his last disastrous voyage on the same day of the year as his embarkation for his first voyage at Hull.

When Crusoe, after the shipwreck and his fight with the waves, at last "clambered up the cliffs of the shore and sat me down upon the grass, free from danger, and quite out of the reach of the water," he instinctively thanked God for his extraordinary escape, showing that he was not altogether reprobate. But soon after, his fleeting and superficial gratitude gave way to a transport of despair; his regeneration will be a long process. During the night, Crusoe's prospects are bettered through the ship's having been washed up near enough to the island to be accessible to a swimmer. He makes no mistake and takes every advantage of the profit offered him. After several journeys to and from the ship

> I had the biggest magazine of all kinds now that ever was laid up, I believe, for one man; but I was not satisfied still, for while the ship sat upright in that posture, I thought I ought to get everything out of her that I could.

There is a beautiful irony in Crusoe's setting himself without delay to recreate in his desert that feeling for home and settlement which, as the very core of the middle way of life, he had abandoned and despised. Back from his last expedition to the ship before it broke up, he writes,

> But I was gotten home to my little tent, where I lay with all my wealth about me very secure.

But not so secure really; and from acquisition Crusoe goes naturally on to make sure of what he has acquired. That done, he begins the long process of improving his lot through using the chances the island provides him; and with that process Defoe interweaves the other process of his spiritual rehabilitation. As Crusoe masters from the bare elements many of the attributes of civilised life, so he progresses from a bare instinct through reason to a faith in God. I doubt if Defoe consciously intended any symbolism, but unconsciously he was led to give Crusoe's culminating triumph in learning to grow corn, to make bread, and to bake pots for storing it some concurrent mental significance, to the incalculable benefit of his book. Anyhow, it was during Crusoe's highest inventive activity that through the earthquake and the fever God awakened his conscience and caused him to progress from the realm of reason to that of faith. Defoe manipulates this progress skillfully. He refers back to Crusoe's instinctive but fugitive religious feeling after being saved from the sea, and he contrives that as Crusoe had several chances to lead a good life and rejected them, so he fails to act on several incipient motions of piety. And as those rejected chances led up to the shipwreck, so the neglected motions led up to the awful dream.

As Crusoe comes to possess more of his mind, so he not only masters more techniques but he ranges farther afield in his island and takes a legitimate pride in being the master of it. But he has not altogether shed his old nature, and even after his regeneration he has wild thoughts of escape. These lead him to the folly of making a huge canoe he is unable to launch and of trying to circumnavigate the island in a small one. Barely escaping with his life, he accepts his reproof. He now governs his temper better, he has learnt to make his pots more efficiently, with a wheel, and he is shown (and this is the culmination of one part of the book) as the monarch of the island with his fortress home and his two plantations.

Thus Crusoe learnt to cope with solitude and with a life now devoid of violent turns and surprises. But that is a different matter from coping with society and its ways. And to that second aptitude he must be educated. It is this further education and the use to which Crusoe puts it that is the theme of the second half of the book. Defoe passes to this second half with perfect art. He does so, well before we are sated with the development of the first theme; and, just because we are not sated, we are open to the great stroke of surprise through which he makes the transition. This is the passage that follows immediately on the above account of Crusoe's solitary and sheltered prosperity:

> It happened one day, about noon, going towards my boat, I was
> exceedingly surprised with the print of a man's naked foot on the
> shore, which was very plain to be seen in the sand.

The stark and yet somehow stealthy simplicity of this reminds me of another great stroke of the imagination, in Defoe's predecessor, Bunyan. In the *Holy War*, following directly on the ecstatic account of Mansoul's felicity after Emanuel has entered and reformed it, Bunyan introduces a sinister new character, marking a major turn in the story, with no more ado than

> But there was a man in the town of Mansoul, and his name was
> Mr Carnal Security; this man did, after all the mercy bestowed
> on the Corporation, bring the town of Mansoul into great and
> grievous slavery and bondage.

I speak roundly of Defoe's *art*, because the single footprint is poetic not literal truth; a probable impossibility, after Aristotle's fashion. Physically it was impossible that there should be but one footprint; artistically it is perfect that the vestige of society that Crusoe first encounters after his years of solitude should be minimal: the emphasis here will be in inverse proportion to the extent of the human manifestation. Even if Defoe had substituted no more than a detached foot, left over from one of the cannibal feasts, the effect, though more gruesome, would have been less profound; the very insubstantiality of the print awakens the imagination more and the reason less than any solid physical evidence would have done. Once aroused to the exclusion of reason, the imagination takes charge and pushes the horror to the extreme.

At first Crusoe seems in his terror to lose all the benefit of his preceding discipline. But he comes to accept the consequent profound change in his condition on the island, though never at ease in mind and ever prone to invading anxieties. Another great stroke of Defoe's art is that he waits before following up the footstep by more substantial ingressions of men. Crusoe resumes his work on the island; and the effect of the footstep is allowed to soften. It is only after a lapse of two years that he meets the remains of a cannibal feast. For two years more he has no other aim than to live close and escape notice. Then he grows bolder and considers action against the savages. More years elapse during which he learns to convert his first, instinctive, bloodthirsty thoughts of vengeance to the resolution, at once safer, more reasonable, and more pious, to leave vengeance to God and to abide the event. Having done so, he reaches a position of comparative stability. This slow timing is very remarkable in Defoe, who elsewhere tends to crowd his events thick, and it adds incalculably to the dignity of what happens on the island. It is as if the mood of reflection the island has come to signify is so profound that it must not be disturbed and abandoned too quickly. It must be partially prolonged into the period after the active life has begun. And there is great beauty in Crusoe's attaining this comparative stability of mind; for it recalls his previous more thorough but actually more precarious stability and at the same time, being comparative only, foretells future change.

That change occurs when the savages land, against custom, on Crusoe's side of the island, and when, soon after and against the reader's expectation, a new human element is introduced, the wreck off the island of a European ship. Nothing could be better than this ship's introduction just as our expectations are thoroughly concentrated on the savages. And nothing is more powerfully conceived in the whole book than Crusoe's yearning for human society, roused by the sight of the wreck:

"Oh that it had been but one!" I believe I repeated the words,
"Oh that it had been but one!" a thousand times; and the desires
were so moved by it, that when I spoke the words my hands
would clinch together, and my fingers press the palms of my
hands, that if I had had any soft thing in my hand, it would have
crushed it involuntarily; and my teeth in my head would strike
together and set against one another so strong that for some time
I could not part them again.

And the incident is followed by the double irony of his finding the "one" in
the form of the dead boy washed up from the wreck, and then, later, when
he has given up hope and in the form he least expected, the second "one"
in the living man, Friday. There was no sin in Crusoe's longing for a companion any more than there was in Milton's Adam when he felt there was
something lacking in Paradise and God put things right by creating Eve. On
the contrary, it was now proper that Crusoe should be no longer content
with the easiness of his confined life. All the same he was wrong still to toy
with desperate plans of escape, yielding once more to his old sin of not being
satisfied with the station God had set him in and of embarking on ill-con-
sidered ventures. He had spent two years in this state, when God intervened
to help him. There is nothing finer in the book than the account of Crusoe,
in good health, unable for no apparent reason to sleep, his mind and memory
working with uncommon speed and clarity, reviewing all his past life, mar-
velling at his blessed and providential security during the years before he
saw the footprint and truly grateful to God for it, but finally worked up into
a feverish desire to venture to sea on the slender hope of a rescue. Worn
out, he fell asleep and had a dream, prophetic of later happening, of saving
a captive savage and of finding in him a companion and pilot in escape. To
this dream's direction he then turned his thoughts; but God, slow to show
his utmost favour as he had been slow to wrath, keeps Crusoe waiting a year
and a half before the prophecy is fulfilled and Friday becomes his slave.

Blessed by Friday's society, Crusoe acts virtuously in teaching him the
rudiments of Christianity and in so doing consolidates his own faith. He has
now served his penance and experiences real felicity. But things do not quite
follow the indications of the dream. Crusoe had planned to go with Friday
to join the Spaniards who, Friday told him, were living with his own people;
but a new landing of cannibals interrupts the plan and leads to the rescue
of Friday's father and a Spaniard. There are now four on the island, and it
is not for nothing that Defoe reiterates the theme of kingship:

My island was now peopled, and I thought myself very rich in
subjects; and it was a merry reflection, which I frequently made,

how like a king I looked. First of all, the whole country was my own mere property, so that I had an undoubted right of dominion. Secondly, my people were perfectly subjected. I was absolute lord and lawgiver; they all owed their lives to me, and were ready to lay down their lives, if there had been occasion of it, for me. It was remarkable, too, we had but three subjects, and they were of three different religions. My man Friday was a Protestant, his father was a Pagan and a cannibal, and the Spaniard was a Papist. However, I allowed liberty of conscience throughout my dominions.

This is, of course, "a merry reflection"; and aptly so, because we are beginning to get back to the world of men. But it is more: it marks a point in Crusoe's mental growth. He has reached a higher stature than when he was a king among his animal dependents, about to be thrown into confusion by the sight of the footprint. Nor should we overlook the mention of property. According to the kind of Protestantism with which Defoe was familiar, it was right that a good state of mind should receive a material reward.

Hereafter the action moves quicker. Crusoe acts wisely and humanely when the ship arrives and the mutineers land. His pretence of his being His Excellency the Governor with a bodyguard of fifty men both serves the plot and intensifies the idea of kingship. It has a tinge of comedy like the passage just quoted, and yet it connotes a still greater mental stature in Crusoe. Having defeated the plans of the mutineers, he obtains a passage for himself and Friday on the ship and provides for the settlement of the island. When he returns to Europe, he acts justly to the Portuguese captain and the English widow who had helped him, and disposes wisely of the wealth God had blessed him with. He ends having learnt his lesson and at peace with the middle way of life.

Suggestiveness

I do not assert that the fullness and good order of the plot of *Robinson Crusoe* imply a great deal by themselves. It is when we add them to the other literary qualities Defoe commanded that we can estimate their full weight. They imply an intensity in the way he apprehended his story, a steady seriousness, unique in his novels.

Defoe may, as I have pleaded, conduct his story with great art. But it is, for all that, a simple story with few characters and no very great diversity of events. Only through making these simplicities pregnant could he achieve the richness of content necessary for the epic effect. And that was precisely what he was able to do. None of the characters strikes our imagination powerfully except Crusoe himself; and he is so limited (you have only to think of Hamlet to admit this) that you wonder why he so impresses. But impress he does; and in two quite different ways. James Sutherland was right in saying that Crusoe "is first of all an Englishman of the lower middle classes making the best of things"; and Coleridge was also right in saying that Defoe's excellence was "to make me forget my specific class, character and circumstances and to raise me, while I read him, into the universal man." And the reader feels like that because Crusoe himself becomes universal man. Further, even in his first, narrower capacity Crusoe embraces both the elements, the adventurous and the domestic, of contemporary puritanism. At the beginning he is dominated by the first, but this does not mean that the second is not there underneath. On the contrary, the moment unmitigated adventure has reached its logical, disastrous end, all Crusoe's energy is turned to making a home for himself, and out of seemingly intractable materials. Defoe stages his union of the two elements with consummate skill. He could, of course, have embodied them in two characters, one bred to seafaring adventure, the other to trade at home, and allowed them to live the lives to which their breeding pointed. Instead, he uses a single character and makes him interesting through his contrariness and pugnacity. Crusoe chooses adventure and chance when it was easy for him to be mercantile and domestic; he fights for domestic security when it was easier for him to fall into a despairing inertia and to accept whatever chance or adventure put in his way. He thus satisfies the two human instincts of being for and against the government. More narrowly he disinfects of their deadliness the deadly virtues of industry, thrift, sobriety, and punctuality. Over and above all this, Crusoe in the great crises ceases to embody the great qualities of contemporary puritanism and becomes the type of man himself in his struggle with circumstance. No character in eighteenth-century fiction embraces so much as Robinson Crusoe.

This richness of the protagonist's character is matched constantly by the rich suggestiveness of the incidents. All recognise Defoe's special gift of making the reader believe, through the utter confidence with which he goes into details, in the facts he presents. Most writers are content that the reader should suspend willingly his disbelief; Defoe is different in sometimes compelling the reader a little in the direction of positive belief in the happening. Defoe's method in itself is no better than the usual one; indeed it would stale quickly if widely affected. But it suited Defoe and gave him his special flavour. Now, in *Robinson Crusoe*, as nowhere else, Defoe used his special kind of verisimilitude to achieve a rare emotional intensity. His ep-

itaph on his comrades who perished in the shipwreck from which only he
was saved is:

> I never saw them afterwards, or any sign of them, except three
> of their hats, one cap, and two shoes that were not fellows.

It is, of course, the last detail that compels Defoe's peculiar kind of credibility.
But it does more. It brings home the commonplace of the insensitiveness
and disorderliness of mere nature (the sea couldn't even bother to wash up
a *pair* of shoes); and it renders that heightened state of the human mind,
when it not only experiences momentous feelings or makes wide general
decisions but simultaneously notices the most trivial details. And, in so
rendering, it stirs the mind of the reader to a state of uncommon
receptiveness.

Defoe's observation of the two shoes' disparity is one of many such in
Robinson Crusoe, and these, as well as having their immediate emotional effect,
combine in making us see events through the eyes of the narrator. We tell
ourselves not merely that these happenings are singularly lifelike but that
Crusoe was an exceptionally observant man; so much so that we surrender
ourselves willingly to see things through his eyes. In other words, we have
the least possible sense of the author's presence and personal opinions, and
a correspondingly strong dramatic sense of events happening to the narrator
or seen through his eyes.

This general remark on *Robinson Crusoe* was provoked by a sentence that
commemorated pitifully Crusoe's lost companions. Take now a passage in
a different mood to illustrate the richness of art still further. It describes
Crusoe's return to the island after his second expedition to the wreck:

> I was under some apprehensions during my absence from the
> land, that at least my provisions might be devoured on shore; but
> when I came back, I found no sign of any visitor, only there sat
> a creature like a wild cat upon one of the chests, which, when I
> came towards it, ran away a little distance, and then stood still.
> She sat very composed and unconcerned, and looked full in my
> face, as if she had a mind to be acquainted with me. I presented
> my gun at her; but as she did not understand it, she was perfectly
> unconcerned at it, nor did she offer to stir away; upon which I
> tossed her a bit of biscuit, though, by the way, I was not very
> free of it, for my store was not great. However, I spared her a
> bit, I say, and she went to it, smelled of it, and ate it, and looked
> (as pleased) for more; but I thanked her, and could spare no more,
> so she marched off.

Such a passage is profoundly puzzling. How, one asks, did Defoe reach such perfection of description? how did he crowd much into a minute space through so simple and direct means? Did he picture the incident with so precise a vision that he wrote his words without a pause? or did he study his effects, for "effects" there are? For instance, he gives the effect of anxiety by using the word *devoured* and not *eaten*: the loss of his stores would be a disaster, to which the stronger word is appropriate. Again, *tossing* denotes a more leisurely action than throwing and corresponds to Crusoe's mood of idleness and amusement. No poet has made sound echo sense in a more masterly way than Defoe when he wrote "ran away a little distance, and then stood still." And near the end *smelled of it*, with its suggestion of a slower caution, fits the nature of cat better than the more abrupt *smelt it* would have done. And, in general, who has conveyed the essentials of cat behaviour in so short a space: with such economy of means and with so much implied? He does not tell us, for instance, that the cat held her tail erect when she left, but the abrupt stiff rhythm of the last words forces that picture on us. The whole little account takes us by surprise; we feel, as we read it, like a very small boy who has lighted on a newly minted half crown. But, for all the surprise, it has its own organic justification. The cat, though technically wild, behaves like a tame one—had Crusoe spared more biscuit he might have kept her—so that she reinforces the domestic theme which Defoe introduces as soon as the opposite theme has reached its logical end in disaster. The passage also makes credible or softens the absence of wild beasts on the island. Some wild life there must be, or we should be incredulous; but violent and dangerous beasts, such as Crusoe encountered before on the African coast and after in the Pyrenees, were out of place. Such skill in both setting off the passage by surprise and bringing it in so pat to forward the action or make credible the situation is as puzzling as the nature of the passage itself. This has the air of pondered and deliberate art; and yet such art is the last thing we expect of Defoe. However, the puzzlement is secondary. What matters is that the passage illustrates both the richness of content and the constructional skill that Defoe commanded in *Robinson Crusoe*.

Allegory

As soon as we assert (or admit) that Crusoe is something more than the chief figure in a lively narrative, being the type both of the merchant adventurer of his own day and of mankind itself in certain difficulties, we have to decide whether to push such multiple significances farther. Present fashion tempts us to push them much farther, and my own temperament may be too ready to acquiesce in it. Making what allowance I can for these two factors, I cannot escape the conclusion that *Robinson Crusoe* is nearer to the sort of thing you get in Bunyan before and Kafka after than are any other of the chief novels of the eighteenth century. Tom Jones is a satisfactory comic hero, but in no way mankind; Mrs Shandy cannot be bettered as a recognisable female character in a book of a certain kind, but has not begun to be Mother Eve simultaneously; and (extend the eighteenth-century mode into the next age) Jane Austen's young women have no other dimension than that of the dramatic fiction in which they exist. Crusoe is nearer to Milton's Adam and to Bunyan's Christian than to any of these. Nor is it surprising in view of Defoe's familiarity with the works of his Puritan predecessors. We can therefore expect some kind of multiple meaning not only in the protagonist but in some of the events of *Robinson Crusoe*.

The question is: in which? Edwin Benjamin goes so far as to see symbolic meanings in the two sides of the island and in the shoots of green barley that spring from the fortuitously scattered grain. The lush side of the island with its grapes, its turtles, and its steamier climate is said to stand for the luxurious temperament. Crusoe rightly decides to remain on the less lush and austerer side, which has its corresponding moral significance. The shoots of barley are also the shoots of grace newly sprung in Crusoe's heart. I do not believe in such precise and detailed symbolism, which could hardly exist without the author's conscious intention. On the other hand, I agree (as I conveyed in describing the plot) with Benjamin's more general theory of a connection between Crusoe's victory over nature and his victory over himself. Because he progressively mastered himself he had the strength to master nature; and some of his physical victories are at the same time symbols of mental triumph. But, again, which? There is enormous force in Defoe's account of Crusoe making his pots. Should we see here the biblical allegory of God the potter and man the pot? is Crusoe's success in making the pot his own success, through God's help, in remaking himself? Again, I am reluctant to admit anything so worked out, so precise. And if Crusoe's potting is anywhere symbolic it is later, when, just after saying that his thoughts were "very much composed as to my condition and fully comforted in resigning myself to the dispositions of Providence," he says that he arrived at unexpected perfection in his earthenware, having learnt to use a wheel. There may well be some correspondence here between the good order of Crusoe's thoughts and the regular motion of the potter's wheel. But as for the first, difficult triumph in pot-making, it should not be separated from the larger process of making and storing bread. Of that process it is the most difficult and perhaps the culminating part, but it is subordinate to the whole. On the other hand, I cannot confine the meaning of the total process of making and storing bread to the mere acts that are necessary to it. Bread is here the token of the civilised life and of the pure essentials, not the trimmings, of that life; and when Crusoe has learnt to grow the grain, to make the bread, and to store it he has made good, as he could not have done through any other act.

This symbolic act of making bread unites with other things in the book to take the action out of its own day and to extend it back in time. On firing his first shot on the island, Crusoe's thoughts fly backward, for he comments: "I believe it was the first gun that had been fired there since the creation of the world." That is a homely way of putting it, and yet the sentiment is the romantically imaginative one of Tennyson's

> wind, that shrills
> All night in a waste land, where no one comes
> Or hath come, since the making of the world.

It is because Defoe commands this kind of imagination that his Crusoe represents both the middle-class pioneer of his own day and earlier man painfully inventing the arts of civilisation.

All in all, the precise limits of Defoe's symbolism do not matter much, if some sense of proportion is preserved. What does matter to the highest degree is that Defoe creates in a careful and unprejudiced reader that sharpened state of mind that knows it must be ready for the unusual and the richly significant.

What I have written so far has been meant to demonstrate among other things that the literary kind to which Defoe tends is the epic rather than tragedy, comedy, melodrama, satire, and so forth. He voices the "accepted unconscious metaphysic" of a large group of men, and he qualifies as their spokesman by revealing a much more capacious mind than they themselves possess. But tending and arriving are different: and in the end I have to face the matter of Defoe's general quality of writing, for on that quality will depend his position on the road between setting forth and arriving.

It must be admitted first that the quality of style in *Robinson Crusoe* is not constant. Here, for instance, is a very poor piece of writing:

> While we were in this condition, the men yet labouring at the oar to bring the boat near the shore, we could see when, our boat mounting the waves, we were able to see the shore, a great many people running along the shore to assist us when we should come near. But we made but slow way towards the shore, nor were able to reach the shore till, being past the lighthouse at Winterton,

the shore falls off to the westward towards Cromer, and so the
land broke off a little the violence of the wind. Here we got in,
and, though not without much difficulty, got all safe on shore.

Here the repetitions of the word *shore* could have been avoided with a little
care and are very ugly. But such lapses are rare; and in general Defoe slides
easily back and forth from full and expressive simplicity to high eloquence
or great intensity. It has been difficult for readers to do justice to the eloquence of Defoe's moralisings through being suspicious of Defoe's sincerity.
Granting him imaginative sincerity, which is alone to the point, we should
overcome that difficulty and recognise the genuine power of passages like
the following:

How strange a chequer-work of Providence is the life of man!
and by what secret differing springs are the affections hurried
about as differing circumstance permit! To-day we love what to-
morrow we hate; to-day we seek what to-morrow we shun; to-
day we desire what to-morrow we fear, nay, even tremble at the
apprehensions of. This was exemplified in me, at this time, in
the most lively manner imaginable; for I, whose only affliction
was that I seemed banished from human society, that I was alone,
circumscribed by the boundless ocean, cut off from mankind,
and condemned to what I called silent life; that I was as one who
Heaven thought not worthy to be numbered among the living,
or to appear among the rest of his creatures; that to have seen
one of my own species would have seemed to me a raising me
from death to life, and the greatest blessing that Heaven itself,
next to the supreme blessing of salvation, could bestow; I say,
that I should now tremble at the very apprehensions of seeing a
man, and was ready to sink into the ground at but the shadow
or silent appearance of a man's having set his foot in the island.

This is a kind of sustained eloquence that issues with perfect propriety from
Defoe's norm, while being very different from it. For emotional intensity
Crusoe's recollection of his uncontrolled passions in his early days on the
island are a sufficient illustration:

Before, as I walked about, either on my hunting, or for viewing
the country, the anguish of my Soul at my condition would break
out upon me on a sudden, and my very heart would die within
me, to think of the woods, the mountains, the deserts I was in,
and how I was a prisoner, locked up with the eternal bars and

bolts of the ocean, in an uninhabited wilderness, without redemption. In the midst of the greatest composures of my mind,
this would break out upon me like a storm and make me wring
my hands and weep like a child. Sometimes it would take me in
the middle of my work and I would immediately sit down and
sigh and look upon the ground for an hour or two together; and
this was still worse to me, for if I could burst out into tears or
vent myself by words, it would go off, and the grief, having
exhausted itself, would abate.

Defoe's qualities of writing are, indeed, great; but we must recognise
his limitations. I first mentioned Pope along with Defoe, because Pope's *Iliad*
and *Robinson Crusoe* belong to the same years; and I remarked how different
were the two societies that the two authors span. It comes as a shock to
reflect that Pope was the younger man by a whole generation, so that it is
hardly fair to use one of the two to illustrate the deficiency of the other. It
comes as an equal shock to reflect that Congreve, whom we associate with
Restoration drama, was nine years *younger* than Defoe, whom we associate
with the eighteenth-century novel. But we shall be justified in using Congreve
rather than Pope as the measure of what Defoe could not compass. The
matter presents itself to me best in terms of flexibility and rigidity. It is not
that Defoe had a rigid mind. On the contrary, Sutherland is right in speaking
of his puckish spirit in his satire, the *Consolidator*:

> Defoe was the awkward boy who will persist in asking questions;
> the difference is that he knew quite well that he was being awk-
> ward . . . A bourgeois who delights to *épater les bourgeois*.
>
> (*Defoe*, London, 1937)

Nevertheless, Defoe cannot overcome the rigidity of his given material. If
he is to remain true to his choric task (a task, of course, not consciously
conceived as such) of voicing the dissenting habit of mind, he cannot be too
critical, he must identify himself with it. And the type of religion in question
with its simple elections, interventions, rewards, admonitions, and punish-
ments, and the type of mercantile morality in question with its surface justice
and its ruthless self-seeking, could not be made flexible by however sensitive
and imaginative an observer. Congreve's Mirabel and Millamant, with their
affectations of frivolity and heartlessness advanced to screen much seriousness and warmth of feeling, betoken a world where mind can move with
greater freedom, between more distant extremes. Defoe has his advantages.
He can oscillate between present and past, between actual contemporary

people and mankind in abstraction or mankind in a primitive phase of culture; but within his own contemporary province his oscillations are a good deal more confined. The styles of the two authors, so well attuned to their substance, confirm the contrast. Defoe's simplicity can compass the homeliness of the day and the timelessness of abstracted human nature, but it lacks the subtle elegance, the diversified tempo, and the overtones and undertones of Congreve. This comparison is not a complaint that Defoe was not other than he was; it merely attempts to point out that however much we like Defoe and feel enthusiastically about him we must avoid the temptation of inflating his genius. I believe *Robinson Crusoe* to be an epic, but an epic having some of the limitations of the middle-class ethos whose choric expression it was.

MARTIN PRICE

The Divided Heart: Defoe's Novels

The rise of the novel in the eighteenth century is the triumph of the particular, however we may explain the novel's coming into being. Two major tendencies feed into the central event. The mock-heroic of Cervantes and his followers subjects the heroic image to the punishing presence of the commonplace. And the marvelous is naturalized as the saint's life, the rogue's picaresque career, the pilgrimage of the individual soul, are all enmeshed in the business of daily existence. The heroic may survive its punishment, but it takes on a new form. The allegorical translucency of the saint's life or of the pilgrim's progress may survive to some extent, but saint and pilgrim alike have now become first of all people with familiar names and addresses, with aunts and cousins, and the elaborate costume of a social existence. Saints become Clarissa Harlowes; pilgrims become Robinson Crusoes; and rogues become—instead of the resilient heroes of a hundred escapades— characters disclosed in the long, disorderly memoirs of Moll Flanders.

The triumph of the particular is the triumph of formal realism, a realism used to a different degree and for a different end by each of the great novelists of the century. The novel provides a spacious vehicle, with its slow rhythm of disclosure, its opportunities for dialogue, description, commentary. None of these is new in itself. They appear in epic, in romance, and in the genres of drama—but the mixture is new. The novel allows a rapid alternation between the character's internal thought and his action; between his view of himself and the author's view of him; between the intense scrutiny and the

From *To the Palace of Wisdom: Studies in Order and Energy from Dryden to Blake.* © 1964 by Martin Price. Southern Illinois University Press, 1964.

panoramic view. The novel gains fluidity by its prosiness. It sacrifices the concentration of poetic language for a new fusion of the poetic and the documentary, and for a more thoroughgoing involvement of the significant in the circumstances where it must find its life and from which it must wrest its values. The novel is the medium in which we can see the spirit of man in its most problematic form—not in lucid contests of principle but (in Lionel Trilling's words) "as it exists in the inescapable conditions which the actual and the trivial make for it" (*The Opposing Self*, New York, 1955).

Defoe's novels—written late in a career given over to journalism and pamphleteering—have always been a puzzle to the critic. Defoe draws upon forms of autobiography as far apart as criminals' sensational narratives of their careers and Puritan preachers' records of their transactions with God and the devil, factual narratives of sea discoveries, and pious accounts of miraculous providences. Running through this compound is the troubled conscience of a Puritan tradesman, aware of the frequent conflict between the demands of commercial gain and those of spiritual salvation. It is this troubled conscience that gives his characters their depth. They are tremendously efficient and resourceful in meeting the difficulties of their "trade," and Defoe catches the excitement of their limited but genuine art. But they are also nagged by doubt and a sense of guilt, by an awareness of what they have ignored or put by in their single-minded commitment. These pangs are not, in most cases, very effectual, but they are none the less authentic. Defoe's characters participate, as often as not, in what Iris Murdoch calls the "dialectic of those who habitually succumb to temptation."

In the novels I shall consider Defoe gives us the great myth of the isolated man bringing order out of unfamiliar materials (the first part of *Robinson Crusoe*), the outlawry of a woman whose social isolation makes her a freebooter in the center of London (*Moll Flanders*), and the recovery of a man from the life of crime into which he is plunged as a child (*Colonel Jack*). All these characters aspire to some kind of morality; all have a glimpse of some idea of redemption. Without these aspirations, they would be near successors to the picaresque heroes of countless jestbooks, coming through dangerous scrapes with wily dexterity. If the aspirations had fuller control of their natures, they might become the heirs of those spiritual heroes who find their way at last from the City of Destruction to the Land of Beulah. But their lives remain curiously unresolved and open. As Ian Watt has said, "Defoe presents us with a narrative in which both 'high' and 'low' motives are treated with equal seriousness: the moral continuum of his novels is much closer than was that of any previous fiction to the complex combination of spiritual and material issues which moral choices in daily life customarily involve" (*The Rise of the Novel*).

Defoe remains a puzzle because he imposes little thematic unity on his materials. Usually the writer who is content to give us the shape of the tale itself has a shapely tale to tell; a tale with its own logic, its awakening of tensions and expectations, its mounting repetition, its elaborate devices for forestalling too direct a resolution, and its satisfying—perhaps ingeniously surprising—way of tying all its threads in one great stroke. Such a tale need not leave those gaps in its narrative that are occasions for us to consider its meaning or theme. In Defoe's narratives the inconsistencies are such that we want to find a significant design, yet they hardly accommodate our wish.

Some critics have found consistent irony in a work like *Moll Flanders* by trimming away troublesome details, hardening the central character, and importing a moral stridency Defoe does not invite. Dorothy Van Ghent finds in Moll "the immense and seminal reality of an Earth Mother, progenetrix of the wasteland, sower of our harvests of technological skill, bombs, gadgets, and the platitudes and stereotypes and absurdities of a morality suitable to a wasteland world." This seems to me at once a great deal more fastidious and more vehement than the attitudes that underlie Defoe's conception of his heroine. The fact that Moll measures her success by money does not necessarily mean that money is her only object. Nor does Moll's indifference to the sensuousness and concrete texture of experience make her "monstrously abnormal" (*The English Novel: Form and Function*, New York, 1953).

Moll Flanders is the chronicle of a full life-span, told by a woman in her seventieth year with wonder and acceptance. In one sense, she is the product of a Puritan society turned to worldly zeal. Hers is very much the world of the Peachums, and in it Moll is the supreme tradeswoman, always ready to draw up an account, to enter each experience in her ledger as profit or loss, bustling with incredible force in the market place of marriage, and finally turning to those bolder and franker forms of competitive enterprise, whoredom and theft. To an extent, she is the embodiment of thrift, good management, and industry. But she is also the perverse and savagely acquisitive outlaw, the once-dedicated servant of the Lord turned to the false worship of wealth, power, success.

Her drive is in part the inevitable quest for security, the island of property that will keep one above the waters of an individualistic, cruelly commercial society. Born in Newgate, left with no resources but her needle, she constantly seeks enough wealth or a wealthy enough husband to free her from the threat of poverty and the temptations of crime. But she finds herself fascinated by the quest itself, by the management of marriages, the danger of thievery. When she has more money than she needs, she is still disguising herself for new crimes, disdaining the humble trade of the seamstress. When she finally settles into respectability, it is with a gentleman, not a merchant; her husband is a rather pretentious, somewhat sentimental highwayman, who is not much good as a farmer but is a considerable sportsman. Moll is no simple middle-class mercantile figure; nor is she another Macheath. Yet she has elements of both.

There is still another dimension of Moll Flanders. Her constant moral resolutions, her efforts to reform, her doubts and remorse cannot be discounted as hypocrisy or even unrealistic self-deception. Moll is a daughter of Puritan thought, and her piety has all the troublesome ambiguities of the Puritan faith. Her religion and morality are not the rational and calculating hypocrisy of the simple canter—the Shimei of Dryden's *Absalom and Achitophel*, for example. They are essentially emotional. She has scruples against incest, but they take the form of nausea, physical revulsion. She intends virtuous behavior and is astonished to discover her hardness of heart. Moll's life is a career of self-discovery, of "herself surprised," surprised by herself and with herself. Just as for the earlier Puritan, the coming of grace might be unpredictable, terrifyingly sudden, and very possibly deceptive, so for Moll the ways of her heart are revealed to her by her conduct more than by her consciousness, and even her most earnest repentance arouses her own distrust until it can well up into an uncontrollable joy. Personality is not something created or earned; the self is not the stable essence the Stoic moralist might seek. It is something given, whether by God or the devil, always in process, eluding definition and slipping away from rational purpose. Even at her happiest, with the man she has long missed, and in the late autumn of her life, Moll can think of how pleasant life might still be without him. It is a wayward thought, a momentary inclination, as real as her devotion and no more real.

What we find in Moll Flanders is not an object lesson in Puritan avarice or in the misuse of divinely given talents. Moll has all the confusion of a life torn between worldliness and devotion, but what remains constant is the energy of life itself, the exuberant innocence that never learns from experience and meets each new event with surprise and force. Moll, like the secularized puritanism she bespeaks, has the zeal that might found sects as well as amass booty, that might colonize a new world as readily as it robbed an old one. And the form of the old zeal, now turned into a secular world, needing the old faith at least intermittently as the new devotion to the world falters with failure, gives us a pattern of character that is one of the remarkable creations of fiction. Defoe, we are told, seems not to judge his material; Defoe must be a brilliant ironist. Both assertions imply a set of values thinner and more neatly ordered than Defoe can offer. He is aware of the tension between the adventurous spirit and the old piety; he can see the vitality of both religious zeal and worldly industry; the thrifty efficiency and the reckless outlawry that are both aspects of the middle-class adventure; the wonderful excitement of technology as well as its darker omens. And seeing all of this, he does not seem to see the need to reduce these tensions to a moral judgment. Like Mandeville, who struts much more in the role, he is one of the artists who make our moral judgments more difficult.

Ultimately, one might call Defoe a comic artist. The structure of *Moll Flanders* itself defies resolution. In giving us the life-span, with its eager thrust from one experience to the next, Defoe robs life of its climactic structure. Does Moll face marriage to the brother of her seducer, a seducer she still loves? It is an impossible tragic dilemma. Yet the marriage takes place, the husband dies, the children are placed; and Moll is left taking stock as she enters the marriage market again. Does she face the dreadful fact of incest? This, too, passes away; she cannot reconcile herself to it, but she can make a settlement and depart in search of a new and illegal marriage. The commonplace inevitably recurs; we have parodies of tragic situations.

Moll herself is not contemptible in her insensitivity. She is magnificently unheroic; and yet there is a modest touch of heroism in her power of re-cuperation, her capacity for survival with decency. In her curiously mean-ingless life, there is a wonderful intensity of experience at a level where affection, inclination, impulse (both generous and cruel) generate all the motions that are usually governed, or perhaps simply accompanied, by a world of thought. We have Defoe's own account of this process in his *Serious Reflections of Robinson Crusoe*:

> There is an inconsiderate temper which reigns in our minds, that hurries us down the stream of our affections by a kind of invol-untary agency, and makes us do a thousand things, in the doing of which we propose nothing to ourselves but an immediate sub-jection to our will, that is to say, our passion, even without the concurrence of our understandings, and of which we can give very little account after 'tis done.

This way of reading *Moll Flanders* imposes its own straitening on the untidy fullness of the book. Ian Watt has made a decisive case for the comparative artlessness of Defoe; there are too many wasted emphases, too many simple deficiencies of realization to make the case for deliberate irony tenable. But one can claim for Defoe a sensibility that admits more than it can fully articulate, that is particularly alert to unresolved paradoxes in human behavior. Watt dismisses in passing the parallel of a work like Joyce

Cary's *Herself Surprised*. There is point in this dismissal, for Cary has raised
to clear thematic emphasis what is left more reticent in Defoe. Yet the
relationship is worth exploration. Few writers have been so fascinated as
Cary with the ambiguities of the Protestant temper. In a great many characters—among them the statesman, Chester Nimmo, in the political trilogy
and the evangelical faith-healer Preedy in the last novel, *The Captive and the
Free*—Cary studied the shimmering iridescence with which motives seem,
from different angles, dedicated service and the search for grace or the most
opportunistic self-seeking. Cary was not interested in "rationalization" but
in the peculiar power achieved by the coincidence of religious zeal and
imperious egoism. Preedy, for example, seduces a young girl and makes her
virtually his slave; but he is convinced that his power to win her love is a
sign of grace—that a love so undemanding and undeserved as hers can only
be a sign of God's love in turn. Preedy is monstrous in one aspect, terrifying
but comprehensible in another; the difference lies in what we recognize to
be his object.

     Cary's effects are so adroit and so carefully repeated that we have no
doubt about calling them ironic. Defoe's are less artful and less completely
the point of his tale. Yet his awareness of them seems no less genuine. Defoe's
characters have secularized old Puritan modes of thought. Moll Flanders is
constantly taking inventory and casting up her accounts as she faces a new
stage of her life. Crusoe, too, keeps an account book, and, more like the
earlier Puritans, an account book of the soul. The doctrine of regeneration,
we are told, caused the Puritans "to become experts in psychological dis-
section and connoisseurs of moods before it made them moralists. It forced
them into solitude and meditation by requiring them continually to cast up
their accounts" (Perry Miller, *The New England Mind*, New York, 1939). In
the diary, particularly, the Puritan might weigh each night what he had
experienced of God's deliverance or of Satan's temptation during the day.
"It was of the very essence of Puritan self-discipline that whatsoever thoughts
and actions the old Adam within had most desire to keep hidden, the very
worst abominations of the heart, one must when one retired to one's private
chamber at night draw into the light of conscience. . . . Having thus balanced
his spiritual books, he could go to bed with a good conscience, sleep sound
and wake with courage" (William Haller, *The Rise of Puritanism*, New York,
1938).

     The "other-worldliness" of Puritan theology was, as Perry Miller puts
it, "a recognition of the world, an awareness of a trait in human nature, a
witness to the devious ways in which men can pervert the fruits of the earth
and the creatures of the world and cause them to minister to their vices.

Puritanism found the natural man invariably running into excess or intemperance, and saw in such abuses an affront to God, who had made all things to be used according to their natures. Puritanism condemned not natural passions but inordinate passions."

This concern with the uses of things places emphasis not on their sensuous fullness but on their moral function, and the seeming bleakness of Defoe's world of measurables derives in part from this. Characteristically, when Defoe in his *Tour* praises the countryside, it is for what man has made of it: "nothing can be more beautiful; here is a plain and pleasant country, a rich fertile soil, cultivated and enclosed to the utmost perfection of husbandry, then bespangled with villages; those villages filled with these houses, and the houses surrounded with gardens, walks, vistas, avenues, representing all the beauties of buildings, and all the pleasures of planting. . . . So, too, the natural scene of Crusoe's island "appeals not for adoration, but for exploitation" (Ian Watt). It is not the things we care about but the motives or energies they bring into play: they may satisfy needs, or call forth technical ingenuity, or present temptations. The physical reality of sensual temptation need not be dwelt upon, for moral obliviousness or self-deception is Defoe's concern (as in the account of Moll's going to bed with the Bath gentleman). If Moll's inventories seem gross, they may also be seen as the balance of freedom against necessity; poverty is the inescapable temptation to crime. And her inventories are, in an oblique sense, still account books of the spirit.

What might once have served the cause of piety becomes a temptation to exploitation. This is the dialectic of which Perry Miller speaks: the natural passion insensibly turns into the inordinate passion. Each of Defoe's central characters at some point passes the boundary between need and acquisitiveness, between the search for subsistence and the love of outlawry. And it is only in the coolness of retrospect that they can see the transgression. Defoe does not play satirically upon their defections; he knows these to be inevitable, terrifying so long as they can be seen with moral clarity, but hard to keep in such clear focus. His characters live in a moral twilight, and this leads to Defoe as a writer of comedy.

We must also keep in mind the essential optimism of the Puritan creed. The Puritans could not, Perry Miller tells us, sustain the tragic sense of life. "They remembered their cosmic optimism in the midst of anguish, and they were too busy waging war against sin, too intoxicated with the exultation of the conflict to find occasional reversals, however costly, any cause for deep discouragement. . . . Far from making for tragedy, the necessity [for battle] produced exhilaration." The battle against sin is not, of course, the only battle in which Defoe's characters are involved, but the struggle in the

world demands the same intense concentration and affords the same exhilaration. If there is any central motive in Defoe's novels, it is the pleasure in
technical mastery: the fascination with how things get done, how Crusoe
makes an earthenware pot or Moll Flanders dexterously makes off with a
watch. The intensity of this concentration gives an almost allegorical cast to
the operation, as if Crusoe's craftsmanship had the urgency of the art by
which a man shapes his own soul. It is beside the point to complain that
these operations are "merely" technical and practical; undoubtedly the man
who invented the wheel had beside him a high-minded friend who reproached
him with profaning the mystery of the circle by putting it to such menial
uses. The delight in mastery and in problem-solving may be a lower and
less liberal art than those we commonly admire, but it is a fundamental
experience of men and a precious one.

Even more, the energy of spirit that is concentrated in these operations
is a source of joy. One might wish that Moll Flanders had founded a garden
suburb with the force she gave to robbing a child, and at moments she feels
so too; but the strength she brings to the demands of life is at worst a
perversion of the spiritual energy the Puritan seeks to keep alive. It is in
doing that he finds himself and serves himself, and Moll Flanders reaches
the lowest point of her life when she falls into the apathy of despair in
Newgate: "I degenerated into stone, I turned first stupid and senseless, then
brutish and thoughtless, and at last raving mad as any of them were; in
short, I became as naturally pleased and easy with the place as if indeed I
had been born there." She loses her sense of remorse:

> a certain strange lethargy of soul possessed me; I had no trouble,
> no apprehensions, no sorrow about me, the first surprise was
> gone. . . . my senses, my reason, nay, my conscience, were all
> asleep.

In contrast is the recovered energy that comes with her repentance:

> I was covered with shame and tears for things past, and yet had
> at the same time a secret surprising joy at the prospect of being
> a true penitent . . . and so swift did thought circulate, and so
> high did the impressions they had made upon me run, that I
> thought I could freely have gone out that minute to execution,
> without any uneasiness at all, casting my soul entirely into the
> arms of infinite mercy as a penitent.

These moments of spiritual despair and joy have their counterparts in her secular life as well. After the death of her honest husband, she is left in poverty:

> I lived two years in this dismal condition, wasting that little I had, weeping continually over my dismal circumstances, and as it were only bleeding to death, without the least hope or prospect of help.

With the pressure of poverty and the temptation of the devil, she commits her first theft and runs through a tortured circuit of streets:

> I felt not the ground I stepped on, and the farther I was out of danger, the faster I went. . . . I rested me a little and went on; my blood was all in a fire, my heart beat as if I was in a sudden fright: in short, I was under such a surprise that I knew not whither I was going, or what to do.

This is the energy of fear, but it is a return to life; and before many pages have passed, Moll is speaking with pleasure of her new art.

The benign form of this energy is that of the honest tradesman whom Defoe always celebrates: "full of vigor, full of vitality, always striving and bustling, never idle, never sottish; his head and his heart are employed; he moves with a kind of velocity unknown to other men" (*Complete English Tradesman*). As R. H. Tawney has written, "a creed which transformed the acquisition of wealth from a drudgery or a temptation into a moral duty was the milk of lions" (*Religion and the Rise of Capitalism*, London, 1926). Yet, as Tawney recognizes, the older Puritan view of the evil of inordinate desires still survived. Defoe may call gain "the tradesman's life, the essence of his being" (*CET*), but gain makes it all the harder for a tradesman to be an honest man: "There are more snares, more obstructions in his way, and more allurements to him to turn knave, than in any employment. . . . [For] as getting money by all possible (fair) methods is his proper business, and what he opens his shop for . . . 'tis not the easiest thing in the world to distinguish between fair and foul, when 'tis against himself" (*CET*). This candid recognition of the traps of self-deception leads Defoe to a considerable degree of tolerance. He cites the golden rule, "a perfect and unexceptionable rule" which "will hold for an unalterable law as long as there is a tradesman left in the world." But, he goes on, "it may be said, indeed, where is the man that acts thus? Where is the man whose spotless integrity reaches it?" He offers those tradesmen who "if they slip, are the first to reproach themselves with it; repent and re-assume their upright conduct; the general tenor of whose lives is to be honest and to do fair things. And this," he concludes, "is what we may be allowed to call *an honest man;* for as to perfection, we are not looking for it in life" (*CET*).

More fundamental is the "paradox of trade and morality" that Defoe recognizes as well as Mandeville: "the nation's prosperity is built on the ruins of the nation's morals"; or, more cogently, "It must be confessed, trade is almost universally founded upon crime." By this Defoe means what Mandeville means: "What a poor nation must we have been if we had been a sober, religious, temperate nation? . . . The wealth of the country is raised by its wickedness, and if it should be reformed it would be undone" (*CET*). Of luxury, Defoe could write "However it may be a vice in morals, [it] may at the same time be a virtue in trade" (*The Review*). As Hans H. Anderson (from whose study I have drawn several of these quotations) points out, Defoe does not try to shock his readers as Mandeville does by insisting upon the irreducible paradox; he tends to abstract issues and to exclude "ethical considerations by the simple expedient of restricting his discussion to what he called the 'Language of Trade.' " But, although Defoe does not take pleasure in the difficulties he creates for the moralist, he shows a keen awareness of the difficulties his characters encounter.

When Robinson Crusoe voices his satisfaction with his island, he finds it a place where the dangerous paradox is happily resolved.

> I was removed from all the wickedness of the world here. . . . I had nothing to covet; for I had all that I was now capable of enjoying. . . . There were no rivals; I had no competitor. . . . But all I could make use of was all that was valuable. . . . The most covetous griping miser in the world would have been cured of the vice of covetousness, if he had been in my case; for I possessed infinitely more than I knew what to do with.

In short, Crusoe's island is the utopia of the Protestant Ethic (as Ian Watt puts it) in a double sense. It is a place where Crusoe holds undistracted to his work and where his work is rewarded; but it is a place, too, where his tradesmanlike energy remains innocent, with no danger of inordinate desires leading to dishonesty. Only in the overambitious project of the *periagua* does Crusoe exceed the limits of utility, and the only consequences are the futility of wasted effort.

All of Defoe's other major characters yearn at one time or another for this freedom from the "necessity" embodied in temptation. The only other character who comes close to Crusoe's freedom is Colonel Jack in his management of slaves. Jack is concerned with the exploitation of his fellow men. Jack's master, the slaveowner, must exact obedience in order to realize the value of his property, but he would prefer to win voluntary service. Jack introduces a policy of mercy that wins the obligation of gratitude from the slave, Mouchat, and thus Jack reconciles trade (or here expediency) with morality and eliminates cruelty:

> if they were used with compassion, they would serve with affection as well as other servants . . . but never having been let taste what mercy is, they know not how to act from a principle of love.

Significantly, when Jack encounters a slave who will not learn this desirable lesson, he sells him off; he can achieve his reconciliation only within the limits of the plantation, as Crusoe can his only in the isolation of his island kingdom. Both these scenes are, in effect, islands of ideal social order.

Later, when Jack is instructed in religious matters, he is made to see how God's mercy acts upon all men just as his own mercy has worked upon the slaves. The sense of mercy "seizes all the passions and all the affections, and works a sincere unfeigned abhorrence of the crime as a crime, as an offence against our Benefactor, as an act of baseness and ingratitude to Him who has given us our life . . . and who has conquered us by continuing to do us good when He has been provoked to destroy us." The "scholar" who instructs Jack proposes, somewhat in the spirit of Shaftesbury, that if men could see with full clarity the nature of both heaven and hell, "the first would have a stronger and more powerful effect to reform the world than the latter." This conception of a grateful man rejoicing in a merciful God is an ideal vision that Defoe would like to sustain. "But," as Jack remarks as he leaves home to wander in the world, "man is a short-sighted creature at best, and in nothing more than in that of fixing his own felicity, or, as we may say, choosing for himself." We are back to Crusoe's "original sin" of leaving his father and the middle station of life, and in fact to all those expansive, restless efforts that are both the glory of the tradesman and the occasion for his temptations. The alternatives to this energy may be deadness of spirit or that serenity that at last confers "the leisure to repent." This leisure is given Defoe's characters intermittently in the course of their lives; only with age is it steadily achieved. Only after seventy-two years of a "life of infinite variety" does Crusoe fully "know the value of retirement, and the blessing of ending our days in peace."

Defoe's characters are all technicians, rational masters of their art, on one level, and creatures of impulse or obsession on another. When the young Robinson Crusoe hears his father's moving speech about the need to keep to the middle station of life, he is—as he tells us—"sincerely affected with this discourse . . . and I resolved not to think of going abroad any more, but to settle at home according to my father's wish." Then follows that verb that runs through Defoe's novels: "But alas! a few days wore it all off. . . ." When a year later he goes to Hull, it is done "casually, and without any purpose of making an elopement that time"; yet on a sudden prompting he finds himself on board a ship bound for London. After escaping a dreadful storm that reveals all the horror and dangers of a life at sea, Crusoe is divided: he cannot face the shame of returning home, but he is still vividly aware of his career as a Jonah:

> An irresistible reluctance continued to going home; and, as I stayed awhile, the remembrance of the distress I had been in wore off; and as that abated, the little motion I had in my desires to a return wore off with it, till at last I quite laid aside the thoughts of it, and looked out for a voyage.

This pattern is typical: the power of the impulse or obsession, the lack of clear decision; conflicts are settled in Crusoe or for him, not by him. Throughout his stay on the island, we see these fluctuations. Is the island a prison, or is it a deliverance from the sinful life he led in the world? Is the fate God has brought upon him an act of divine goodness, or is it fearfully inscrutable? All the trust he has achieved deserts him when he finds the footprint in the sand, and it is slowly regained. As he turns to Scripture and lights upon a telling verse, he finds comfort. "I thankfully laid down the book, and was no more sad," he tells us; and then adds, "at least, not on that occasion." There is always this note of reservation in Defoe's characters—as they prudently conceal some part of their fortune or story. It may be a note of mistrust, but, even more, it shows a sense, in the midst of joy or pleasure, that the mind of today need not be that of tomorrow, and perhaps cannot.

Moll Flanders, like Crusoe, is a creature of mixed and unstable motives. She goes to Bath, she tells us, "indeed in the view of taking what might offer; but I must do myself that justice as to protest I meant nothing but in an honest way, nor had any thoughts about me at first that looked the way which afterwards I suffered them to be guided." It is sincere enough, but the moral twilight is clear, too. She lodges in the house of a woman "who, though she did not keep an ill house, yet had none of the best principles in her self." When she has become the mistress of the gentleman she meets at Bath, she remarks that their living together was "the most undesigned thing in the world"; but in the next paragraph she adds: "It is true that from the first hour I began to converse with him I resolved to let him lie with me."

The surprise has come in finding that what she had been prepared to accept through economic necessity, she has encouraged through "inclination."

Earlier in America, when Moll discovers that she is married to her brother and the disclosure drives him to attempt suicide, she casts about:

> In this distress I did not know what to do, as his life was apparently declining, and I might perhaps have married again there, very much to my advantage, had it been my business to have stayed in the country; but my mind was restless too, I hankered after coming to England, and nothing would satisfy me without it.

Here, too, the motives are a wonderful mixture of concern, prudence, and impulse. What is most remarkable about Moll Flanders is her untroubled recognition of her motives, her readiness to set them forth with detachment, at least to the extent that she understands them. She recalls those Puritans who scrutinize their motives as if they were spectators beholding a mighty drama. When Moll robs a poor woman of the few goods that have survived a fire, she records:

> I say, I confess the inhumanity of the action moved me very much, and made me relent exceedingly, and tears stood in my eyes upon that subject. But with all my sense of its being cruel and inhuman, I could never find it in my heart to make any restitution: the reflection wore off, and I quickly forgot the circumstances that attended it.

Fielding was to make something beautifully ironic of this kind of mixture of motives. Defoe uses it differently; candor disarms the moral judgment that irony would require. The stress is more upon the energy of impulse than upon its evil. And the energy is such that it can scarcely be contained by a single motive or be channeled long in a consistent course.

JAMES SUTHERLAND

The Relation of Defoe's Fiction
to His Nonfictional Writings

Defoe is not unique in having taken to writing fiction when he had almost reached his sixties: William de Morgan was even older when he wrote *Joseph Vance* and the other novels that succeeded it. Yet such a development so late in life is certainly unusual; and one can only suppose that the interest in human behaviour and circumstances which led to the writing of fiction was always there, but that other activities claimed the writer's attention and kept his creative gifts in suspense. In De Morgan's case those gifts were fully satisfied by the demands of a flourishing pottery business in which he was actively engaged for over thirty years. The case of Defoe is not strictly comparable (even if we remember the odd parallel of his running a brick and tile factory at Tilbury); for although he had been trading actively, he had also been writing on a wide variety of topics for more than thirty years before he published *Robinson Crusoe*. When he took leave of the readers of *The Review* in his final number (June 11, 1713), he treated them to a discourse on "the modish, tho' abominable Vice of MODERN WHORING":

> And what Whore are you for, said one that stood at my Elbow when I wrote this—Why, I'll tell you my Case in a few words; Perhaps this Paper has been *my Whore*, at least formerly, when it pleased you; if so, then like the *Israelites*, that put away their strange Wives, I have resolved to part with her, and so I escape the lash of my own Satyr. Writing upon Trade was the Whore I really doated upon.

From *Imagined Worlds: Essays on Some English Novels and Novelists*, edited by Maynard Mack and Ian Gregor. © 1968 by James Sutherland. Methuen, 1968.

Writing on trade may indeed have been his permanent whore, but he was almost equally susceptible to the seductive charms of politics, religion, military affairs, and much else. One obvious result of all this varied literary composition was that when he turned to fiction in 1719 he was already a trained writer whose "mind and hand went together," and who uttered whatever he had to say with an easiness and readiness that have rarely been equalled in English prose.

It may still be thought odd that he had reached his sixtieth year before his first work of fiction appeared. Yet this is true only in a limited sense. A strong element of fiction is present in many of his earlier writings, and it gives to them much of their effectiveness and their lasting appeal. We may pass over *The Consolidator: Or, Memoirs of Sundry Transactions From The World in the Moon* (1705); for although this satirical piece is fiction of a sort, and has some ingenious allegorical effects, it represents in Defoe's writing something of a dead end. More important for our present purpose are those pieces in which he makes use of a persona. Like many of his contemporaries he often employed some form of indirect utterance when he engaged in the risky business of political and religious controversy. His earliest extant pamphlet, which need not detain us here, carried the title, *A Letter to a Dissenter from his Friend at the Hague, Concerning the Papal Laws and Test . . .* (1688). The fiction of "his Friend at the Hague" was no more than a conventional disguise designed to protect the real author, although it may also be said to have given the arguments used the judicious impartiality of an outsider looking on at the English scene in 1688. The first occasion on which Defoe's use of a persona was genuinely integrated with the argument and affected the presentation of it occurs in *The Poor Man's Plea* of 1698. The plea of the Poor Man is made "in relation to all the proclamations, declarations, Acts of Parliament, etc., which have been, or shall be made, or published, for a Reformation of Manners, and suppressing immorality in the nation"; and his argument is that one law for the rich and another for the poor will never lead to any effective reform of national vices. The Poor Man is an honest, steady sort of person; and in spite of what he has to say about some of the clergy and magistrates, he writes more in sorrow than in anger, knowing his place and not offering to take too great liberties with his betters. Since Defoe is on this occasion addressing himself primarily to "gentlemen and others," he does not risk alienating the well-to-do or educated reader by allowing his Poor Man to write in an illiterate fashion, or to use low and vulgar colloquialisms. Yet he does succeed, at least intermittently, in suggesting the natural, uninhibited speech of the English middle class:

> The Parson preaches a thundering Sermon against Drunkenness,
> and the Justice of the Peace sets my poor Neighbour in the Stocks,
> and I am like to be much the better for either, when I know
> perhaps that this same Parson, and this same Justice, were both
> drunk together the Night before.

Here the "thundering" sermon and the ironical "I am like to be much the better for either" have the authentic sound of middle-class conversation. Again, the Poor Man makes his points with some admirably homely illustrations, calculated to come within the range of the common man's experience. In support of the argument that the poor man's vices affect only himself, whereas those of a rich man affect a whole neighbourhood, he gives us this:

> If my own Watch goes false, it deceives me and none else; but if
> the Town Clock goes false, it deceives the whole Parish.

If it is objected that this is really Defoe's own personal style, the answer cannot be a flat denial, for it is undoubtedly *one* of the styles of writing natural to Defoe—in *The Review*, for instance, but also elsewhere in some of his pamphlets. Yet it is quite a different style from that of *Giving Alms no Charity*, a pamphlet addressed to "the Parliament of England" and accordingly written in a more elevated manner, and different again from that of *The Shortest Way with the Dissenters*. In *The Poor Man's Plea* Defoe may sometimes have forgotten the persona he has assumed, but for the most part the forthright and earnest voice we hear is that of the humble citizen who is his spokesman.

What he had done effectively enough in this piece he went on to do with disastrous success in *The Shortest Way with the Dissenters*. Here the persona is a High Church clergyman of immoderate views, prepared to go to almost any length to stamp out nonconformity. When a satirist has to deal with intolerance so extreme as to be hardly credible, the simplest way to expose it is to let it speak with its own voice. This is a sort of jiu-jitsu method by which the satirical victim is thrown by his own weight and impetuosity. Defoe caught the imperious tone of the High Church fanatics so successfully that many of them welcomed *The Shortest Way* as a powerful and unambiguous statement of their views, and, on the other side, many of the Dissenters believed that the author was really and truly calling for them to be "hang'd, banish'd, or destroy'd, and that the Gallows and the Gallies should be the Penalty of going to a Conventicle." To the Dissenters Defoe might well have cried, "I am Cinna the poet! I am Cinna the poet!" What, in fact, he did say, some time after the event, was a good deal more cutting:

All the Fault I can find in my self as to these People is, that when I had drawn the Picture, I did not, like the Dutch Man, with his Man and Bear, write under them, *This is the Man*, and *This is the Bear*, lest the People should mistake me.

(*The True-Born Englishman*)

Defoe, in fact, had identified himself so absolutely with his persona that *The Shortest Way* was almost indistinguishable from the Highflyer outburst it purported to be. If that compels us to have some reservations about his pamphlet as a piece of normal satire, it only serves to underline his ability to assume an imaginary personality and to render it convincing by the verisimilitude of the expression.

Over the years Defoe put forth his ideas under various disguises. He was at different times a Quaker, a stockjobber, a Scots gentleman, an "honest Tory," and so on. So little had he learnt from the traumatic experience of *The Shortest Way* that towards the end of Queen Anne's reign he was again in serious trouble for writing three pamphlets on the succession. Two of these, with the provocative titles of *Reasons against the Succession of the House of Hanover*, and the still more inflammatory *And What if the Pretender should Come? Or, Some Considerations of the Advantages and Real Consequences of the Pretender's Possessing the Crown of Great Britain*, were written by an apparent Jacobite who was in favour of restoring the Old Pretender to the throne of his father when Queen Anne should die. But the "reasons" and the "consequences" were so patently, and at times heavily, ironical that any Jacobite who really thought those were good reasons or desirable consequences must have been out of his mind. Still, the persona was made sufficiently plausible to effect at least a temporary deception, and to enable Defoe's Whig enemies to procure his arrest and imprisonment.

Before considering the effect on Defoe's fiction of this ingrained tendency to make-believe I shall mention another marked feature of his nonfictional writing that is relevant here: on a surprising number of occasions (and sometimes in the most unlikely contexts) he has a way of slipping into a passage of dialogue. One such passage occurs in *The Poor Man's Plea*, where, in stressing the point that the gentry not only tolerate heavy drinking, but even make it their way of "expressing their Joy for any publick Blessing," he suddenly gives us an illustration:

Jack, said a Gentleman of very high Quality, when after the Debate in the House of Lords, King William was voted into the Vacant Throne; *Jack* (says he) *God damn ye, Jack, go home to your Lady, and tell her we have got a Protestant King and Queen, and go*

make a Bonfire as big as a House, and bid the Butler make ye all Drunk,
ye Dog.

From the first Defoe had a quick ear for the varied speech of his fellow countrymen. In the pages of *The Review* there are some spirited passages of dialect conversation, as in the account of a country election (June 8, 1708), or in the sarcastic comments of the mercer, the milliner, the draper, and the barber's boy while the knight and the peer, who have failed to pay the tradesmen for the clothes and wigs they are wearing, go past their shops (January 17, 1706), or in the discussion between two west-country rustics (April 12, 1712) about the peace negotiations "at a great vurdern place yonder, over the zee":

> JOHN: What, 'tis'n Youtrich, is it, William?
> WILL: . . . 'tis zome zuch Name, I do think; it is *You-trik* or
> *We-Trik*, or zomething like that, but shure I doon't
> remember, vor I doon't use those Outlandish Words
> much.

When, in 1715, Defoe brought out the first part of *The Family Instructor* he was exploiting the resources of dialogue much more fully. This highly popular work was, in effect, a series of didactic domestic plays, in which groups of middle-class characters, young, adolescent, and middle-aged, converse in language appropriate to their age, sex, and station. Dialogue enters even into the *Tour thro' the Whole Island of Great Britain* and, much more extensively, into *The Complete English Tradesman* (1725). Those passages of lively and idiomatic dialogue, which to the modern reader of *The Complete English Tradesman* are perhaps the most interesting parts of the book, were so little to the liking of the editors of the 1738 revision that they lopped most of them out, on the ground of their supposed tediousness, and because they were "on too particular a case to be generally useful." If we think of that work solely as a practical handbook, we may have to agree with the editor's decision; but by 1725, with most of his works of fiction now behind him, Defoe had become so used to the particular case that whenever an opening occured he slid naturally into a treatment of his topic in terms of men and women, engaged here in the very human occupation of buying and selling.

If we now turn to Defoe's fiction, we find him invariably throwing his stories into the form of autobiography, in which the chief character is simply a more sustained and more fully developed persona than those he had made use of from time to time in his earlier nonfictional writing. Although critics vary in the extent to which they think they can see Defoe himself in *Robinson*

Crusoe or *Moll Flanders*, Crusoe and Moll are not Daniel Defoe, but characters he has imagined, and in whose shoes he has tried (successfully for the most part) to put himself. It has been objected by Ian Watt that in *Robinson Crusoe* Defoe disregarded "the actual psychological effects of solitude," and that Crusoe's behaviour is very unlike that of those actual castaways whose stories were almost certainly known to Defoe. "What actually happened to the castaways," Professor Watt points out, "was at best uninspiring. At worst, harassed by fear and dogged by ecological degradation, they sank more and more to the level of animals, lost the use of speech, went mad, or died of inanition" (*The Rise of the Novel*). To this it might be answered that the ordinary reader of *Robinson Crusoe*, with no critical axe to grind, is so far from finding Crusoe's behaviour unconvincing that the whole desert-island sequence of events leaves a sharp impression on the mind of historical actuality. Much, indeed, is made by Defoe of the effect of solitude; Crusoe's fear of the savages is fully realized; and the frustrations of a solitary man trying to do work that requires many hands are expressed again and again: everything is there, except that deterioration of mind and character that Professor Watt sees as inevitable in the circumstances. What Defoe himself would have done if he had ever been cast away on a desert island it is no doubt impossible to say; but it is a fair guess that he would have behaved very much like Crusoe. This is another "particular case," but prose fiction deals in particular cases. At all events, there seems every reason to believe that in *Robinson Crusoe* (*a*) Defoe was putting himself in the place of someone else, and (*b*) the someone else behaved in the sort of way that Defoe himself would have behaved (or believed he would behave) in the same circumstances, and (*c*) this persona was therefore some sort of unconscious adjustment between an objectively realized character and Daniel Defoe's idea of Defoe. The same may be said again of the Saddler in *A Journal of the Plague Year*. Yet when this substitution process becomes more difficult, either because the personality of the imagined narrator is very different from his own (as with Moll Flanders and Colonel Jack), or even repellent (as with Roxana), he can still create a credible character.

A shipwrecked tobacco-planter, the daughter of a convicted thief who becomes a thief herself, a London saddler, a boy stolen from his family by gypsies who turns pirate, another boy boarded out as an infant with a foster mother and growing up as a thief, a French refugee who marries an eminent London brewer and becomes "the fortunate mistress": all these narrate their lives to us in Defoe's fiction. Does he make any attempt to individualize his different heroes and heroines by the way in which they tell their story? It must be admitted that there is a strong resemblance between the colloquial prose of each and every one of them, and that they all write in a reasonably educated style, not unlike one of the more habitual styles of Defoe himself.

> Well, their Warrant being executed, I came readily with them. The Officer, who presently saw himself imposed upon, and that there was not the least occasion of Violence, admitted me very frankly, being very much Indisposed, to ride on Horse-back, while they came all after on Foot, sometimes a quarter of a Mile behind; nothing had been easier than for me to have rid away from them all, if I had thought fit; but I had not Guilt enough to make me think of an Escape. The next Project was, that all this was of a Saturday, that they might Triumph over me, and keep me in their Custody two Nights in suspence, without any Release. On the Monday I tendred Bail; the scandalous Endeavours a Set of Men made use of to fright and deter Friends that were willing to Bail me, will deserve a particular Narration, and shall not want it.

Is this Moll Flanders telling us about how she was arrested for picking a pocket or stealing a parcel of lace? It could well be just that; but in fact it is Defoe himself telling the readers of *The Review* (April 18, 1713) about his own arrest for writing the three ironical pamphlets already mentioned. Defoe wrote at speed, and he wrote for a public that would scarcely have appreciated a long story told in the style of, say, an eighteenth-century Augie March. In any case, his various heroes and heroines had either had a normal middle-class education or were self-educated. Crusoe had not been "bred to any trade," but was intended by his father for the law; Moll Flanders grew up in the family of the Mayor of Colchester, and had "all the advantages for [her] education that could be imagined," learning to write, to dance, to speak French, and so on; Colonel Jack was "born a gentleman" and made considerable efforts when he grew up to acquire an education suited to what would have been his class if he had not been an illegitimate child farmed out on a foster parent.

Yet when he can legitimately introduce a more individualized speech idiom Defoe sometimes avails himself of the opportunity. When Moll, lying ill upstairs, hears the Colchester family talking about her, he gives us the sort of authentic middle-class dialogue, nicely varied for each member of the family, that he had already written for *The Family Instructor*. A little earlier Moll has recorded an equally natural conversation between herself, aged eight, and her old nurse; and in *Colonel Jack* there is again a successful attempt to reproduce the language of childhood and to enter into the mind of a child.

The language of Will the Quaker in *Captain Singleton* is particularized with
the appropriate "thou's" and "thee's" and the vocative "Friend." The conversation of Xury and Friday in *Robinson Crusoe* and of Mouchat in *Colonel
Jack* indicates at least a rather crude attempt on Defoe's part to imitate the
sort of pidgin English he may have heard spoken by negro slaves in London.
(It is worth remembering that in *The Royal Slave* Mrs. Behn's Oronooko and
Imoinda speak nothing but standard English.) What is perhaps odd is that
Defoe makes no use in his fiction of the various English dialects with which
he had shown himself to be familiar in the pages of *The Review*, nor, when
Colonel Jack is in Scotland, does Defoe make any attempt to reproduce the
speech of the local inhabitants, although, again, he must have known it well.

As early as November 1, 1718, a writer in *The Weekly Journal; Or, British
Gazetteer* anticipated a good deal of later criticism of Defoe by referring
superciliously to "the little art he is truly master of, of forging a story, and
imposing it on the world for truth." For Leslie Stephen and other nineteenth-
century critics this process began with *A True Relation of the Apparition of one
Mrs. Veal to one Mrs. Bargrave* (1706), which was generally regarded as perhaps
the earliest example of "the fictions which he succeeded in palming off for
truths" (*Hours in a Library*, London, 1899). But the investigations of twentieth-century scholars have shown that there are very few facts in this celebrated ghost story that cannot be authenticated. Whatever Mrs. Bargrave
saw, or thought she saw, when she opened the front door of her house at
noon on September 8, 1705, she certainly existed; and so (until September
7) did her friend Mrs. Veal. Mrs. Bargrave told her story to various people,
and by September 13, when the first extant report of it was written down
in a letter from one E.B. of Canterbury to an unknown correspondent, it
was all over the town. Other surviving letters from Canterbury, dated Oc-
tober 9 and November 15, add a few facts and omit others; and by December
24 the story was in print, when *The Loyal Post* gave an account of the whole
strange incident, based on "Several Letters . . . from Persons of Good Credit
. . . , besides Relations we have by Word of Mouth."

So fully authenticated has Mrs. Bargrave's story now become, that one
hesitates to make claims for Defoe's version that may only be shown to be
unjustified by the discovery of still more contemporary evidence. But the
True Relation differs from all earlier accounts by being more circumstantial,
by suppressing any evidence that would tend to discredit Mrs. Bargrave's
reliability as a witness (Defoe is in fact at some pains to establish it), and by
giving almost all the rather dreary conversation between the two women in
oratio recta. *The Loyal Post* had observed that "there are abundance of Particulars of the two hour Discourse which Mr. Bargrave relates too tedious to

be here inserted." But to the author of the *True Relation*'s tediousness (or, at any rate, detailed particularization) was a guarantee of truth; and in his account of their conversation the two ladies ramble on more or less inconsequentially (but of course all the more naturally for that reason), and in its very flatness their talk seems to be utterly authentic. The narrator, too, introduces fresh matter with an "I should have told you before," and towards the end of his narrative he jumps without any logical sequence from one afterthought to another. Here, as elsewhere with Defoe, it is hard to tell whether we have to deal with the artlessness of a conscious artist, or whether the carelessness and lack of a consistently sequential narrative are due to nothing more than Defoe's haste. But on at least two occasions—both turning on the all-important fact that Mrs. Veal is not there *in the flesh*—we seem to see the hand of Defoe giving an added touch of vividness. The three earliest accounts all mention the fact that when Mrs. Bargrave opened her front door and saw her old friend standing there she offered to kiss ("salute") her. Mrs. Veal's way of evading the kiss is expressed in the three accounts as follows:

> But Mrs. V. clapp'd her down in a Chair, by wch she concluded her not willing, & so forbore.

> and went to salute her, but she rushed by her, and sat herself down in a great armed Chair, and fell into discourse of severall things y^t had hapned w^n they lived together at Dover.

> asked her to Come in and offerd to salute her upon which she sat herself down in a Chair Saying she was very weary.

All three make the point that Mrs. Bargrave had come very near to kissing a ghost, but Defoe obviously felt that this was such a dramatic moment that it deserved to be lingered over and left uncertain till the last possible moment. His account therefore varies significantly from the others.

> Madam, says Mrs. Bargrave, I am surprized to see you, you have been so long a stranger, but told her, she was glad to see her and offer'd to Salute her, which Mrs. Veal complyed with, till their Lips almost touched, and then Mrs. Veal drew her hand cross her own Eyes, and said, *I am not very well*, and so waved it.

The second occasion concerns Mrs. Bargrave's offer of a cup of tea to Mrs. Veal. The first three versions are more or less together on this episode, although the third introduces some new material:

> And in their discourse Mrs. B. ask'd her to drink some Chocolate, & whether She would Eat something? Mrs. V. said if She talk'd of eating or drinking She would be gone.

> Mrs. B. askt Mrs. Veal if she would drink any Coffee or Tea,
> she told her y^t if she talkt of eating or drinking she would be
> gone.

> Mrs. B. then asked Mrs. V. if she would Drink any tea to which
> she Replied now [qy. noe (?)] but if I Would you have no fire to
> make it to which she replied that she wold sone have her fire nay
> said Mrs. Veal if you talk of drinking I am gon.

Defoe's treatment of the incident comes nearest to the last of those three
statements, but again there is a significant difference:

> Mrs. Bargrave asked her, whether she would not drink some Tea.
> Says Mrs. Veal, *I do not care if I do: But I'le Warrant this Mad
> Fellow* (meaning Mrs. Bargrave's Husband) *has broke all your
> Trinckets.* But, says Mrs. Bargrave, *I'le get something to Drink in
> for all that*; but Mrs. Veal wav'd it, and said, *it is no matter, let it
> alone*, and so it passed.

Mrs. Veal's "I do not care if I do" is of course affirmative; its modern
equivalent, "I don't mind if I do," is the standard reply in an English pub
to the offer of a drink. Defoe's Mrs. Bargrave has again been brought to the
verge of discovering that her apparently material visitor is in fact immaterial
(ghosts don't drink tea), and again the discovery is avoided at the last moment
because Mrs. Veal changed her mind and "wav'd it." One or two other small
touches of the same kind might be noted; but for the most part Defoe seems
bent on establishing the absolute truth of the story by dwelling on trivialities
and recording conversations verbatim, with all their irrelevant and insignif-
icant detail. It is (let us face it) a wasteful method of convincing a reader,
but it works; and it was the method that Defoe was to employ again and
again in his works of fiction. For the purpose to which he put it, the insig-
nificant becomes significant, and the irrelevant takes on relevance because it
is helping to authenticate the fictitious and make it pass for truth. It would
be easy to exaggerate the influence of the *True Relation* on the development
of Defoe's fiction; it was only another small piece knocked off in the course
of a phenomenally busy life. Yet, as Defoe saw it, the problem presented
by Mrs. Bargrave and her ghostly visitor and that presented by Robinson
Crusoe on his desert island must have seemed much the same: it was the
problem of how to give complete credibility to the basically incredible; how
to succeed in "imposing it on the world for truth."

Defoe is a good deal more interested in human character and human
behaviour than he is usually credited with being, and in short episodes he

has often the power to make us enter into a situation and share the feelings of his characters. But what ultimately interests him is the individual human being coping with circumstances, adjusting himself to changes of environment or fortune, striving in one fashion or another to make a living—*gagner sa vie*. His preoccupation with the problems of earning a living is not an indication of some sordid economic bias in his mind; it is the expression of a serious concern with something which he believed to be fundamental, and which gives shape and significance to most human lives. If his characters are often criminal types, they only serve the better to let him explore the problem which seems to have interested him above all others—that of *necessity*; the will to survive that comes into collision with economic facts, that natural morality which is often in conflict with law and order. As he once put it, in one of his many pronouncements on necessity, "Men rob for Bread, Women whore for Bread: Necessity is the parent of Crime." With such considerations uppermost in his mind, the autobiographical form was the one best suited to his purpose. "Who would read a novel if we were permitted to write biography—all out?" The man who asked that question was not Defoe, but H. G. Wells [in his *Experiment in Autobiography*]: the two writers have much in common. Both wrote voluminously, both were teeming with new ideas, both had interests that overflowed the bounds of the conventional novel, and both wrote rapidly and at times carelessly. "Indisputably the writing is scamped in places," Wells admitted in a discussion of his novel *Marriage*. "It could have been just as light and much better done. But that would have taken more time than I could afford . . . The fastidious critic might object, but the general reader to whom I addressed myself cared no more for finish and fundamental veracity about the secondary things of behaviour than I." These words, *mutatis mutandis*, might have come from the pen of Defoe. Again, when Wells says that what he was insisting upon in his novels was "the importance of individuality and individual adjustment to life," he might be Defoe writing of *Robinson Crusoe* or *Moll Flanders*. When, finally, he tells us: "I was disposed to regard a novel as about as much an art form as a market place or a boulevard. It had not even necessarily to get anywhere. You went by it on your various occasions," we recognize a conception of the novel that may not at present be fashionable, but that runs through much of English fiction from the time of Defoe to the present day. In such fiction what we read, and enjoy, is as much the author as the work. Those who wish to sneer at H. G. Wells may also sneer at Defoe. But should they?

MANUEL SCHONHORN

Defoe's Journal of the Plague Year: *Topography and Intention*

Until very recently Daniel Defoe's *Journal of the Plague Year* received little commendable scholarly attention. Critics felt disposed to argue single-mindedly either the *Journal*'s absolute faithfulness to the historical record or its inventiveness; and in so doing concluded by minimizing its artistry or its reliability. Mr. Frank Bastian, in his reconsideration of the work [in *The Review of English Studies* 14, 151–73], has rectified the generalizations about the book's historical worth and the picture of Defoe as an unreliable recorder of the plague year. He has dismissed the possibility that "a large part of Defoe's information was actually derived from some diary, or manuscript observations, communicated to him by a member of his very family" (Brayley, *Defoe's Journal of the Plague Year*, London, 1835); he has shown that the *Journal*'s facts, "when they can be tested, prove to be neither recklessly invented, nor simply borrowed from previously published works"; and he has revealed the historical reality of the characters appearing in the *Journal*. The full extent of Defoe's indebtedness, of course, can never be completely known. The plague, as a catastrophic event reshaping the lives of the society and recurring with deadly frequency, came down to Defoe's time with a body of anecdotal appendages and carried within itself the seeds of a mythology.

All previous examinations of Defoe's *Journal* have been either historical or biographical, or both; the examination which follows is topographical. In addition, I should like to present some considerations about Defoe's handling

From *The Review of English Studies* 19, no. 76 (November 1968). © 1968 by Oxford University Press.

of details which he found in his sources, and which have only been alluded
to in passing by his commentators. His modifications of his sources, and the
implications of his tonal variations, have never been fully understood.

I

The peculiar and historical nature of the topographical problem which
faced Defoe in his reconstruction of the plague year of 1665 should be clearer
once the reader considers the structure and composition of the *Journal*. Supposedly the author is one H. F., a saddler, now buried in Moorfields, and
the journal is said to be based on his "memorandums" of his experiences
during the plague, written down as they occurred, and later assembled into
a coherent narrative. Writing in 1721, then, primarily to take advantage of
the public interest in and apprehension arising from the Marseilles epidemic
of the previous year—still, as Defoe's own periodical journalism reveals, a
source of anxiety for Londoners—Defoe, projecting himself imaginatively
into the plague scene, had to do more than simply reconstruct the London
of nearly fifty years before; he had to recreate a London consumed by the
Great Fire of 1666, which had swept away much of the area affected by the
plague. Of the 448 acres within the walls of the ancient city,

> the Buildings on 373 Acres were utterly consumed, by that late
> dreadful Conflagration; also 63 Acres without the Walls, in all
> 436 Acres, 89 Parish-Churches, and 13200 Houses, besides that
> vast Cathedral of St. *Paul*'s, and divers Chappels, Halls, Colleges,
> Schools, and other public Edefices, whereof the whole Damage
> is hardly to be computed or credited.
> (E. Chamberlayne, *Angliae Notitia; or, The Present State
> of England*)

While there were prefire inns and alleys, edifices and landmarks standing in
1721, Jacobean London had virtually disappeared. In addition, its disappearance had been accelerated by a mass of minor changes which were
ordered and carried through by the many royal and civic commissions and
committees set up for the rebuilding of London after the fire. Perhaps I
should not overestimate the problem facing Defoe, as he distinguished for
his readers the older, plague-ridden London from the eighteenth-century
city. Major changes were rare; razed streets were widened, or straightened,
not obliterated. But "although no comprehensive scheme of improvement
was carried out at the time, and the streets were rebuilt for the most part
on their old sites, yet they *were* rebuilt as *streets*, with some definite line of

frontage, and not as footways to and from individual houses" (H. A. Harben, *A Dictionary of London*, London, 1918). While it would be fair to say that London had been restored, rather than replanned, there were, as a modern historian of the city concludes, striking changes. "The new city, if not unrecognizable, was very different from the old" (T. R. Reddaway, *The Rebuilding of London after the Great Fire*, London, 1940).

Defoe's object was, as Mr. Bastian has stated, "to pass off the *Journal* at its face value as a genuine record of the plague, able to stand the scrutiny of those who could themselves recall those days. It was his interest as well as his inclination to deal almost exclusively in facts." Defoe himself was aware, as his text reveals, of the verification or refutation which could greet his historical fiction. H. F., remarking about the numbers buried at the Great Pit at Aldgate and its location, admits that "there may be some ancient persons alive in the parish who can justify the fact of this, and are able to show even in what place of the churchyard the pit lay better than I can." Obviously there were others who were also able to verify the facts of the topographical references to pre-Fire London. To indulge thoughtlessly in anachronisms could easily lead to the same kind of suspicions which Defoe himself had directed at a contemporary physician in his tract published five weeks earlier than the *Journal*, the hastily compiled *Due Preparations for the Plague, as Well for Soul as Body*. In that plague piece Defoe noted, "it is strange this gentleman should take upon him to write that which so many people now alive can contradict." For reasons, then, or verisimilitude and for acceptability by a suspicious reading public, Defoe had to take into account the changes which had occurred since the plague year of 1665. Parish boundaries had been revised, theatres rebuilt, and churches destroyed; some temporary names applied descriptively had gone out of fashion, and others had come into use. It is thus too simple to argue that, "with a London map before him, together with his accurate acquaintance of the town, Defoe should have had little trouble in evolving his history" (Nicholson, *The Historical Sources of Defoe's Journal of the Plague Year*, Boston, 1919). At every stage in the description of the plague scene, as Defoe traced the steps of his seventeenth-century saddler, there was possibility for error. A comparable situation would be for a writer today to venture a concocted autobiography of a young American growing up in a New York City neighbourhood during the 1930s. The neighbourhood scene by the writer in the present would not bear the slightest resemblance to that of the bygone period. Gone would be the narrow but empty streets and the corner shops of an earlier time. The dark alleys and the private backyards and the brownstone houses which would have been the protagonist's terrain have given way to thoroughfares, enclosed playgrounds, and the high-rise project developments of the postwar period. To dwell on the latter would be to make a fantasy of what purported to be realistic fiction. A contemporary map in this situation would do little more than record the street locations of that earlier period. All the landmarks which give the sense of the scene would have been obliterated, and well-nigh unrecoverable.

The manner in which Defoe spoke from the genuine past while establishing his "presentness" to his contemporary reader should reduce—it cannot completely dismiss—superficial comments about his carelessness. On the simplest level, the eighteenth-century reader is given the sense of the past by the spaced sprinklings of "thens" and "nows" as the older London is recalled for him by a man who had "lived to see a further increase, and mighty throngs of people settling in London more than ever." Again, more than a dozen times, Defoe's narrator, by his arguments for civic reform and better plague-control, deduced from lessons of the past in language appropriate to the present, shows his public concern and narrows the gap between his time and the reader's. More importantly, the supposed author of the *Journal* is fully aware of the physical changes which have occurred in London between the time of his "original" memorandums and his later ordering of them for his published narrative. I have examined almost ninety topographical references in the *Journal of the Plague Year* to structures such as churches, inns and taverns, hospitals, monuments, pesthouses, prisons, markets, and docks; to streets, lanes, alleys, and courts; and also to a scattering of loosely defined topographical locations. In nearly every instance I have found that Defoe has concentrated upon landmarks and conspicuous objects of the London scene of 1665, all therefore chronologically relevant to the *Plague Year*; at the same time, these locations and structures were still part of the London scene of 1720. In only seven instances which I have been unable to pinpoint with comfortable accuracy does there remain the possibility for error.

Three of these streets, which cannot be definitely proved to have been in existence in 1665—Butcher Row, Harrow Alley, and Moses and Aaron Alley—are located in the parish of St. Botolph, Aldgate, the parish not only of Defoe's fictitious narrator in the *Journal* but also of Henry Foe, Defoe's uncle. Here it is quite likely that Defoe is recollecting scenes of early childhood visits or repeating what he perhaps heard from his uncle, thus reducing the possibility of error. In fact, if Defoe's topographical entries are plotted on a London map, it will be found that, while he touches the periphery of London at every point, from a mention of Stillyard on the south to Newgate on the west and Moorfields on the north and reaching to Aldgate parish on the east, the largest number of references are concentrated in two localities.

The first is H. F.'s parish of St. Botolph, Aldgate. This would support that argument that a good deal of Defoe's anecdotal detail, not available in the published sources, must have been transmitted to him orally by his uncle, who was still alive in Defoe's fifteenth year. Defoe was also fortunate in the fact that Aldgate parish, home of the relative upon whom he imaginatively fathered the *Journal*, was one of the eastern areas untouched by the Fire, and thus remained with its topography unviolated. The second area of concentration is the parish of St. Stephen, Coleman Street. In this area was located the warehouse of H. F.'s brother, to which the *Journal* narrator went and near which some lengthy actions of the *Journal* take place. In this area Defoe mentions a dozen or so alleys and courts, some of which came into existence at some time subsequent to the plague, a fact which he always calls to his reader's attention. Now Mr. Bastian has discovered that Defoe's merchant father was living in the parish as early as 1667; the house and warehouse described in the *Journal* anecdote are thus the house which was Defoe's home for part of his boyhood, and Defoe is thus remembering alleys and courts, then unnamed perhaps, which he trod as a child.

By sensibly restricting his topographical particulars to the northern and eastern outskirts of London, to those parts without the old walls which had escaped the fire, and within the city to sections he knew from boyhood experiences, Defoe was obviously reducing the chances for error. For example, of the six inns and taverns mentioned by name in the *Journal*, five— the Angel, Pye, Pied Bull, Three Nuns, and White Horse—are outside the walls of the burnt city, and the sixth—the Bull Head—was at Gracechurch and Leadenhall, at the eastern edge of the Fire line and untouched. While Defoe was careful about topographical anachronisms, he was also deliberate in restricting his remarks to those edifices which still existed in 1720. For example, he notes a half-dozen of London's churches. While all antedate the fire, all remained standing into the eighteenth century, untouched or restored. Thus, the *Journal* is like so many others of Defoe's reconstructed historical works not derived from abundant contemporary documents. There is no true fidelity to the past in the volume, no reminder here of the thirty-three churches destroyed in the Great Fire and never rebuilt, nor of the ancient city of Elizabeth's with its narrow streets and overhanging alleys. Nevertheless, Defoe's historical consciousness helps to support the most modern claim that the "*Journal* thus stands closer to our idea of history than that of fiction" (Bastian). Defoe's conventional but in this case unusually complex impersonation has not been distorted by topographical inaccuracies which could have seriously damaged the *Journal*'s authenticity and its reception in its age.

II

Led astray by their preoccupation with the factual or fictional aspect of the *Journal*, all of the critics in their study of the sources of Defoe's volume have minimized the nature of Defoe's modifications of those sources. Even Watson Nicholson, who had sensibly noted Defoe's variations and divergences from the earlier accounts, concluded that "Defoe transcribed the facts without alteration and equivocation." Nicholson's contention is not exactly correct. For what is clearly evident to one examining those facts and Defoe's transcription from them is that in every instance in which Defoe parts company from them, he is found tempering the harsh extremes of human nature, apologizing for the graceless actions of panicky civilians and flattering the response of the authorities as they attempted to relieve the population. Dr. Nathaniel Hodges in his examination of the pathology of the plague, *Loimologia* (1720), which became one of Defoe's principal sources, remarked on the deep-seated malignity of the infected who deliberately carried the disease to the innocent and the healthy. Defoe picks up this point, often remarking about the great debates among the physicians, "namely that there was a seeming propensity or a wicked inclination in those that were infected to infect others," "that they did not take the least care, or make any scruple of infecting others." At first Defoe can only say that "there might be some truth in it too, but not so general as was reported." But immediately after he makes a disclaimer:

> What natural reason could be given for so wicked a thing at a
> time when they might conclude themselves just going to appear
> at the bar of Divine Justice I know not. I am very well satisfied
> it cannot be reconciled to religion and principle any more than
> it can be to generosity and humanity; but I may speak of that
> again.

And when he does, in every case he is defending the integrity of the distraught people. The reports are really false, for the infected people ran from one place to another "in their desperation." Their carelessness derived from fear, for,

> having been driven to extremities for provision or for entertain-
> ment, they had endeavoured to conceal their condition, and have
> been thereby instrumental involuntarily to infect others who have
> been ignorant and unwary.

Further on, in his more extended discussion of the problem, Defoe completely rejects any argument favouring malignity in the nature of man or accounting it a "corruption of human nature." He chooses to give the debate a different turn,

> and answer it or resolve it all by saying that I do not grant the fact. On the contrary, I say that the thing is not really so, but that it was a general complaint raised by the people inhabiting the outlying villages against the citizens to justify, or at least excuse, those hardships and severities so much talked of.

Defoe concentrates always on the ignorance of those who propagated the disease being utterly unmindful of their own condition; and the *Journal* includes a number of cases of those who, rather than carelessly disseminating the disease to those around them, "showed the contrary to an extreme," and voluntarily withdrew to their deaths, rather than infect others.

Concerning the inhuman behaviour of those who looked after the dying people, the sources are in complete agreement. The nurses in particular are singled out for the harshest abuse. While the rich were able to flee, Thomas Vincent tells us, the poor through their poverty were forced to stay behind, infected, shut up in their houses, "and none suffered to come in but a nurse, whom they have been more afraid of, then the Plague itself" (*God's Terrible Voice in the City*, London, 1667). Dr. Hodges can only speak of them "in the most bitter terms." Defoe, true to his sources, has to repeat the reports of smotherings, robberies, and murders, but his judgements are significant and extensive:

> I must say I believe nothing of its being so common a crime as some have since been pleased to say, nor did it seem to be so rational where the people were brought so low as not to be able to help themselves, for such seldom recovered, and there was no temptation to commit a murder, at least none equal to the fact, where they were sure persons would die in so short a time, and could not live. . . . But these stories had two marks of suspicion that always attended them, which caused me to always slight them, and to look on them as mere stories, that people continually frighted one another with. First, that wherever it was that we heard it, they always placed the scene at the farther end of the town, opposite or most remote from where you were to hear it.
>
> In the next place, of what part soever you heard the story, the particulars were always the same, . . . so that it was apparent, at least to my judgment, that there was more of tale than of truth in those things.

The scandal told of the buriers, that they stripped the corpses and carried them naked to the burial mounds, Defoe is also unable to accept, and can only leave the charge undetermined, "as I cannot easily credit anything so vile among Christians." This refusal to condemn, this tempering of any adverse judgement of the populace and authorities, is the most characteristic quality of the *Journal*. In almost every case the participants are exonerated from any charge of cruel behaviour or offensive conduct. If watchmen took bribes, permitting the healthy citizens who were quarantined to flee in the night and possibly infect others unknowingly, Defoe confesses them to be accessories to

> the most innocent corruption or bribery that any man could be guilty of, and therefore could not but pity the poor men, and think it was hard when three of those watchmen were publicly whipped through the streets for suffering people to go out of houses shut up.

Conversely, violence done to the watchmen by the quarantined could itself not be condemned, nor could a tolerant observer expect less. The people shut up or imprisoned were guilty of no crime, and any and all stratagems were excusable in those disordered times. Defoe implies that only those who were "injurious and abusive" were murdered:

> and consequently, if they brought mischief upon themselves by such an undue behaviour, that mischief was upon their own heads; and indeed they had so much the hearty curses of the people, whether they deserved it or not, that whatever befell them nobody pitied them, and everybody was apt to say they deserved it, whatever it was.

Even the parish officers who gave such undependable accounts of the progress of the plague in their weekly bills of mortality, faking the statistics to misrepresent the strength of the infection, are blameless: "let any one but consider how men could be exact in such a time of dreadful distress, and when many of them were taken sick themselves, and perhaps died in the very time when their accounts were to be given in." The country folk, so severely rebuked by all of Defoe's predecessors, are downrightly defended. One village's refusal to permit a poor citizen to set up in an empty house brings no censure from Defoe. He admits the hardship of the case. "But there was no remedy; self-preservation obliged the people to those severities, which they would not otherwise have been concerned in." And then he continues in a more apologetic vein:

I know that the inhabitants of the towns adjacent to London were much blamed for cruelty to the poor people that ran from the contagion in their distress, and many very severe things were done, as may be seen from what has been said: but I cannot but say also that, where there was room for charity and assistance to the people, without apparent danger to themselves, they were willing enough to help and relieve them.

Defoe's sustained and temperate commentary on all of the unpleasant aspects of the plague scene is well calculated to allay the latent and potential panic and hysteria of the population should another epidemic strike, as was the case in 1721. But perhaps something more can be said about Defoe's deliberate emphases and his modification of his source material which give the *Journal* its most distinctive tone. If one accepts Defoe's latest biographer's general contention, that the *Journal* was "intended partly as propaganda to support the administration of Sir Robert Walpole" (Moore, *A Checklist of the Writings of Daniel Defoe*, Bloomington, 1960), that is, as something more than a simple and narrowly conceived defence of the quarantine measures instituted by the government the previous summer of 1721, one's admiration for Defoe's achievement increases enormously. For while composing an historical fiction which more and more we are compelled to class as a reliable document of the time, Defoe at the same time has so carefully manipulated his tone that the *Journal* stands as a quiet yet authentic testimony of a city's victory in the face of a disaster of frightful proportions. Throughout the experience Defoe's London has triumphantly asserted its illustrious qualities.

In his speech that autumn of 1721, at the opening of the new session of Parliament, the King had asked for a renewal of England's past glory, to be built now by "extending our commerce upon which the riches and grandeur of this nation chiefly depend." It was a "positive and creative policy, a clarion call to London and the principal merchants" to redirect their private interests for the public good (J. H. Plumb, *Sir Robert Walpole: The Making of a Statesman*, London, 1956). I would like to suggest that it is possible to conceive of the *Journal of the Plague Year* as an article of persuasion which abets that policy. As a writer for *Applebee's Journal* during the summer of 1721, Defoe had been able to incorporate in the midst of the terrifying plague news he was reporting from the Continent a lengthy essay of primary economic interest: *Essay to Revive Trade and Credit*. While such a blatant and uncalled for commercial approach would have been unthinkable in the *Journal*, Defoe was still able to present a subtle reminder to Londoners of the inherent decency possible even in times of the greatest stress. While giving life to fleshless statistics and recording with uncompromising detachment the devastation of Restoration London, Defoe has yet written a song of praise to an older England which could not have gone unnoticed by his eighteenth-century readers. The plague history which Defoe's contemporaries read early in 1722 contained a programme for civic reform "in case the like public desolation should happen" again, indicating in the clearest way imaginable the safety and strength which lie in rightly channelled energies. Defoe's plague journal is a reminder of the prodigious charity and benevolence of the London citizenry in the past. And above all it is a clearly stated plea for sanity and tolerance in religious matters. For one memorable time those breaches of charity and Christian union were overcome. Spiritual differences were reconciled and barriers to religious peace removed. The extraordinary zeal of the people obliterated distinctions and fostered for a moment the union of all men of good will. Defoe recurs again and again to religious themes—as of course we would expect him to—but what is clearly obvious is the scrupulous impartiality with which he relates both church history and the churches' history during plague time. There is no rebuke for those churchmen who fled, making no provision for their sick and poor left behind. There is no wrathful condemnation over the lack of Christian benevolence. No profession is accused of wilful neglect; no sect is reviled for deserting its flock.

Near the end of his volume Defoe repeats an abusive paragraph from Vincent's somewhat haughty jeremiad, indicative of the raw comments made upon those ministers who had fled the city. The people wrote verses and composed scandalous reflections on the fleeing ministers, Vincent notes, and frequently pamphlets were flung about the streets, "*of Pulpits to be let. . . .*" Defoe elaborates this in the *Journal* into a pointed though moderate attack on the government's harassment of the Dissenters after the plague and of the Dissenters' disdainful reproach of those ministers of the Anglican faith who had deserted their pulpits, and concludes with a sympathetic statement of the frailty of human nature and a tribute to the many of all professions and employments who did endanger their lives for the safety of the commonweal:

> Upon all these accounts, I say, I could wish, when we were recovered, our conduct had been more distinguished for charity and kindness in remembrance of the past calamity, and not so much a valuing ourselves upon our boldness in staying, as if all men were cowards that fly from the hand of God, or that those who stay do not sometimes owe their courage to their ignorance

and despising the hand of their Maker, which is a criminal kind
of desperation, and not a true courage.

We are always aware of the steady, moderate, and tolerant mind behind
the journalistic presentation. Always thoughtful, decently emotional, Defoe,
with his temperate and judicious reconstruction of the past, forces the present-day reader to consider those elements of the *Journal* which account for
its endurance. Part of the volume's greatness would seem to lie precisely in
this tone of reason and judgement and its artful incorporation with the
accurate historical scene, which together have presented posterity with a
journal which is something more than a transcription of reality and an anecdotal account of an epidemic. Given its redirections of emphasis and the
historical circumstances of 1721, Defoe's volume can be read as a quiet tribute
to England's capital city, a low-keyed record of the vitality of a great people
under the most insufferable hardship they had known in modern times.
Everything has been seen in the best possible light. The plague may be the
angry voice of God, but it has not materially damaged the energy and fibre
of the people. While making full use of the expected horror of the situation,
Defoe in his recitation has inculcated a feeling of pride without in any major
manner distorting the situation's historical truth.

HOMER O. BROWN

The Displaced Self in the Novels of Daniel Defoe

I. NAMES

"A fine Story! says the Governess, you would see the Child, and you would not see the Child; you would be conceal'd and discover'd both together."
—*Moll Flanders*

Names, false names, absence of names seem to have special importance for Daniel Defoe's novels. None of his fictional narrators, with the exception of Robinson Crusoe, tell their stories under the name he or she was born with. The narrator of *A Journal of the Plague Year* is anonymous, signing his account at the end with the initials H. F. In the other novels, the narrators receive their names in something like a special christening. Bob Singleton is given his name by one of the series of "mothers" through whose hands he passes after being kidnapped from his true parents. Colonel Jack receives the name John from the nurse who is paid to take him by his real parents, who are unmarried "people of quality." Unfortunately, all three of the nurse's sons, one of them really hers and the other two paid for, are named John.

Moll Flanders's real name is too "well known in the records, or registers, at Newgate and in the Old Bailey," so she chooses to write under the alias "Moll Flanders" and begs the reader's patience "till I dare own who I have been, as well as who I am." It is by the revelation of this true name (to Moll but not the reader) that Moll recognizes her real mother, who had also adopted

From *ELH* 38, no. 4 (December 1971). © 1971 by the Johns Hopkins University Press.

an alias, and discovers that she has married her own brother. Moll Flanders is the name she takes during her time as a thief in London, when, though already a middle-aged woman, she falls under the tutelage of a woman who refers to her as "child" and whom Moll calls "mother." The title page of *Roxanna* is a veritable catalog of her aliases throughout her career. Curiously, the name Roxana is the name she bears for the shortest time and one she did not give herself. She received it, in the presence of the king, from the spontaneous cry of a group of men at a masked ball in appreciation of the costume she was wearing. But Roxana is a special case, for the reader does learn at least her true Christian name because it is also the name of her daughter, who pursues her through the last part of the book.

At the moment of narration few of Defoe's narrators are living under the name by which they "sign" their stories. Secrecy seems to be an absolute precondition of self-revelation. Or, to put it in a less perversely contradictory way, these narrators seem under a double compulsion to expose and to conceal themselves. Certainly it is a literary convention, a premise of fictional narration, aimed at convincing the reader of their veracity, since Defoe published all these books as the "real" memoirs of their narrators. But it is a curious convention, since it goes beyond a mere premise of narration and becomes an important theme in the narration, an event in the story itself.

Moreover, literary convention cannot explain this practice of conceal-ment in the life of the true author of these fake memoirs, Daniel Defoe, which was not, incidentally, his real name. Before and even after he took up the writing of these books at the age of sixty, Daniel *Foe* served as the agent of various interests, parties, governments, writing and acting under innumerable assumed names and points of view, to the extent that it is difficult to separate fact from fiction in our knowledge of his own life and impossible to go beyond certain limits in ascertaining what he actually wrote.

Robinson Crusoe is a somewhat special instance of Defoe's habit of con-cealing the true name of his narrators. Robinson has purportedly related the events of his own life under his own name through two volumes—*he* at least has committed no crime and requires no secrecy. In the preface to the third volume, however, Robinson hints that if the events he has narrated are not strictly true they are allegorically true and that perhaps Robinson Crusoe is not his real name. Many readers have taken this hint to mean that Defoe had written his own spiritual autobiography under the metaphor of the shipwrecked and isolated Crusoe. The question has never been decided. The double project of revelation and concealment of this least sophisticated of novelists was successful. The "real" Daniel Defoe has disappeared into the absence of an irrecoverable time.

We can only probe for the meaning of the double compulsion in the written world of his novel and perhaps ponder the relationship of that compulsion to the project of writing lies that look like truth. Our hopes are limited: if on the one hand we are reduced to a search for the meaning of the name he withheld from us, we know that in the end we will have to content ourselves with no more than the name alone.

What will we find to explain this curious game of names? In a sense it cannot be completely explained or understood because the only real evidence lies in the books themselves and also because, since it is a literary convention, we are touching upon a cultural symptom as well as a personal one and all such symptoms are overdetermined. Two provisional explanations, however, will emerge from an examination of Defoe's fiction. One has to do with a strong fear of the menace of other wills, a pervasive fear in these novels. Another explanation has to do with the way the self becomes somebody else in conversion. In this discussion I will place special weight on *Robinson Crusoe*, for while it provides less mystery about names than the other novels, it offers itself as a kind of myth to explain the fear of exposure, detailing the consequent strategies of the self. In order to discuss this impulse at the source of Defoe's fiction, I will have to defer consideration of the intense fascination with the factual, the most pervasive and already much discussed characteristic of Defoe's writing—defer it, I would hope, only to recover it in a new light.

These provisional explanations might help also to illuminate what is involved in the constitution of imaginary novelistic characters.

II. THE MYTH OF SINGLENESS

In my youth, I wandered away, too far from your sustaining hand, and created of myself a barren waste.
> —AUGUSTINE, *Confessions*

Defoe's novels are based on a notion of radical egocentricity. Robinson wonders why his isolation on the island was "any grievance or affliction" since "it seems to me that life in general is, or ought to be, but one universal act of solitude":

> The world, I say, is nothing to us but as it is more or less to our relish. All reflection is carried home, and our dear self is, in one respect, the end of living. Hence man may be properly said to be alone in the midst of the crowds and hurry of men and business.

All the reflections which he makes are to himself; all that is
pleasant he embraces for himself; all that is irksome and grievous
is tasted but by his own palate.

What are the sorrows of other men to us, and what their joy?
Something we may be touched indeed with by the power of
sympathy, and a secret turn of the affections; but all the solid
reflection is directed to ourselves. Our meditations are all solitude
in perfection; our passions are all exercised in retirement; we love,
we hate, we covet, we enjoy, all in privacy and solitude. All that
we communicate of those things to any other is but for their
assistance in the pursuit of our desires; the end is at home; the
enjoyment, the contemplation, is all solitude and retirement; it
is for ourselves we enjoy, and for ourselves we suffer.

(*Serious Reflections*)

Robinson's thirty years of solitude on a desert island is the metaphor of this
selfishness. In fact, his story is based on the etymological metaphor
"islanded"—isolated. When Robinson was in Brazil, he "used to say, I lived
just like a man cast away upon some desolate island that had nobody there
but himself." The whole book has to do with the progressive materialization
of spiritual metaphors for what is implicit in Robinson's condition from the
beginning, in the same way that the book itself is a factualization of the
metaphors of the whole tradition of spiritual autobiographies.

Selfish, isolated, but is he really alone? Other Defoe narrators are just
as solitary in the midst of society. Robinson's island isolation is after all only
a metaphor for the solitary selfishness of all men. This seemingly impenetrable selfishness, however, is a Hobbesian "state of nature," transposed into
a social world, atomistic, volatile, where the mere existence of another person, for Robinson even the *possibility* of the existence of another person, is
a threat to the self. Even Robinson in his wilderness, through all those years
of never encountering another human being, is constantly haunted by a sense
of menacing otherness. He must always be on guard. He never loses the
agonizing sense of being watched. Far from only being a representation of
Robinson's egocentric isolation, the book is peopled by *signs* of the constant
presence of the other—Robinson's fear, the footprint of a man, the hand of
God, the constant presence of the older Robinson in the double perspective
of the narration, the presence of the spectator-reader before whom Robinson
rehearses his solitude. In a sense, no Defoe character, not even Robinson,
is ever alone.

The need for secrecy at the moment of narration for most of Defoe's "autobiographers" is no mystery. With the exception of Robinson and H. F., they have committed crimes for which they can be called to justice. Near the beginnings of their stories, however, they also are all bereft of family and protection and are thrown into a harsh and dangerous world of deceptive appearances, whose inhabitants are indifferent, conniving, menacing. Some, like Robinson or H. F., orphan themselves seemingly by choice. Others, like Colonel Jack and Bob Singleton, are virtually cut off from their origins, and so, from their true names. Roxana, even as a young girl, long before she is deserted by her husband and left to protect herself and her family, is removed from France and her childhood, bringing with her nothing, "but the Language." The separation from any guardian structure is sharp. Their isolation is complete.

No wonder, then, that Defoe has been said to have discounted the importance of personal relationships in his novels. There is no richly complex conflict between wills more or less equal in strength in his fictional world. The Defoe character has to struggle against all the others, against a harsh necessity. There is no sense of an individualized other consciousness confronting the protagonist as there is in Richardson's world or Austen's or George Eliot's. The paradigm is Moll in a crowded London street; her survival depends on her ability to take "the advantages of other people's mistakes" while remaining unseen herself. The value of her story for the reader will be in its warning "to Guard against the like Surprizes, and to have their Eyes about them when they have to do with Strangers of any kind, for 'tis very seldom that some Snare or other is not in their way." Otherness for a Defoe character is generic, anonymous. Individual antagonists like Roxana's landlord, or even her Amy, Moll's various men, Robinson's Moorish captor or Friday can be tricked or subordinated without much apparent difficulty, but a single, anonymous footprint in the sand seizes Crusoe's mind with uncontrollable terror. However easily any Defoe "I" can deal with any individual menace, the unnamed dread remains. Perhaps the most striking example is the London of the plague. The "others" of the *Journal* are anonymous numbers of dead and dying. Any conversation, even the slightest human contact, carries the risk of death.

When Robinson finds himself shipwrecked, almost his first act is to begin to build a wall around himself. He further insulates himself; he creates an island within the island. His action is obsessive. He spends almost three and a half months building the wall—"I thought I should never be perfectly secure 'till this Wall was finish'd." Although he longs for deliverance from his solitude, he is compelled to hide his presence so "that if any People were to come on Shore there, they would not perceive any Thing like a Habitation." So, in the midst of a threatening and unknown space, Robinson creates for himself an ordered interior, crowded with things which can be listed and enumerated to his satisfaction. He "furnishes" himself with many things," as a chapter title phrases it. Like the fallen angels, Robinson sets about to build and secure his own Pandemonium, following the advice of Mammon to "seek / Our own good from ourselves, and from our own / Live to ourselves, though in this vast recess, / Free, and to none accountable" (*Paradise Lost* 2.252–55). But, of course, their self-reliance is a sham, their Pandemonium is a parody of Heaven, founded upon denial of the divine Other, whose power they can never escape. Like the angels, Robinson's concern with things is a symptom of his fall. Robinson's brave statement, "I build my fortress," echoes ironically Luther's famous hymn based on the Ninety-first Psalm.

Moll Flanders in disguise in the middle of a crowded London street, H. F. in his "safe" house surrounded by the plague, Robinson in his fort— the image is a recurrent one. Earlier in Robinson's account, in Brazil he carves out a plantation "among Strangers and Savages in a Wilderness, and at such a Distance, as never to hear from any Part of the World that had the least Knowledge of me." Still earlier, there is Robinson quavering in the hold of the ship that takes him from home, surrounded by a raging sea.

At the beginning of the book Robinson's father points out to him that his "was the middle State, or what might be called the upper Station of *Low Life*, . . . that this was the State of Life which all other People envied" because

> the middle Station had the fewest Disasters, and was not expos'd
> to so many Vicissitudes as the higher or lower Part of Mankind
> . . . that this Way Men went silently and smoothly thro' the
> World, and comfortably out of it, not embarrass'd with the La-
> bours of the Hands or of the Head, not sold to the Life of Slavery
> for daily Bread, or harasst with perplex'd Circumstances, which
> rob the Soul of Peace and the Body of Rest; not enrag'd with the
> Passion of Envy, or secret burning Lust of Ambition for great
> things; but in easy Circumstances sliding gently thro' the World,
> and sensibly tasting the Sweets of living, without the bitter,
> feeling that they are happy, and learning by every Day's Expe-
> rience to know it more sensibly.

Then, at the outset, Robinson already possesses the kind of security, freedom from exposure, that most other Defoe narrators and later even Robinson himself long for. What is given to Robinson is suddenly taken from other Defoe protagonists by circumstances over which they have no control. Moll Flanders and even H. F. must expose themselves to danger in order to survive. Why does Robinson give up so easily what the others have to struggle so hard to gain? In a sense, this is the same question implicit in the beginning of this essay: expressing so strong a desire for concealment, why do they offer their confessions at all? This is as difficult a question as asking why Defoe wrote novels. The desire for concealment could have been easily satisfied by silence, by writing or publishing no books at all. The obvious answer to so manifestly impossible a question—that Defoe wrote books to make money, that is to say, like Moll or H. F., to survive—is less satisfactory than it might at first appear. There were other ways to make money, many of which Defoe tried. Much of the other writing Defoe did involved the need for secrecy or masking.

Defoe's narrators seem obsessed with concealing themselves, but the impulse leading them towards exposure appears equally strong. Complete concealment is impossible, perhaps not even desirable. On the one hand there is the insistence on building a faceless shelter around the self, but, on the other, a recurring compulsion to move out into the open. This double compulsion can be expressed as a double fear. When an earthquake makes him fear the security of his cave, Robinson writes that "the fear of being swallow'd up alive, made me that I never slept in quiet, and yet the Apprehensions of lying abroad without any Fence was almost equal to it." These two fears, however—fear of being swallowed up by the earth, fear of lying in the open—are the same at bottom. Why does Robinson fear sleeping without the protection of a wall? He is afraid of ravenous beasts and cannibals. If one is caught abroad with one's guard down, unconscious (sleeping), one risks loss of self. But the dangers are as great apparently if one never ventures out. Both fears are basically fears of engulfment: one, the fear of being lost in the recesses of one's own nature (the earth), fear of solipsism and anonymity; alternately, fear of being captured, "eaten" by the other. Perhaps behind both, Defoe's fear of imprisonment. Fear of forms, equally strong fears of the formless. The fear of being devoured recurs throughout Robinson's narrative. At the beginning, he is afraid of being swallowed alive by the sea. Near the end, he defends himself against the devouring wolves.

Besides fear or biological need, there are other reasons apparently for venturing abroad. Curiosity forces H. F. constantly to risk infection. Moll learns that the others betray moments of unconsciousness from which she can profit: "a Thief being a Creature that Watches the Advantages of other Peoples mistakes." Why does Robinson surrender his initial security? The reasons are intentionally vague to point to the fact that his motivation is beyond his understanding and ambiguously beyond personal choice, for the reasons are generic and at the same time subject to his accountability. His motivation or lack of justifiable motivation, involving disobedience of the father, is a restlessness of spirit which is simultaneously culpability and its own punishment. He describes the sources of his "meer wandering Inclination" as "something fatal," a "Propension of Nature," symptoms of what he shares with general man, the heritage of the fall. "Design'd" by his father "for the Law," he "would be satisfied with nothing but going to Sea," great symbol of the unformed. The opposition could not be more clear. What is most threatening is also most alluring. Throughout his life, even after his conversion, Robinson will feel the compulsion to leave behind the preformed, the already-given world of law, and face the unknown and undifferentiated, full of menace for the self and simultaneously full of promise. Unable to accept the given definition of himself, the will and legacy of his father, the world of law, Robinson experiences himself as incomplete and searches mistakenly for completion in the world outside. He does not possess himself but is scattered among a world of things. He must externalize himself in the world. He must create a self out of the formless sea of pure possibility, out of the surrounding, anonymous wilderness. The world is for him to make something of—his own.

Here is the source of his egocentricity. His feeling of loneliness in Brazil at being "at such a Distance as never to hear from any Part of the World that had the least Knowledge of me" suggests that this distance is an alienation from a part of himself held in thrall by the world outside. This alienation and his longing for companionship through his years of isolation on the "Island of Despair" and his fear of the other all testify to his continuing sense of incompleteness but also reveal the lie behind the way he has sought fulfillment.

Fear of the other, determining need for concealment; necessity, allurement of the world offering some form of completion to the self, determining the impulse to risk exposure. This is the explanation of the concealment and exposure or guarded exposure of Defoe's narrators that is revealed by the play of names. Hiding behind the disguise of Robinson and his factual-seeming narrative, Defoe is doing what Robinson does—constructing and hiding inside a "natural" fortification which cannot be perceived as a "habitation" from the outside. In a sense this is as close as we can get to an answer to the problem formulated at the beginning. Pursuit of the mystery might, however, give a fuller sense of the implications of this strategy for the development of the novel.

III. THE NECESSITY OF BECOMING OTHER

I preferred to excuse myself and blame this unknown thing which was in me but was not part of me. The truth, of course, was that it was all my own self, and my own impiety had divided me against myself.

—Confessions

After fifteen years, after his material and spiritual security has seemed complete, and his only confrontation has been hearing unexpectedly his own name pronounced by his parrot, Robinson experiences the incredible shock of seeing the "naked footprint of a man." The hidden self-other structure of the book is brought into the open. The footprint is the merest sign of the *near* presence of another human being—yet shouting significance for Robinson in the very fact of its inadequacy of signification.

It is the sheerest kind of accident, almost miraculous, as he realized, that he has seen it. Characteristically he sums up the odds: " 'twas Ten Thousand to one whether I should see it or not, and in the Sand too, which the first Surge of the Sea upon a high Wind would have defac'd entirely." A footprint in the sand—a partial signature whose power lies in its mystery and ambiguity. A sign of transience—in both the sense that it is the mark of action and also that it is temporary, contingent; it is the static trace of a human movement and a recent movement at that. But rather than being any signal to Crusoe's hopes—of company or of deliverance—in a flash the footprint destroys all his hopes and all his security.

The contradiction between Robinson's desire to externalize himself and his fear of being seen receives sharp definition:

> The first Thing I propos'd to my self, was, to throw down my Enclosure, and turn all my tame Cattle wild into the Woods, that the Enemy might not find them; and then frequent the Island in Prospect of the same, or the like Booty: Then to the simple Thing of Digging up my two Corn Fields, that they might not find such a Grain there, and still be prompted to frequent the Island; then to demolish my Bower, and Tent, that they might not see any Vestiges of Habitation, and be prompted to look farther, in order to find out the Persons inhabiting.

Seized by this terror at the possible presence of another human being, Robinson wants to remove all traces of himself from the island at the cost of destroying all that he has worked for, all that he has created of himself in things. He wants to disappear, to be invisible, to see without being seen. When he recovers his reason, he will try to accomplish this same end by more practical means. He will build a second wall, further enclosing himself; he will go out of it only rarely, when it is necessary, and then only with the greatest caution and circumspection; and he will go to great lengths to provide armed vantage points, hiding places where he can spy on intruders without himself being seen.

Before he conceives of the idea of erasing all trace of himself from the island by destroying his possessions, he imagines more reasonably such destruction by those who left the footprint:

> Then terrible Thoughts rack'd my Imagination about their having found my Boat, and that there were People here; and that if so, I should certainly have them come here again in greater Numbers, and devour me; that if it should happen so that they should not find me, yet they would find my Enclosure, destroy all my Corn, carry away all my Flock of tame Goats, and I should perish at last for meer Want.

When he considers doing the same thing to himself, it is almost as if he would be acting in place of the others, doing to himself what he most fears at their hands. At this point in his narrative, in a confused way, a dialectic between self and other begins to emerge.

At first Robinson thinks the footprint must have been made by the devil to frighten him. This idea removes the element of the contingent from the sign, gives it purpose *for* him. Curiously, his idea also mitigates the otherness of the sign. Later, when he is frightened by the dying "he-goat" in the cave, he comments "that he that was afraid to see the Devil, was not fit to live twenty Years in an Island all alone; and that I durst to believe there was nothing in this Cave that was more frightful than my self." In the *Serious Reflections*, he notes the old proverb "that every solitary person must be an angel or a devil." Here the same association is implicit, for he moves from the idea that it is the devil's footprint to the persuasion that it is a "meer Chimera of my own; and that this Foot might be the Print of my own Foot." If this is true, "I might be truly said to start at my own Shadow," but he is unable to convince himself completely of this solution. He records his terrors when he leaves his shelter as if he were seen by someone else: "But to see with what Fear I went forward, how often I look'd behind me, how I was ready every now and then to lay down my Basket, and run for my Life, it would have made any one have thought I was haunted with an evil

Conscience." Roxana also thinks of herself as being haunted by her own evil conscience when the daughter named after her reappears in her life.

All these speculations—the chimera, his own foot, his own shadow, an evil conscience, the curious ability to see himself as another would see him—amount to a confusion between the self and the other. The island, which is an extension of himself, has dark areas Robinson has never explored; he is constantly startled by versions of himself, the voice of the parrot, the dying goat. In the same way, the other holds a dimension of himself which Robinson has ignored, a reflection of himself that in his selfishness he has not recognized, and more, the other holds a part of himself in thrall, in an interdependence to which he has been blind. There is also an otherness *in* him. At this point, a brief comparison with an earlier autobiographer might be illuminating. The young Augustine was alienated from himself in his acceptance of the Manichean belief that evil was a foreign substance in the soul: "The truth, of course, was that it was all my own self, and my own impiety had divided me against myself" (*Confessions*, bk. 5, sec. 10). As a result of this blindness toward the true location of himself, he had fragmented and scattered himself among the objects of the world. Similarly, Robinson is unable to account for whatever it is in him that constantly leads him to his own misery and destruction, his "foolish inclination of wandering abroad," which leads to his scattering of self among the objects of his desire and fear.

Recognition of the nature of this otherness and its relation to himself comes gradually as he is exposed to the other in a series of very strange stages over a number of years: first, the footprint, then human bones—"all my Apprehensions were bury'd in the Thoughts of such a Pitch of inhuman, hellish Brutality, and the Horror of the Degeneracy of Humane Nature"—and then finally the sight of the cannibals themselves from a distance. He is so horrified by them that he thinks of slaughtering them, making himself God's agent of justice, but he realizes both the presumption of this notion and its dangers for himself, so he decides to hold himself hidden and apart from them. To attack the cannibals without direct provocation to himself would not only question the design of God's providence for all creatures but it would also mean that he would be matching their barbarity with his own. Such an action on his part, he realizes, would be like the cruelty shown by the Spaniards in America, "a meer Butchery, a bloody and unnatural Piece of Cruelty, unjustifiable either to God or Man; and such, as for which the very Name of a *Spaniard* is reckon'd to be frightful and terrible to all People of Humanity, or of Christian Compassion." The irony of this identification of the enemy as Spaniards and cannibals, both outside the pale of what is human, should be apparent, for Crusoe's first friends on his island, the first human subjects of his "commonwealth," are two cannibals and a Spaniard. He will not only be forced to recognize their humanity, but also will be driven to acknowledge their barbarity in himself or at least in those with whom he identifies.

For the moment, Robinson's two fears of exposure and of being devoured are now focused on this one representative of a cannibalistic nature which is ambiguously human. When another ship wrecks off his island and the entire crew is apparently lost, Robinson is given a strong sense of the possibilities in his own condition. One of his fantasies about the fate of these men is that they might have tried to make the shore in their boat but instead were carried out by the current "into the great Ocean, where there was nothing but Misery and Perishing; and that perhaps they might by this Time think of starving, and of being in a Condition to eat one another." So, there are circumstances which could turn shipwrecked sailors like Robinson into cannibals. This possibility is reinforced when he and Friday witness the treacherous cruelty of the English mutineers—"O Master!" Friday says, "*You see* English *Mans eat Prisoner as well as* Savage *Mans.*"

On the other hand, it is the humanity of Friday and later of the Spaniard that Crusoe comes to know. The discovery of Friday's loyalty and devotion causes Robinson to reflect that even on savages God has bestowed

> the same Powers, the same Reason, the same Affections, the same Sentiments of Kindness and Obligation, the same Passions and Resentments of Wrongs; the same Sense of Gratitude, Sincerity, Fidelity, and all the Capacities of doing Good, and receiving Good, that he has given to us; and that when he pleases to offer to them Occasions of exerting these, they are as ready, nay, more ready to apply them to the right Uses for which they were bestow'd, than we are.

Robinson must come to see himself in the other and the other in himself. His "social contract," the statement of his subjects' dependence on him, is his covert admission of dependence on them since it is he who insists on it. He also comes to a greater self-knowledge by seeing himself and his works reflected in their eyes. Earlier he had seen himself from the outside as another, totally unsympathetic and possibly hostile, might have seen him. Now he sees himself from the perspective of a friendly providence in the misery of the English seamen who are about to be beached by the mutineers: "This put me in Mind of the first Time I came on Shore, and began to look about me; How I gave my self over for lost; How wildly I look'd round me: What dreadful Apprehensions I had: And how I lodg'd in the Tree all Night for fear of being devour'd by wild Beasts." This time he sees his despair in some one else and from the point of view of their and his deliverance. He reflects that just as he did not know that first night that the storm would drive the ship close enough to land for him to receive supply for his needs "so these three poor desolate Men knew nothing how certain of Deliverance and Supply they were, how near it was to them, and how effectually and really they were in a Condition of Safety, at the same Time that they thought themselves lost, and their Case desperate." Now, more than twenty-five years after Robinson's shipwreck, he knows that the same thing had been true of him, that he had been "in a Condition of Safety" when he had thought himself lost.

IV. THE CONVERSION OF CONVERSION

The good which I now sought was not outside myself. I did not look for it in things which are seen with the eye of the flesh by the light of the sun. For those who try to find joy in things outside themselves easily vanish away into emptiness. . . . But it was in my inmost heart where I had grown angry with myself, where I had been stung with remorse, where I had slain my old self and offered it in sacrifice, where I had first purposed to renew my life and had placed my hope in you, it was there that you had begun to make me love you and had made me glad at heart.

—*Confessions*

Crusoe's ability to stand outside himself is related here to his understanding of the providential meaning of experience. That he is able to see the other Englishmen from the standpoint of a providence of which he is now the agent results from his discovery of the plan of his own life much earlier in the book, when he was still alone on the island. This "objectivity" of the self and the corresponding vision of time's plan, transcending the experience of the isolated self, are the consequences of a conversion which in Defoe never seems a single moment, a sudden and total turning which restructures the self for all time, as it is, for example, in Augustine's *Confessions*. Crusoe does experience something like that moment—there are the misunderstood providential warnings, the despair about his isolation, the new warnings in the storm, earthquake, and dream, the sickness that is symbolic of death, the discovery of the biblical message, the prayer and conviction of spiritual deliverance. But in time his certainty is dissipated as if by time itself. And each discovery of a new danger, for example, Crusoe's discovery of the footprint, at least temporarily wrecks all certainty.

Conversion is a recurrent need, a revelation followed each time by another lapse, a forgetting that is like an absence, requiring a new dialectical struggle. Not a completely new conversion, actually—Crusoe must be brought back to the self discovered in the initial conversion and by that movement freed from self-deception, freed in a sense from self. And this must happen again and again. He will suffer the consequences of the original fall, the restlessness, the "foolish inclination to wander abroad," as long as he lives. He must constantly refound himself in Christ and His providence, placing all his reliance on Him.

It is just here that resides buried the curious message of the episode of the corn, curious because it never became completely explicit and because it holds great meaning for Crusoe's egoism. When the corn sprouts first appeared, Robinson thought them miraculous, divine suspension of the laws of nature for his benefit. When he remembered that he had shaken out a bag of chicken feed in the place where the barley and rice were growing, "the Wonder began to cease; and I must confess, my religious Thankfulness on God's Providence began to abate too upon the Discovering that this was nothing but what was common." In the perspective of the narration, Robinson's judgment on the vacillations is that

> I ought to have been as thankful for so strange and unforeseen
> Providence, as if it had been miraculous; for it was really the
> Work of Providence as to me, that should order or appoint, that
> 10 or 12 Grains of Corn should remain unspoil'd (when the Rats
> had destroy'd all the rest,) as if it had been dropt from Heaven;
> as also, that I should throw it out in that particular Place where
> it being in the Shade of a high Rock, it sprang up immediately;
> whereas, if I had thrown it anywhere else, at that Time, it had
> been burnt up and destroy'd.

Critics who, like Robinson, attribute spiritual significance to his experience regard the episode as symbolic of the "seeds" of grace. In this context of Robinson's egoistic blindness against which the episode renders judgment, the implications of the passage seem to be more probing. Surely the scriptural reference is to John 12:24–25: "Except a corn of wheat fall into the ground and die, it abideth alone: but if it die, it bringeth forth much fruit. He that loveth his life shall lose it; and he that hateth his life in this world shall keep it unto life eternal." Robinson must die to himself and place all his reliance on God.

Radical individualism in all its isolated inwardness was implicit in Christianity from its beginning; in its emphasis on the brotherhood of all men, the message of Christ explicitly cut across the limits of family, tribe, or nation. One expression of the subjectivist implications of Christianity was in the intense self-exploration of Augustine's *Confessions*, a work which informs Defoe's fictional project. The implications of this individualism were worked out in the Renaissance and in a more radical way in the Reformation, of whose puritan strain Robinson is a well-known representative. Yet Christianity was also provided with this antidote to the narcissism that threatened it—the notion of the symbolic death of the self. Robinson's resistance to God's call manifested itself in one way in his obsessive fear of the loss or death of self involved in being "swallowed up" or devoured by his beginnings, by the unformed chaos of the sea, by the other. Robinson does undergo a sickness unto death, literally and figuratively, a symbolic death of the self from which he emerges with a truer if temporary understanding of God's plan for him. And as the text from John suggests, and as it was for Augustine, in his sacrifice of self Robinson is given himself for the first time.

The nature of this gift is expressed more explicitly in Moll's conversion in Newgate. Her experience is at first wayward fluctuation between repentance and selfishness. When she discovers that her Lancashire husband is bound to be hanged for a highwayman, she is so overwhelmed by grief for him and by reflections on her own previous life that "in a Word, I was perfectly chang'd, and become another Body." But this transformation is a return to self: "The wretched Boldness of Spirit, which I had acquired, abated, and conscious Guilt began to flow in my Mind: In short, I began to think, and to think indeed is one real Advance from Hell to Heaven; all that harden'd State and Temper of Soul, which I said so much of before, is but a Deprivation of Thought; he that is restor'd to his Thinking, is restor'd to himself." Inasmuch as she is still concerned about her own fate, she is still selfish and the Moll who narrates doubts the sincerity of her repentance at this point. Finally, when she receives the condemnation of this court it is "a Sentence to me like Death itself" and she feels "real Signs of Repentance." Like Augustine and Robinson, she sees the things of this life in a new way: "I now began to look back upon my past Life with abhorrence, and having a kind of View into the other Side of Time, the Things of Life, as I believe they do with every Body at such a Time, began to look with a different Aspect, and quite another Shape, than they did before."

In his conversion, Augustine is also given a "view into the other side of time." He also is transformed into "another body," which paradoxically is a matter of being "restored to himself." Restored to himself first in this sense, as he says: "O Lord, you were turning me around to look at myself. For I had placed myself behind my own back, refusing to see myself. You were setting me before my own eyes so that I could see how sordid I was, how deformed and squalid, how tainted with ulcers and sores." But he is also restored to himself in a larger sense. Augustine's last doubts before giving himself over to Christ were his doubts concerning his ability to accept continence. For this, he must throw himself on Christ's strength, not try to rely on his own. By being made capable of continence by God, Augustine is given himself, for as he explains: "By continence we are made as one and regain that unity of self which we lost by falling apart in the search for a variety of pleasures."

The similarities between Defoe's fictional memoirs, particularly Robinson's, and their ultimate model, Augustine's *Confessions*, are striking, but their differences are of signal importance. Both Augustine and Robinson have relied upon themselves, upon their own strength and reason, in important, though differing, ways. Each experienced himself initially as incomplete. The early life of each was a wandering, yet for each, every erring step was guided by Providence bringing him to the moment of salvation. To each the command of God comes by discovery of a chance word in a Sortes Biblicae. Each is brought by the symbolic death of conversion to an understanding of time and to a self-knowledge, the "proof" of which lies in the act of confession or narration.

For Defoe, however, the gift of self is as "symbolic" as the sacrificial death. Self will continue to reassert itself and be lost consequently in distraction. For it is Defoe's insight that the essential characteristic of a symbolic death is that it is only symbolic and must be repeated *endlessly*. *All* solutions in this life are symbolic, perhaps "figural" is a better word, and fallen man is never free of the consequences of Adam's sin until he suffers its original punishment, actual death. If he can be "justified" only by God, the promise figured by Providence can be fulfilled only in heaven. From this point of view, Providence is sight cast forward, into the not yet. Is it too commonplace to say that modern realism is born in the split between the symbolic and the actual, in the despair over the real efficacy of the symbolic?

One consequence is that there is a necessary discrepancy between the allegorical truth and the fact of the story. For example, Tom Jones calls father a man named Allworthy, who is squire of Paradise Hall, from which he evicts Tom for his wrongdoing. But Allworthy is not omniscient and Tom has not done what he has been accused of. Instead he is a victim of deceit, treachery, and misunderstanding—certainly no orthodox allegory of man's fall. Moreover, in the course of the novel, Tom must acquire worldly wisdom and aspires to Sophia who is not (at least in this novel) wise. Similarly, Richardson's Clarissa disobeys an inexplicable demand of her father and is seduced from her garden by the serpentlike Lovelace. Of course, in this case, the demand of the father is not only inexplicable, it is also patently unjust and Clarissa runs away with Lovelace to escape that injustice. The pattern is there, however, but from this point of view, the realistic story, life in this world, is an incomplete, distorted shadow of its spiritual truth. Hence the traditional dissatisfaction with the "allegory" of *Robinson Crusoe*. The point is not that these writers tried and failed to write novelistic allegories but that life could not be reduced or raised to a spiritual meaning.

The experiences of both Augustine and Robinson find their clear focus against a scriptural and sacred background. For example, the pear tree of Augustine's adolescence, the garden where his struggle with salvation takes place, and the fig tree under which he is saved are types of Adam's tree of forbidden fruit, the garden of Gethsemane, and Christ's "tree" or cross under which man is redeemed. Robinson's story is the story of Jonah and of the Prodigal Son. But it is the "real" Augustine who is offered in the *Confessions* by way of these stories, the real Augustine purged of the accidents of a purely personal life and revealed in the figural patterns of the Scriptures. On the other hand, Robinson is not a real person—the fact of his memoirs is their factitiousness. If, as Robinson insinuates in his *Serious Reflections*, his story is only allegorically true, then it is either true as some have thought of Defoe's own life, or the truth of the story is offered as the general truth of everyman's life. If it is Defoe's truth, then the accidents of his own life are given in what is *essentially* true in Robinson's adventures. If it is a general truth, then another reversal has taken place, for this universal essence is offered as the *actuality* of a very eccentric individual life. Symbol and fact are united in Augustine's *Confessions* but forever divided in Robinson's.

This split is demonstrated in a striking way when Robinson appears to the English mutineers "as another Person": "So that as we never suffered them to see me as Governour, so I now appear'd as another Person, and spoke of the Governour, the Garrison, the Castle, and the like, upon all Occasions." Here it is his metaphoric or spiritual condition (as "governor" of the island, "viceroy to the King of all the earth" [*Serious Reflections*]), which is held aside, while his disguise, the *other* person he becomes, is his *actuality*, in all the fantastic garb of an eccentricity which has survived almost thirty years of isolation. His disguise is almost like the lies of Odysseus—more plausible than the fantastic adventures he has undergone in the *Odyssey*. I have said that the split is between the symbolic-essential and the accidental-actual, but here the value of these poles has been reversed and the actual has become "other" than the truth. The split in Robinson's being in this passage is also, and not incidentally, the same as the split between the bourgeois *legal person* and the unique individual.

Through his conversion Augustine gains both the true order of life and his true self—one and the same thing in confession, which is the *full* giving of self in speech whose truth is guaranteed by the presence of the divine omniscient other. The "real" self of Defoe's various "memoirs," however, is a fictive self. Defoe's confessions are not *his* confessions at all. The pattern of Christian truth has become the design of a lie masked as actuality, the plot of a novel. The symbolic death of the Christian pattern has become truly symbolic on another level, inasmuch as even actual death in fiction is still a symbolic death. And the symbolic deaths of Robinson's or Moll's conversions are the doubly symbolic deaths of surrogate selves.

The full implications of this death by proxy are revealed in the story of Roxana, where the death is carried a step more distant and conversion is either impossible or no longer necessary. Roxana makes her escape into the curious oblivion of the end of that book disguised by the clothes and sanctimonious speech of a Quaker, symbols of a conversion she cannot attain. The split in Roxana, indicated by disguise, is more complicated than Robinson's self-division. She appears as the self she would like to be (her "spiritual truth") at the same time she is confronted by her past self projected onto the form of her daughter, who bears Roxana's true name, whom she deserted as a child, and who later appeared again as her servant at the moment she became the notorious Roxana. Now, it is this poor scapegoat of a daughter, the alter ego of a fictional character, yet the only truly individualized "other" of any of Defoe's fictions, who is made to suffer a sacrificial death for which Roxana will never be forgiven.

The death is brought about in a curious way—curious, in the light of the dialectic between self and other in Defoe's novels. The witness to Roxana's first crime against morality was her servant Amy. Roxana felt compelled to force Amy to sleep with her seducer: "As I thought myself a Whore, I cannot say but that it was something design'd in my Thoughts, that my Maid should be a Whore too, and should not reproach me with it." As witness to her crime, Amy would become the dangerous other—seducers or seducees never seem to have enough self-consciousness to appear as threats to the self in Defoe. The witness is the dangerous other. Roxana, by watching Amy's seduction by the same man who has ruined her, has rendered Amy "safe." She has made her an accomplice, an adjunct to her own will. When, at the end of the book, Amy does away with the daughter by some means that Roxana can't bear to think about, Amy has become like an element of Roxana's personality, capable of acting autonomously (somewhat like the daughter herself). That Amy is enacting Roxana's secret will is proved by Roxana's overwhelming sense of guilt. The book ends in the uncertainty of the unspeakable. It is either the most resolved of all the dialectical struggles between self and other in Defoe's fiction or the most unresolvable.

What is certain is that the symbolic death has been moved a step farther away from the "I" who narrated all of Defoe's books. The conversion has disappeared completely, although Roxana, beyond her Quaker costume, does become another person. Near the beginning of her account of her life, but speaking from the obscurity into which she disappears at the end, Roxana says: "Being to give my own Character, I must be excus'd to give it as impartially as possible, and as if I was speaking of another body." What has replaced the conversion is the act of narration itself.

And what can be said of Defoe? In the preface to *Roxana*, he describes himself as the "Relator" who will "speak" the words of the Beautiful Lady. Unable to give a true account of the self, he is doomed to speak the words of "another-body" as if they were his own, putting on the disguise of one fictive self after another.

V. PROVIDENCE AND WRITING: A NATURAL HABITATION

Roxana's maxim, "That Secrets should never be open'd, without evident Utility."
Robinson's maxim, "The prudent man forseeth the evil and hideth himself."

"Speech was given to man to disguise his thoughts."

                                                          —TALLEYRAND

When Robinson began to ponder the mystery of the footprint found on the beach, he discovered that he could not be certain that he had not left the print himself. Like the mystery of causality itself, the footprint is a trace of an intentional act seen from the outside: "Again, I consider'd also that I could by no Means tell for certain where I had trod, and where I had not; and that if at last this was only the Print of my own Foot, I had play'd the Part of those Fools, who strive to make stories of Spectres, and Apparitions; and then are frighted at them more than any body." The enigmatic footprint is like a ghost story, a genre most interesting to Defoe, whose power is great enough to deceive even its own teller. The footprint then is similar to a myth, told by an individual who yet cannot claim authorship, like the dream barred from its source by disavowal. In short, the footprint is a figure for the book of Robinson's adventures. Did Robinson leave the footprint or was it left by the threatening other? Are the adventures authored by Defoe, who disavowed them, by the Robinson who signed them, or by the other in whose constant presence they are structured and who is their destination?

Perhaps there is already on Defoe's part a glimmer of that suspicion of the concept of the unified and identifiable "subject" with which it has been

seen by later thinkers, particularly by Nietzsche and Freud and more recently
by Derrida. For Defoe's project seems to have involved the creation of more
or less autonomous voices, themselves without a center, that is to say, ir-
redeemably ec-centric voices. Or, rather, voices whose center is a felt lack
of center, the absence of which could be explained by the *insertion* of the
myth of fallen man, yet voices created without the distance or structure of
a consistent irony, a fact which has troubled the criticism of Defoe's books.
Voices calculating a world of facts but who are themselves fictions after all.
Books whose ambiguity is deep, thorough, and finally unresolvable.

The problem of Defoe criticism is well stated by the title of an early
twentieth-century study, William Trent's *Daniel Defoe: How to Know Him*.
My strategy has been to chip away at the hard flint of that ultimately un-
answerable question in the hope that the sparks would illuminate, if only
slightly, the surrounding terrain.

How can Robinson tell for certain where "I had trod and where I had
not?" Time, the shifting sand on the beach, how indeed can they afford a
true history or a stable identity to a mind isolated in a subjectivity, the
subject of which is so elusive? An heir of Adam, Robinson has lost the
opportunity of "sensibly tasting the sweets of living, without the bitter"
offered by his father at the beginning of the book. He can only come to
knowledge dialectically, by contraries. He can only know good, his good,
by experience of evil. Robinson's obsession with reason as *ratio*, measure-
ment, his sometimes comical "accounting," point not only to his empiricism
but also to the curse of fallen man. All evaluations of his condition are relative.
When he considers himself ruined, he must acknowledge that there are others
who are worse, just as in the beginning when his father tried to convince
him he was set up for life, he thought he could become better. In order to
account for his condition after the shipwreck, he *has* to draw up the famous
profit and loss sheet, the spiritual bookkeeping for which he (and Defoe with
him) has been so often derided. The curiosity of this debit-credit sheet lies
in its slipperiness. One *fact* is not registered against another. The facts are
the same on both sides of the sheet; each side merely interprets the fact in
a different way. There are no true alternatives present. Instead of representing Robinson's ingenuous calculation, the sheet does give a true account
of the flux of moods, moods considered as facts, the dizzying back and forth
of a subjectivity deprived of an external gauge of truth.

Robinson's journal itself is another form of this spiritual bookkeeping.
If one cannot gauge the meaning or portent of each moment, perhaps the
pattern formed over longer periods of time would reveal the truth. Such an
accounting might provide a true profit and loss tally of the spirit. Crusoe's

journal not only documents his recall of day by day events as he recounts them more than thirty years later, it also represents an attempt to give the shifting moments of a subjective time something like a spatial ordering in the same way that he carves notches into a post to mark each day he is on the island. The journal is an attempt to define a situation by ordering the present as it becomes the past. Writing also means to Robinson a deliverance from the agonizing and confusing impact from momentary impressions about his condition: "I now began to consider seriously my Condition, and the Circumstance I was reduc'd to, and I drew up the State of my Affairs in Writing, not so much to leave them to any that were to come after me, for I was like to have but few Heirs, as to deliver my Thoughts from daily poring upon them, and afflicting my Mind."

Robinson wants what Sartre's Roquentin, one of his heirs, desires: "I wanted the moments of my life to follow and order themselves like those of a life remembered. You might as well try and catch time by the tail" (*Nausea*). Crusoe's journal, like the greater account of which it is a part, is an attempt to do precisely that—catch time by the tail. The events of each day are recorded into the journal, already culled and selected, already abolished by the past tense of language and presented to us, a legacy to heirs that the Crusoe *living* each moment could not expect. We can never, however, get close to the lived moment and neither can Robinson capture it. Even the journal shows signs of a later editing, at the time of the principal narration, from the perspective of a story already closed. Moreover, such a perspective inheres in the narrative past tense. As Roquentin observes, "You have started at the end . . . and the story goes on in the reverse: instants have stopped piling themselves in a lighthearted way one on top of the other, they are snapped up by the end of the story which draws them and each one of them in turn, draws out the preceding instant." The whole book is caught up on a past tense suggesting an end which renders significant each sentence.

Crusoe's story, however, goes backwards in more obvious senses than that meant by Roquentin and Sartre. We are given no fewer than four accounts of Robinson's first days on the island, each differing in some small detail: the main account in Robinson's narrative, *two* journal accounts, and finally when Robinson relives his plight as he watches the English mutineers and their victims. First, we have the account in the chronological course of Crusoe's narrative, written years later, long after even his return from the island to civilization.

The second version is composed at the same time. This is the journal that might have been, if he had started it when he first landed on the island, and it curiously is the one most different although it is ostensibly contemporaneous with the narration of the book. The reason that he did not begin the journal the first days was that he was too busy then making himself secure but also that he was "in too much discomposure of mind, and my journal would have been full of many dull things." The writing of the journal then is the result of the *composition* of his mind, and although it has precedence in time over the other two versions, it is still separated from the event by an extensive period of time, for Robinson doesn't begin it until he is more or less settled on the island—perhaps six weeks after the shipwreck, after he finished the table and chair, probably November 12 according to the journal itself.

The differences between these accounts of his first days, mainly concerning whether he wept with joy or with terror, despair or thanksgiving, whether he slept on the ground or in a tree, are less significant than the fact that there *are* differences. What are we to make of this confusion, other than to see it as an emphasis on the elusiveness of even the facts of this narrative and an admission of an irreparable tear between the written account and the naked, lived moment? The journal—trace of the event—is vacant like the footprint. In fact, it is marked by a double absence. The writing of the account releases Robinson from the pain and confusion of experiencing— "to deliver my thoughts from daily poring upon them, and afflicting my mind." The journal serves the same purpose. And it is also removed from the event. It objectifies and orders both Robinson's thoughts and his daily experiences.

The gap cannot be closed. Narrative language removes the contingency and absurd inconsequence of the lived moment by abstracting that moment from the field of open possibility and directing it toward a certain outcome which will define it and give it significance. As Roquentin comments, " 'It was night, the street was deserted.' The phrase is cast out negligently, it seems superfluous; but we do not let ourselves be caught and we put it aside: this is a piece of information whose value we shall subsequently appreciate. And we feel that the hero has lived all the details of this night like annunciations, promises, or even that he lived only those that were promises, blind and deaf to all that did not herald adventure."

Annunciations, promises, and one might add, portents and warnings—for that is precisely the way Crusoe lives, or rather relives in his narrative, each event of his experience. What in the already realized end guarantees the significance of each event is identical with the ordering of written narrative and the opposite of the subjective flux of the lived moment—the discovery of God's plot, His Providence. The point of view of narrative is precisely a providence. In God's plan, Robinson's end *is* in his beginning—each step along the way is either a promise or a warning, but always an annunciation of a divine structure which exists outside of time, but which operates in and through time. Sartre's argument with narrative is that the foundation of the passing moment in narrative language bestows on it a privilege, robes it with a destiny, that is altogether false to experience, but Robinson's discovery of a special providence saves the moment, placing on each moment a heavy burden of significance.

Providence not only underwrites Robinson's narrative, it is also discovered by means of the writing of the journal. The subject caught in the flow of time is blind to the providential meaning of his experience. Crusoe suffers the flickering onrush of momentary sensations and is driven by selfish appetites and fears which change as rapidly as circumstances change: "Everything revolves in our minds by innumerable circular motions, all centering in ourselves" (*Serious Reflections*): "And by what secret differing Springs are the Affections hurry'd about as differing Circumstances present! To day we love what to Morrow we hate; to Day we seek what to Morrow we shun; to Day we desire what to Morrow we fear; nay even tremble at the Apprehensions of" (*Robinson Crusoe*, chap. 7).

Though Crusoe is given many warnings, many chances for repentance, as soon as the warning danger has passed, so dissolve Robinson's resolutions and promises. The Defoe self in isolation is the self of Hobbesian sensationalism. The order revealed one moment is obliterated by the new sensations crowding in the next. It is the function of narrative, with its double perspective, to remember.

By means of his journal, Robinson discovers the startling concurrence of his "fortunate and fatal days":

As long as it [the ink] lasted, I made use of it to minute down the Days of the Month on which any remarkable Thing happened to me, and first by casting up Times past: I remember that there was a strange Concurrence of Days, in the various Providences which befel me; and which, if I had been superstitiously inclin'd to observe Days as Fatal or Fortunate, I might have had Reason to have look'd upon with a great deal of Curiosity.

First, I had observed, that the same Day that I broke away from my Father and my Friends, and ran away to *Hull*, in order to go to Sea; the same Day afterwards I was taken by the *Sallee* Man of War, and made a Slave.

The same Day of the Year that I escaped out of the Wreck of that Ship in *Yarmouth* Roads, that same Day—Years afterwards I made my escape from *Sallee* in the boat.

The same Day of the Year I was born on (*viz.*) the 30*th* of

> *September*, that same Day, I had my Life so saved 26 Years after, when I was cast on Shore in this Island, so that my wicked Life, and my solitary Life begun both on a Day.

Later, when Robinson leaves the Island of Despair, he is "deliver'd from this second Captivity, the same Day of the Month, that I first made my Escape in the *Barco-Longo*, from among the *Moors* of *Sallee*." Robinson will justify our belief in such amazing coincidences by detailing examples in his essay on Providence from the long tradition of such concurrences, beginning with the Scriptures and continuing into modern political history. The scriptural example alone marks the meaning of this pattern in Robinson's life. It is in Exodus (12:41–42) and has to do with the children of Israel leaving their exile and imprisonment in Egypt the same day of the year, 430 years after they entered into it. Robinson's isolation has also been an exile and imprisonment, but the justification has a larger meaning as do all the scriptural parallels. Robinson's exile from himself and from the truth has been a type of the exile of the chosen people and of everyman, but as the real history of a man, as it is presented, it represents a figural truth. In the preface to his *Serious Reflections* when he admits the story is allegorical, Robinson does not give up the claim to its authenticity. He simply claims to have "displaced" its literal truth:

> All these reflections are just history of a state of forced confinement, which in my real history is represented by a confined retreat in an island; and it is as reasonable to represent one kind of imprisonment by another, as it is to represent anything that really exists by that which exists not. The story of my fright with something on my bed was word for word a history of what happened, and indeed all those things received very little alteration, except what necessarily attends removing the scene from one place to another.

One is reminded that among the earliest meanings of *figura* was its usage in rhetoric to conceal the truth (in a figure of speech). It usually had to do with suggesting without actually expressing a truth which for political or tactical reasons or simply for effect could not be expressed openly. This was precisely Defoe's purpose.

Any discussion of the question necessarily collapses into the ambiguity Defoe left surrounding it. No sooner are we satisfied with his admission of allegorical truth in the preface to Robinson's *Serious Reflections* than we discover that among the reflections it prefaces is "An Essay upon Honesty" and another on "the Immorality of Conversation," which contains a section about "Talking Falsely." No oversight on Defoe's part. In case we miss the point, he at first distinguished from the lying tales he is attacking such "historical parables" as those in the Holy Scripture, *Pilgrim's Progress*, or, "in a word, the adventures of your fugitive friend, 'Robinson Crusoe.' " But then he makes the standard puritan attack on realistic fiction: any fiction that offers itself as historical truth is a dangerous and damning lie. Lest we dismiss the discrepancy as mere ingenuousness on the part of Defoe, he adds the following disclaimer: "If any man object here that the preceding volumes of this work seem to be hereby condemned, and the history which I have therein published of myself censured, I demand in justice such objector stay his censure till he sees the end of the scene, when all that mystery shall discover itself, and I doubt not but the work shall abundantly justify the design, and the design abundantly justify the work." Does that settle the issue?

Ambiguity aside, it is possible to say that while Defoe is impersonating Robinson Crusoe, he is also impersonating on another level Providence itself. Just as the double vision made possible by the Christian conversion is replaced by the double vision of narration, the structure of narration has stood in place of providence.

It is no accident and may in fact be "the end of the scene" Robinson alluded to earlier that the last story he tells in his *Serious Reflections* concerns a young man who speaks to an atheist in the voice of a mutual friend and is taken instead for the voice of a spirit, messenger of God and medium of His Providence, by the disbeliever who is thereby saved.

Defoe's fortress is complete, constructed according to the laws of nature and concealing the plot of Providence. It is a natural habitation, in which like Robinson, Defoe can live in the open but unseen and unmolested by devouring eyes. In his essay "Solitude" Robinson countered the voluntary withdrawal into the desert wilderness of the religious hermit by the voluntary exile in the midst of society by means of something like disguise. Peaceful solitude

> would every way as well be supplied by removing from a place where a man is known to a place where he is not known, and there accustom himself to a retired life, making no new acquaintances, and only making the use of mankind which I have already spoken of, namely, for convenience and supply of necessary food; and I think of the two that such a man, or a man so retired, may have more opportunity to be an entire recluse, and may enjoy more real solitude than a man in a desert.

Defoe's fiction has provided him with such a hermitage.

Many novelists who followed Defoe were strangers in a strange land and found means of both concealing and exposing themselves in their novels. Pseudonymity and anonymity haunt the novel throughout the eighteenth and nineteenth centuries. Perhaps these novelists too confronted the necessity of becoming other persons in their narrators. There was Richardson's "editorship," for example, and while Jane Austen's and George Eliot's concealment of their names was perhaps only conventional for lady writers, Stendhal's need for pseudonyms was obsessional. Scott, already a famous author, concealed himself behind the tag of "the author of Waverley" and became the most visible "great unknown" of his day. Defoe's discoveries about the nature of narrative and its plots made the novel an apt genre for a society of isolated and mutually suspicious individuals. Perhaps all novelists begin in anonymity and construct for themselves the personality of their works.

H. DANIEL PECK

Robinson Crusoe:
The Moral Geography of Limitation

Almost everyone agrees that geography yields meaning in a special way in Daniel Defoe's first novel, *The Life and Strange Surprising Adventures of Robinson Crusoe*. Yet there is no wide agreement concerning the way geography actually functions in the narrative. In recent years, two dominant interpretations which attempt to throw light on this subject have emerged. One group of critics seeks to understand the topography of Crusoe's island as a "state of nature" in which "economic" or "political man" makes a new beginning in "pure" surroundings. Ian Watt, in discussing what he calls the economic "myth" of *Robinson Crusoe*, gives the novel's main character the status of culture hero and names him the "ideal prototype" of Western civilization who, faced with a sense of restlessness and isolation, overcomes these feelings by "ceaseless economic activity." The island, in this view, becomes the "utopia of the Protestant Ethic," in which temptations and diversions are lacking and in which "Crusoe's energies cannot be deflected" from productive work (*"Robinson Crusoe* as a Myth," *Essays in Criticism* 1, pp. 95–119).

A variant upon this view is one which posits the island's narrative function as the setting for political development. Maximillian Novak argues that both the *Surprising Adventures* and *The Farther Adventures of Robinson Crusoe* must be seen "as a single work concerned with the political evolution of society in the state of nature . . . " He understands Crusoe's assumption of the title "emperor" as carrying serious implications, illustrating how, in

From *The Journal of Narrative Technique* 3, no. 1 (January 1973). © 1973 by the Eastern Michigan University Press.

stages, Crusoe's island evolves from an absolute to a patriarchal monarchy, and eventually to "what he [Defoe] regarded as the ideal government—a more or less democratic state with most of the power in the hands of the able and diligent" (M. Novak, "Crusoe the King and the Political Evolution of His Island," *Studies in English Literature* 2, pp. 337–50). Both these variants, then, regard the island setting of *Robinson Crusoe* as a type of "pure" or "mythic" landscape in which the complex processes of economic and political growth are demonstrated.

The proponents of a second major interpretation do not see the novel in economic or political terms; rather, they seek to understand the island's geography as a component of a "spiritual biography." In this view, the landscape becomes a moral testing ground in which the conditions of the environment provide a symbolic counterpart for a state of mind. The island becomes not a real place at all, but an allegorical convenience, in which a mental or spiritual battle is waged, as, for example, the physical world is in *The Pilgrim's Progress*. This interpretation is perhaps most convincingly presented by George Starr in his [1965] *Defoe and Spiritual Biography*, where he argues that the action and the outward environment of the novel "present a spiritual condition in concrete terms," and that "spiritual disaffection" is conveyed "through the language of physical distance." Starr, by carefully linking *Robinson Crusoe* with a body of religious literature, attempts to show how the topography of the island is the field for Defoe's depiction of an essentially spiritual conflict.

There is merit in both these interpretations, and they are certainly not contradictory at every point. Yet neither, in my view, effectively comes to terms with the way geography is appropriated and yields meaning in *Robinson Crusoe*. Both make the mistake of approaching the novel initially as "myth" and then working "downward," as it were, toward the concrete details; the inevitable effect of this procedure is to diminish the force of the novel's realism. What is required, it seems to me, is an approach which maintains the environment as a real place, but at the same time deals with the problem of the self.

Defoe's own prolific statements concerning politics, economics and religion have often been used to support the interpretations I have summarized above. But the underlying assumption of this paper is that in the character of Crusoe, Defoe is expressing a level of motivation and meaning that is more fundamental to his experience than either economic or religious theory, one which he may not have been entirely aware of, namely, the need for "place."

The concept of place, as I am using it here, emphasizes the importance of environment to the development of the self. From this point of view, the island is not merely a negative setting of duress in which Crusoe is thrashed into repentence (any threatening environment would serve that purpose), but a specific and positive landscape insofar as Crusoe enters into a willing relationship with it. *Robinson Crusoe* does deal with correspondences between the material world and mental life, but this is not to say that one side of the correspondence is any more "real" than the other. Rather, "place" becomes in the novel not a mythic setting but an active force in "grounding" the hero and creating in him a sense of personal identity.

While this approach to *Robinson Crusoe* differs from economic/political and religious constructs, it does not preclude them and, in a sense, underlies them. For, in this novel, a commitment to place is the necessary first step in the development of economic and political structures as well as the precursor of religious experience. As Novak suggests, the *Surprising Adventures* and the *Farther Adventures* should be examined together, but this should be done with a different emphasis than he recommends. The first volume of the series shows how the forced acquisition of a sense of place in a tightly bounded environment results in the psychological "grounding" of the hero; the second explores the results of Crusoe's having been "liberated" from the island and his subsequent freedom to wander in a geography not of limited horizons but one of vastitude.

Most of the "pre-island" narrative of the *Surprising Adventures* illustrates the hero's propensity to wander and his inability to "stay put." Going to sea to avoid the "middle life" his father espoused and later suffering depression at his plantation in Brazil, Crusoe always sets himself in motion when possibilities arise for identification with a place, even though some of his voyages have been harrowing. The seagoing life offers him the mobility he feels he requires, and both the *Surprising Adventures* and the *Farther Adventures* make symbolic use of the contrasting geographies of land and sea. In the early sections of the first volume, the moral fluidity that sea travel makes possible is clearly demonstrated. The imagery of "floating" on the sea as well as on the surfaces of life is dominant, and it is obvious that voyaging allows Crusoe to avoid "placing" himself in either a moral or a geographic sense. This kind of life has cumulative effects, for the wandering existence involves the subject in a terrible paradox; the more freedom he acquires, the more deeply implicated he becomes in his own errors and is thus "trapped." By contrast, Crusoe's later confinement on the island can be seen as a "liberating" experience.

The island on which the hero is eventually marooned is richly endowed by nature and, as he finally realizes, also richly endowed with opportunities for the moral life. But when he is first stranded there, he fails to recognize either of these possibilities. For Robinson Crusoe, whose identifying characteristic has been an inclination to wander, no situation could conceivably be worse. His initial reaction to this "horrid Island," this *Island of Despair*," is one of a terrible sense of confinement and isolation. Realizing that he has been washed ashore on an island "environ'd every Way with the Sea," that is, totally bounded, he feels "absolutely miserable."

The sea had always permitted Crusoe to operate along the surface, both literally and morally, but this island and its contingencies force him to seek out depth, literally to "work my Way into the Rock." In his attempt to sink his habitation into the earth and to perform other necessities of survival, he discovers that he possesses neither the tools nor the skills to adapt himself to this place. Everything must be done by "inexpressible Labour." His wall, even though it is *"no more than about 24 Yards in Length,"* is only completed by virtue of enormous amounts of effort and time.

Many have seen in Crusoe's "vision" a turning point in the novel. It has been viewed as a moment of dramatic revelation, after which the hero changes the pattern of his life from waywardness to regularity. But in fact, when the island experience is looked upon in terms of place, the vision becomes not so much the occasion for a dramatic turnabout (as significant as it is), as the culmination of a process begun almost the moment Crusoe is washed ashore. Before the vision occurs, he has begun to adapt himself to the requirements of life on the island, and even to resign himself to the conditions of his "imprisonment." This process has, to be sure, been prompted almost entirely by necessity, but this does not deny its effect.

Crusoe's gradual accommodation to place is perhaps best expressed in his own growing awareness that this environment is not totally resistant to his efforts, and that he can, in fact, create a tolerable way of life. In the "pre-journal" narrative, he recounts with some satisfaction the gains he made in this respect: "I had never handled a Tool in my Life, and yet in time by Labour, Application, and Contrivance, I found at last that I wanted nothing but I could have made it."

It is clear that Crusoe himself regards the vision as a religious experience, and I do not wish to deny that this is the case, but rather to emphasize that his "conversion" was preceded by a three-year period in which necessity and accommodation to place had taught him, in his better moments, "not to despair of any Thing." In other words, the rudiments of a sense of place and a concomitant sense of boundaries precede the spiritual event.

While the "postvision" Crusoe may be looked upon as a repentant sinner, he can more accurately be seen, it seems to me, as one who has now assumed a sense of place. Before the vision, it was necessity which developed in him a feeling of resignation. But after this event, it is as though the external bounds formed by the shores of the island have become internalized. His newfound desire to make his life "regular" is a sign that he is self-consciously imposing limitations upon the range of his desires as well as the range of his territory. Before the vision, he looked upon the bounded existence he was forced to lead as a "Prison," but as he tells us, he "learn'd to take it in another Sense." What this signals is that there is now a correspondence between the bounded topography of the island and the terrain of Crusoe's mind. Both are self-limiting and both possess a significant center. Just as he was forced to dig into earth and rock to form his habitation, his experience on this island has also forced him to dig down into his own soul, a process he had always been able to avoid when he was associated with the geography of the sea. It is in these ways that inner and outer landscape are so closely related in this novel.

Significantly, after this change has occurred, Crusoe begins his serious exploration of the island. But it is exploration this time, as never before, with a "Home," or center, to return to. Crusoe suffers occasional lapses in this attachment to place, but inevitably he recovers it. Tempted at first by the more "pleasant fruitful Part of the Island," he momentarily considers moving his habitation there. But it is not long before he acknowledges the desirability of maintaining his center: "I confess this Side of the Country was much pleasanter than mine, but yet I had not the least Inclination to remove; for as I was fix'd in my Habitation, it became natural to me, and I seem'd all the while I was here [on the other side of the island], to be as it were upon a Journey, and from Home." The "old" Robinson Crusoe would have been incapable of expressing such sentiments as these.

With his geographic and spiritual center established, Crusoe begins actively to explore the different parts of the island. As he tells us, "Having now secur'd my Habitation [here we might read *self*], as I thought, fully to my Mind, I had a great Desire to make a more perfect Discovery of the Island, and to see what other Productions I might find, which I yet knew nothing of." The world which he sets out here to investigate is not the relatively boundless world of the high seas where he had performed his earlier "explorations," but rather a bounded world which, nevertheless, is rich and diverse. A world limited in scope but rich and satisfying is, of course, reflective of the inner sense of boundary and self-limitation which Crusoe has acquired. Returning home from his journey, he can contemplate "with great Pleasure the Fruitfulness of that Valley, and the Pleasantness of the Situation" and yet not feel compelled to uproot his habitation.

The experience of exploration has another dimension as well, for it is Crusoe's way of appropriating the whole of this place as his own. It is at this point in the novel that the concept of his "lordship" enters his mind. This is not merely a question of his having arrived upon the island first; his "ownership" is rather the result of having cultivated and finally identified with this place. Later, when Friday, the Spaniard, Friday's father and others arrive, the foundations for Crusoe's political claims to leadership have already been firmly laid. The implications of Crusoe's "kingship" and the political transition from a patriarchal monarchy to a kind of absentee ownership are worked out in the *Farther Adventures*. But suffice it here to say that in order for political development to occur, the vital process of appropriation of and identification with place must be a *fait accompli*.

Crusoe's growing sense of the island as "his" island is primarily a place value and only secondarily a political and economic one. Those critics who declare these more sophisticated concepts the basic levels of meaning in the novel ignore Crusoe's own statements about his "home." His most basic sense of "ownership" of the island is revealed when, during one of his explorations, he is nearly pulled out to sea by a current. Suddenly faced with the loss of this "home," he desperately fears "being driven from my beloved Island," which he sees as "the most pleasant Place in the World." Clearly it is a place and not merely a territory which is at stake here.

After this frightening event, Crusoe settles even more securely into a "sedate retir'd Life" and tells his readers, "I liv'd really very happily in all things, except that of Society." And, of course, after Friday joins him on the island and supplies the "society," the remaining time in this place is deeply satisfying: "the three Years which we liv'd there together [were] perfectly and compleatly happy." But it is significant that even before Friday's arrival, Crusoe has so identified with the island that he tells us, had it not been for the danger of savages, he "could have been content to have capitulated for spending the rest of my Time there, even to the last Moment, till I had laid me down and dy'd, like the old Goat in the Cave."

The island experience has taught Crusoe the virtue of the bounded life and the dangers of a too wide-ranging perspective. If a person lacks a significant center, Defoe seems to be saying, he is likely to dissipate his energies in wasteful activity and never really come to terms with himself. That is, by acquiring a sense of place, Crusoe has also established a sense of self. The tightly bounded and necessitous life on the island has convinced him of the value of setting one's own limits. At one point, as Crusoe reflects on his condition, the design of this argument becomes extremely clear:

> How infinitely Good that Providence is, which has provided in
> its Government of Mankind, such narrow bounds to his Sight
> and Knowledge of Things, and though he walks in the midst of
> so many thousand Dangers, the Sight of which, if discover'd to
> him, would distract his Mind, and sink his Spirits; he is kept
> serene, and calm, by having the Events of Things hid from his
> Eyes, and knowing nothing of the Dangers which surround him.

Crusoe's celebration here of "narrow bounds" sounds like an injunction
against aimless travel, and the real question posed in the *Farther Adventures*
is whether the "liberated" hero, returned to a world of flux, can maintain
his "center" away from the environment which, in a sense, created and
enforced it.

The geography of much of the *Farther Adventures* differs greatly from
the dense and bounded landscape of Crusoe's island. The dominant scenes
are those of expansive oceans and the vast open spaces of the Asian continent.
This immense and open-ended geography is, in many respects, made to
order for a wanderer who wishes to be free of boundaries of any kind.

The *Farther Adventures* begins by detailing what had only been outlined
at the conclusion of the *Surprising Adventures*; it describes how Crusoe, after
a period of indecision, marries, raises a family, tries farming, but finds life
in England unsatisfactory and sets sail again after his wife dies. His motives
for doing so are really double; he feels a deep nostalgia for his island "home,"
but at the same time he is "inur'd to a wandring Life." The two motives
work together to get him to sea again, but after that initial consonance, they
war with each other for the rest of the novel. As Crusoe expresses the dilemma
later, "I thought that by this Voyage, I had made no Progress at all, because
I was come back as I might call it, to the Place from whence I came as to a
Home; whereas, my Eye, which like that, which *Solomon* speaks of, *was never
satisfied with Seeing*, was still more desirous of Wand'ring and Seeing."

Crusoe's return to the island brings him a report of the events that have
occurred since he left ten years before, and he discovers that the diverse
group of Spaniards, Englishmen and natives that he left behind has undergone, in social terms, something of what he experienced alone. After much
conflict they have, because of necessity and common danger, come together
and formed a "Family," a family which continues to regard Crusoe as its
"father."

The case of the wayward sinner who, like Crusoe, resists "grounding,"
is most dramatically worked out in the history of rebellious Will Atkins.

Atkins and some of his English accomplices have repeatedly disrupted the society of the island and threatened, from time to time, its very existence. But eventually, through a set of experiences which includes forced isolation, Atkins and his associates are reformed into model colonists.

Even after an absence of ten years, Crusoe finds that he is still honored as the patriarch and natural leader of the island, and it is clear that his people would welcome his continued presence. Yet despite the fact that he exhibits a genuine love for the island and a sense of responsibility toward its inhabitants, he feels compelled to depart and fulfill the demands of his wandering life. Crusoe's last acts on the island are intended to stabilize the community and to impose the same kind of bounds which had created such a rich life for him when he was on the island. First, he gives his name to a document which sets "out the Bounds and Situation of every Man's Plantation." Second, he conceals from them a "sloop" he had earlier manu- factured for their use, deciding that without easy access away from the island they will be more likely to stay together. Ironically, Crusoe's last activities on the island are intended to impose a "bounded" life upon his colonists, yet he, at that moment, is about to embark upon a series of aimless voyages.

After his departure Crusoe does, of course, think of his island from time to time and occasionally sends his people supplies. But he has, in reality, become an absentee monarch, and it is clear that such a monarch cannot cultivate a genuine society. The implication is strong that Crusoe's virtual neglect of his island is responsible for its community's eventual demise. His failure even to give the place a name reflects his lack of commitment. Later, he acknowledges this fact and muses, with regret, upon what might have been and what has actually happened to his experiment:

> nay, I never so much as gave the Place a Name: but left it as I found it, belonging to no Man; and the People under no Discipline or Government but my own; who, tho' I had Influence over them as Father and Benefactor, had no Authority or Power, to Act or Command one way or other, farther than voluntary Consent mov'd them to comply. Yet even this, had I stay'd there, would have done well enough; but as I rambl'd from them, and came there no more, the last Letters I had from any of them [indicated] . . . that they went on but poorly, were Male-content with their long Stay there; that *Will Atkins* was dead; that five of the *Spaniards* were come away . . . and that they begg'd of him [Crusoe's part-

ner] to write to me . . . to fetch them away, that they might see
their own Country again before they dy'd.

But Crusoe cannot respond to this sad request, for, as he puts it, "I was
gone *a Wild Goose chase.*" The political lesson of this testimony is clear; even
a benevolent monarchy cannot succeed if the monarch does not have a commitment to place, if he is, in fact, *monarch in absentia.*

Shortly after Crusoe sails away from his island for the last time, his
ship is attacked by hundreds of natives in canoes and Friday is killed. With
the death of that living representative of the rich natural world of the island,
Crusoe virtually disassociates himself from it and expresses this disassociation
with a tone of great finality: "I have now done with my Island, and all
Manner of Discourse about it; and whoever reads the rest of my Memorandums, would do well to turn his Thoughts entirely from it, and expect to
read of the Follies of an old Man, not warn'd by his own Harms."

From this point onward, the narrative of the *Farther Adventures* documents the disorienting and morally destructive effects of the loss of a significant center. It is clear from the last quotation that Crusoe's island no
longer has imaginative significance for him, as it did during his ten years in
Europe. He is now effectively cut off from his "home," and therefore will
suffer increasing separation from his own sense of identity. At times the
process of drift and disorientation takes on almost allegorical overtones in
the later sections of the novel. There is not room here to recount every detail
of Crusoe's lengthy voyages that carry him virtually all over the earth. But
a few examples will illustrate well enough what Defoe apparently felt it
means to be a wanderer.

The state of nature in which Crusoe had lived a solitary life on the
island possessed a purity that cannot be duplicated. By contrast, to be in
the world as a wanderer, Defoe seems to be saying, is to collect the world's
guilt. When the crew of Crusoe's ship commits a bloody massacre against
the natives of a village at Madagascar, he is rightly appalled and brings moral
judgment to bear upon the sailors, including his own nephew, the captain:
"I always, after that Time, told them, God would blast the Voyage; for I
look'd upon all the Blood they shed that Night to be Murther in them."
While he did not take part in the massacre and condemns those who did, it
is clear from Crusoe's sense of foreboding that he too, indirectly, is implicated. Later, another case of acquired, or secondhand, guilt makes the pattern
almost transparent. Crusoe and a newly acquired partner purchase a ship
from a group of sailors who have deserted their captain and left him to die.

They have no knowledge of the reprehensible deed and buy the ship in good faith; but because of a case of mistaken identity they are pursued and attacked as the traitors and finally forced to give up the ship in order to discard the "guilt." The predicament is, according to Crusoe, "the most dangerous Condition that ever I was in thro' all my past Life."

But after the tainted vessel is sold on the coast of China and Crusoe embarks upon his land travels over Asia, the quality of his experience doesn't change very much. The expansive and open desert through which he travels functions in the novel very much the same way as the oceans did earlier. In this land setting, Crusoe pursues the same kind of confusing and, at times, desperate course that marked his sea voyages. Unlike his island, which was a bounded but richly endowed area, both the oceans and the desert are geographically and morally open ended. This quality of boundlessness seems to have an even greater effect on Crusoe when he traverses Asia than when he was on the sea. Earlier, his "guilt" was only secondhand, but on the mainland he gets into desperate circumstances because of his own recklessness and overzealous reactions.

In light of the way Crusoe acts toward heathen peoples in Asia, it is interesting to recall how he responded to the cannibals who visited his island many years before. Two cases arose in which he felt outraged at their barbarism, and in each case he vowed to slaughter them. But in the island setting, in which he had acquired a sense of limitation and restraint, he relented both times and took a more humane view. In the first instance, he concluded that he "had taken wrong Measures in my Resolutions to attack the Savages; that it was not my Business to meddle with them, unless they first attack'd me." The second episode occurred after Friday had arrived, and Crusoe was again incensed at the actions of a group of natives on their "inhumane Errand." But once again he tempered his rage with reason: "it occurr'd to my Thoughts, What Call? What Occasion? much less, What Necessity I was in to go and dip my Hands in Blood, to attack People, who had neither done, or intended me any Wrong? Who as to me were innocent."

But on the Asian plain, after a period of relatively pointless wandering, Crusoe's passions fly totally out of control on one significant occasion. In a village of the Tartars, he goes into a "Rage" at the sight of a heathen idol. Ironically, his response is to advocate exactly the kind of massacre of heathen peoples that he earlier abhorred at Madagascar. Attempting to get support from a companion for his plan to destroy the village, he describes that earlier action which he hopes will impress him: "I related the Story of our Men at *Madagascar*, and how they burnt and sack'd the Village there, and kill'd Man, Woman and Child, for their murdering one of our Men, just as it is related before; and when I had done, I added, that I thought we ought to do so to this Village." When this plan is discouraged, Crusoe decides to settle for the destruction of the idol itself, which in turn makes him and his caravan the object of fierce pursuit by Tartar horsemen. And this pursuit, which comes close to bringing disaster to Crusoe and his friends, is not, like the chase on the high seas, a case of mistaken identity. At this point in the *Farther Adventures*, Crusoe is as far from the relatively contented and reasonable figure we knew on the island as he will get.

Very late in the novel, the hero's travels bring him into contact with a character who offers him a last chance to recover something of his former sense of place and inner presence. In Siberia, Crusoe meets an exiled Russian prince who explicates the virtues of the bounded life with such great clarity that it cannot be missed.

In a style that has become increasingly characteristic, Crusoe introduces himself to the prince by boasting of his dominance over his "subjects" on the island: "First, *I told him*, I had the absolute Disposal of the Lives and Fortunes of all my Subjects: That notwithstanding my absolute Power, I had not one Person disaffected to my Government, or to my Person, in all my Dominions." This introduction is interesting because it shows Crusoe concentrating solely upon his power. All patriarchal affection, responsibility and love of place, which he once possessed, are gone. All that concerns him now is the possession of an object.

The prince functions as Crusoe's opposite number on this issue, and it soon becomes apparent that although he is exiled and has lost his territorial holdings, he possesses something far more valuable, his sense of self. Crusoe is not beyond recognizing this and remarks that the prince is "not a Monarch only, but a great Conqueror; for that he that has got a Victory over his own exorbitant Desires, and has the absolute Dominion over himself, whose Reason entirely governs his Will, is certainly greater than he that conquers a City."

The life of exile that the prince and his few companions live is one of great simplicity, just as Crusoe's life on the island was, and it is no less bounded than the island. Yet there is one great difference between Crusoe's past "imprisonment" and the prince's present exile. Crusoe had no choice concerning his twenty-eight-year confinement on the island; the prince has opportunities to escape from Siberia. Crusoe, when he was offered his "liberation," reverted to form and a life of aimless and self-destructive wandering, as the *Farther Adventures* bears out. The prince, on the other hand, has firmly established his own *inner* limits, and when he refuses Crusoe's offer of transport out of Siberia, he explains in full the virtues of self-limitation:

Here I am free from the Temptation of returning to my former
miserable Greatness; there I am not sure but that all the Seeds
of Pride, Ambition, Avarice and Luxury, which I know remain
in Nature, may revive and take Root, and in a Word, again
overwhelm me, and then the happy Prisoner, who you see now
Master of his Soul's Liberty, shall be the miserable Slave of his
own Senses, in the Full of all personal Liberty: Dear Sir, let me
remain in this blessed Confinement, banish'd from the Crimes of
Life, rather than purchase a Shew of Freedom, at the Expence
of the Liberty of my Reason, and at the Expence of the future
Happiness which now I have in my View, but shall then, I fear,
quickly lose Sight of.

There was a time when Crusoe would have perfectly understood such paradoxes as "happy Prisoner" and "blessed Confinement." But now, with his
offer of escape rejected, he is puzzled. He asks the prince if he is sure that
this offer may not be "the Call of Heaven." By this time, we know that it
is typical of Crusoe to confuse the impulse to travel with divine beckoning.
He leaves Siberia as he arrived, an aimless wanderer who once possessed a
"center" but has lost it.

As Robinson Crusoe quickly returns to the European continent and then
England after more than ten years of travel, we are aware that his "adventures" have only served to move him ever "farther," both geographically and
psychologically, from the one place in his experience and imagination that
once granted him the only real satisfaction of his life.

LEO BRAUDY

Daniel Defoe and the Anxieties
of Autobiography

From Apuleius to Norman Mailer writers have written about characters bearing their own names and left the reader with the problem of distinguishing between the two, or at least with the nagging feeling that such a distinction could add to the fuller understanding of their work. Daniel Defoe did no such thing. Although the first-person singular was his favorite literary pose, and he used it in fiction and nonfiction alike, he never spoke in his own voice as Daniel Defoe, the private person. Two voices sound through his work: the public person who speaks in the nonfiction, detailing and explaining his opinions about the issues of the day; and the private impersonation, that first-person voice that gives life to the characters who are the most enduring part of Defoe's legacy as a writer: Robinson Crusoe, Captain Singleton, Moll Flanders, Colonel Jacque, and Roxana.

When critics speak about the psychological side of Defoe's novels, they often complain that his characters never "develop." But in the essay that follows, I would like to consider Defoe's first-person novels (a term less cumbersome than "pseudo-autobiographies") as the record of his exploration of what constitutes human individuality and how to write about it. Many of the great literary changes of the eighteenth century—the new importance of the novel, the disappearance of satire, the fascination with sentiment and sensibility, the exploration of extreme states of feeling—seem to me to be related to an anguish and uncertainty about human character. The question is not "what is human nature?" (too broad and timeless), but "what separates

From *Genre* 6, no. 1 (March 1973). © 1973 by Donald E. Billiar, Edward F. Heuston, and Robert L. Vales.

one individual from another?" and "what is personal identity?" After a lifetime of writing what was largely expository nonfiction, Defoe at 59 began the series of first-person novels for which he is most famous, from *Robinson Crusoe* (1719) to *Roxana* (1724). The power of these novels comes from Defoe's energetic awakening to the implications of speaking in his own voice or masquerading in the voice of another, and within the novels he grapples with the problem of individuality and identity with an energy bordering on obsessiveness. Older forms of autobiography and new possibilities rest side by side in the hollow of Defoe's novels, bound together by his acute sense of the mystery of human separateness, that point beyond which someone, real or imagined, can no longer be "explained."

Although Defoe's works frequently sport didactic aims and exhortations to the reader, their inconclusive endings and elusive tone announce their preoccupation with uncertainty. The heart of Defoe's originality is to introduce uncertainty into autobiography. Few early autobiographies are *about* uncertainty in the same way that Defoe's first-person novels are; in few early autobiographies does the question of whether or not the narrator deserves our trust ever arise. Whatever the differences, say, between *The Golden Ass* of Apuleius and Augustine's *Confessions*, they both deal with false certainty that is transformed into true certainty, abruptly in the first and gradually in the second. *The Golden Ass* requires the active participation of an intelligent reader to make its meaning clear; Augustine more explicitly makes his path a route every man and every woman can follow. But both works assume a continuation and imitation of their precepts in the life of the reader. Modern confessional autobiography—one of the most important descendants of Defoe's work—has little of that kind of didacticism or edification. It seeks to give meaning to a seemingly meaningless life by casting that life in literary form. It seizes upon the uncertainty of the meaning of life as its true subject, and it supplies meaning not by analogy to some supervening spiritual order, but through the self-conscious act of literary self-preoccupation.

Whatever credit is usually given to Defoe in the history of the novel, Richardson tends to be awarded the title of "father" of the psychological novel. He has been taken at his own valuation as the writer without a past or a tradition, untainted by insincerity and "art," who for the first time in literature looks directly at human beings. Defoe, on the other hand, has been denied the ability to create "real" characters because he draws on past autobiographical and biographical traditions. The most common study of Richardson concentrates on characterization; the most typical study of Defoe discusses either what works lie behind his own or what works he actually ransacked to create his own. This kind of critical emphasis disintegrates

Defoe's works into what has influenced them and diverts attention from Defoe to the mass of seventeenth- and early eighteenth-century biographies and autobiographies, whether criminal, political, military, or spiritual. By implication it characterizes Defoe as merely a much more skilled and successful practitioner of the old forms, and tells us little about what Defoe has personally accomplished or the historical moment that helped create the enormous difference in emotional and aesthetic intensity between Defoe's work and what preceded it.

Before Defoe, works that dealt with an individual life usually did not see character as a problem because their intentions were openly didactic. In the spiritual autobiography the writer was in great part offering a model for the individual reader to imitate; in the criminal autobiography the reader was offered a model to abhor. Anything excessively particularizing in the character of the model could possibly debar the reader from the vicarious participation that was essential to the success of the form. Whether they were exemplary or cautionary, the idea of the self in these works is a settled question. Even though the writing of a spiritual autobiography may have been a unique and individual attempt to discover the shape of one's life, the *form* of the work was a purgation of the demons of individuality, and conversion a reacceptance into the fold of general religious truth. In the same way, the final repentance and submission of the criminal made up for the sins of his individualism, so that the reader could enjoy surrogate straying while he was assured of a final security. Whether such "lives" took the form of "do what I do" or "I'll do it so that you don't have to," the presentation of the subject's character was done with as little real individuality as possible. The lives of criminals and saints, military men and whores, followed a preset pattern.

Defoe's first-person novels may make us uneasy because the panoply of didactic sameness coexists with definite personalization. Despite Defoe's own later efforts in *Serious Reflections of Robinson Crusoe* (1720) to make Crusoe into a paradigm and the book an allegory of Defoe's own life as well as the life of everyman, when we read the novel, we feel with great power Crusoe's individual problems, his craziness and his idiosyncrasies. And at the same time we sense Defoe's struggles with the problem of creating a truly separate character in fiction, a character who draws his energies not from the canons of spiritual autobiography (or economic individualism), but from some core sense of uniqueness, even a uniqueness with pathological overtones, that he shares with his creator.

Instead of taking *Crusoe* as a model by which to judge the other works, I would characterize it as Defoe's first and last attempt to align his exploration of the possibilities of autobiography with a settled and traditional paradigm of human life and behavior. Within it is already growing a fascination with the efforts of the individual to define himself in accordance with some preexisting spiritual, social, cultural, or literary pattern. Until the eighteenth century, history-writing, like biography and autobiography, sought primarily to discover the sameness of history, the repetition of patterns. Defoe's novels engage the uniqueness of human identity outside the rhythmic repetitions of public history and the causal control of a verifiable past. Time is basically irrelevant to him, and his heroes and heroines in general have little to do with the cycles of weeks, months, and years, or the events of public history, unless, like the plague of 1666 in *Journal of the Plague Year* or the 1715 Jacobite Rebellion in *Colonel Jacque*, such events are important less for themselves than because they play a role in the lives of his narrators. After *Crusoe* the pressure of genealogy on Defoe's characters also almost vanishes, unless it is genealogy like Colonel Jacque's belief that his origins were "gentlemanly," a self-generated belief again more important than any external reality. Defoe discovers within autobiography its central paradox of eccentricity laid down with universality: the unique self making himself and his ideas palatable for a large audience. Even in *Crusoe* he rejects the solution of spiritual autobiography that egotism should be channeled into a religious paradigm that asserts the basic similarity of everyone's problems and solutions. In *Crusoe* and more markedly in his later novels, he explores the actual anxieties of personal identity and the inability of earlier autobiographical forms to offer sufficient solace.

Defoe developed his first-person style largely as a vehicle for his journalism and nonfiction, and much of the basic solidity of his novels comes from the unhurried power of a matter-of-fact tone that helps enforce belief. Defoe chose the first person to convey an impression of clarity and nonpartisan interest in the plain truth of whatever he was discussing—a reasonable and friendly voice that when it talked about politics or discussed the intricacies of some contemporary economic issue could be believed. The first person is so obviously a conscious style in Defoe's works that it is difficult to believe that it was chosen only for moral reasons, to contrast with the rhetorical flourishes of a more obviously self-conscious style. Defoe made many statements about fiction that seem to align him with Bunyan in a "puritan" hostility to artistry in literature. But a solider motivation for his "plain" style seems to be a distrust of the ability of language to convey with any accuracy the nuances of personality. The straightforward first person has its definite limits: it is fine for conveying the specifiable. The first person of Defoe's nonfiction yields the objective, recording side of the novels: the lists of Crusoe, Moll and Colonel Jacque; the descriptions and statistics of *Journal of the Plague Year*; the military events of *Colonel Jacque* or *Memoirs of a Cavalier* or *Memoirs of Captain Carleton*. The disengaged and detached narrator can successfully convey some fragment of public history to the reader because he is not a public man himself and has no partisan jawbone to swing. But when the focus is on the narrator himself, when the point is not explanation and description of the outside world but self-explanation and self-description, when the list is less a reflection of what is objectively true than a symptom of distress sent up by a confused sense of self, then the plain style becomes a mask like any other style. In late works like *Conjugal Lewdness* (1727), Defoe often talks more about the difficulties of finding the proper words for his delicate subject than he does about the subject itself. The speakers in his novels manipulate the plain style to disguise and dissemble; all of them tend to speak in the same accents on their separate occasions of supposed self-revelation. Unlike many later novelists (who are much easier to discuss critically), Defoe does not use style as a mode of characterization. Behind a seemingly transparent screen of plain talk, his narrators conduct their elaborate evasions.

The energies that brought forth Defoe's novels do not seem rooted in any desire to justify the orders of history, society, or religion, nor do they seem to be merely another expression of the previous clarities of Defoe's first-person method. The power of the novels and their ability to move us even now spring from some darker potentialities in Defoe's earlier works. He senses within the autobiographical form a way to explore eccentricity and uniqueness rather than a way to include the individual within orders larger and more comprehensive than his own understanding. In Defoe's novels the didactic autobiography that deindividualizes its subject gradually gives way to a type of autobiography that searches out the *once* of a human life. Defoe's novels reflect a (frequently inconclusive) search for identity within the confines of the self, and they draw upon such general orders as providential explanation in much the same way that contemporary authors use Freud or that Milton played with Copernican and Ptolemaic theories of the universe—explanations to be tested as much for their literary usefulness as for their truth.

Defoe's characters are not characters the way we usually understand the term, with an inner life so rich and complex that we expect them to leap off the page and onto the psychiatrist's couch. They are more like characters in films, with whom we may share the most intimate moments and who may tell us everything about themselves, but whose essential natures remain elusive because they necessarily are seen and heard only from without. Our sense of their individual reality comes from mystery not complexity, even while they profess to be revealing all.

Many of Defoe's characters, like Moll or Singleton, are in actual flight from legal authority, and therefore have practical reasons for remaining evasive and disguised. But other, less threatened, narrators, like Crusoe and Colonel Jacque, express the same paradoxical mixture of reticence and revelation, self-protection and self-exposure. Play with identity, through disguise and name change, has a specific plot function in many of Defoe's novels. Yet it appears so often that it begins to take on a larger significance. Defoe's narrators combine personal evasion and literary self-assertion to preserve personal identities that often seem precariously defined. Their stories are told under the shadow of a world that threatens their sense of self, less from legal punishment than from the implacable pressure of family, society, or the providential order of the universe. Most of Defoe's narrators are in flight from such a priori definitions of themselves, in much the same way that the new form of his first-person narratives may be attempting to break away from earlier autobiographical forms. Through daring and uncertainty, Defoe's characters try to restore to themselves a sense of personal identity and worth that is constantly in doubt, because of birth as an orphan, or the dehumanizing effects of anonymous poverty, or the uncertainty of a place of final security (or a neatly tied-up last paragraph). After rejecting a frame of traditional values that pinch and push the personality into acceptable shape, Defoe's heroes and heroines find unlimited possibility for self-definition. Faced with such terrifying freedom, the individual must establish an identity to deal with it, simultaneously mediating potential and repression. Part of Defoe's insight about the character in search of security about his identity is his discovery of the similar anxieties of confinement and freedom.

Robinson Crusoe is the main counterexample to the argument I have sketched above: Crusoe, say many critics, revolts against his father and therefore against the entire divine order (taking all authority to be equivalent). Crusoe, they may go on to argue, finally adopts a providential interpretation of history that underlies his reconciliation, repentance, and "conversion." But in fact Crusoe never does return to his father and family, and he becomes rich by the accretions of time rather than his own abilities. Essentially Crusoe is as much a wanderer at the end of his memoirs, whether the *Adventures* or the *Farther Adventures*, as he was when be began, "inur'd to a wandering life," hardly even wondering, as Captain Singleton does, whether there is anything beyond "this roving, cruising life." I suppose that it could be argued that Crusoe can continue his wanderings after "conversion" because now he is more errant than erring, his desire for new places now securely stabilized by the rudder of Providence. At the end of *Farther Adventures of Robinson Crusoe* Crusoe anticipates another journey, this time to heaven:

> And here [in England] resolving to harass myself no more, I am preparing for a longer journey than all these, having lived seventy-two years a life of infinite variety, and learnt sufficiently to know the value of retirement, and the blessing of ending our days in peace.

But Crusoe still sees this final adventure like his other ones, a chance for more movement. Few of Defoe's characters seem happy at rest, and the relative ease with which Crusoe accepts his final retreat seems belied by the inconclusiveness of *Captain Singleton, Moll Flanders,* and *Roxana.* All of them may one time or another talk about themselves in terms of money; as Moll says, "Money's virtue, gold is fate." But money satisfies only society's demand for identity. Movement more keenly satisfies the self. Even H. F., the narrator of *Journal of the Plague Year,* confined by choice in London, tells the utopian story of the three men who escaped, and considers it his duty to be constantly on the go, checking every rumor, while throughout the novel appear images of being buried alive, quarantined, and shut up in locked houses.

"A life of infinite variety" says Crusoe at the end of the *Farther Adventures,* and the phrase is echoed frequently in Defoe's later novels until it even appears in the extended title of *Roxana, The Fortunate Mistress or, a History of the Life and Vast Variety of Fortunes of Mademoiselle de Beleau, afterwards called the Countess de Wintselsheim in Germany, Being the Person known by the Name of the Lady Roxana in the time of Charles II.* But the variety that Defoe's narrators use as a touchstone of value has little to do with the bildungsroman variety of experience through which we watch the narrator grow in character. Once again, our usual ideas of character must be put aside to see clearly the value Crusoe or Moll or Roxana place on variety. Variety and movement complement one another; Defoe's characters achieve authenticity not through learning and development (our usual criteria for judging the "fullness" of a literary character), but some basic sense of *being.* Variety and movement enhance this sense of being because they are the means by which Defoe's characters can change identity, become other people, disguise themselves, and hoodwink others. Defoe does not define his characters through a gradual revelation of their basic natures; his understanding of character is not that settled. He seems instead to view identity as combat, either against the secure identities of others or against definitions of character inherited from tradition and ideology. By their manipulation of many identities, his narrators attempt to solidify the one mysterious identity that belongs to each.

John Richetti has emphasized Defoe's "ability to suggest a world of controlling circumstances, which we can recognize as real, in which at the same time extravagant fantasies of success and conquest can take place." But after *Crusoe*, I would argue, the forces of control have had their exposition, and Defoe begins to explore more fully the individual resistance to control. The decrease in providential language in *Captain Singleton* (1720) is remarkable after the importance of providential language in *Crusoe*, and it implies as well the irrelevance of spiritual biography to Defoe's later explorations of character. *The Life, Adventures, and Piracies of the Famous Captain Singleton* effectively contradicts any complacencies about the ability to understand character that may have been set up by *Robinson Crusoe*. At the end of the novel, in one of the most surrealistic scenes in all "realistic" literature, Singleton sets up his conditions for retirement to England after a life of piracy: (1) his friend William, the Quaker with whom he has carried on most of his adventures, will not reveal himself to any relative (although Singleton later marries William's sister); (2) neither William nor Singleton will remove the Greek beards and the Greek clothes they assumed in Istanbul to pass as merchants; (3) neither will ever speak English in public; and (4) they will live together and pass as brothers. This does not recall the serene "retirement" at the end of *Farther Adventures*, with its Horatian echoes, in which the self takes ease after long toil. Instead of being satisfied by the repentance for a life of piracy that Singleton asserts, we are horrified and fascinated with this vision of perpetual disguise in what is nominally Singleton's native land. Revelation of character isn't a problem in spiritual autobiography because all is ultimately to the glory of God, even what would otherwise be hardly bearable outbursts of egotism. But the final vision of *Captain Singleton* shows the potential clash between the purposeful revelations of spiritual autobiography and the damage to the tender self that may result when revelation goes too far. At one point, William warns Singleton that he should be careful lest he reveal himself accidentally while talking in his sleep. This motif of involuntary self-disclosure appears again in *Moll Flanders*. But in *Singleton*, Defoe seems not yet clear about where he will go. The form of the novel itself changes oddly: it begins as a pirate "biography" and ends as a familiar letter to a friend. Singleton's revelations withdraw from the public stage of writer and audience to a more intimate kind of connection. *Crusoe* barely hinted at the possibility that frankness about oneself held any problems, whether psychological or literary. Its preoccupation with Providence may have been the expression of an actual providential anxiety, a desperate need to assert that God had not left the world behind, even though the orders of society and culture seemed to possess none of their old authority or effectiveness. By *Singleton*, the literal and metaphysical cannibals who come to rob Crusoe of his body and soul have become more intriguing subjects for Defoe than any analysis of the inadequacy of older forms.

In flight from pressures that threaten to distort their sense of identity and faced with a possibly malevolent freedom, Defoe's characters protect themselves principally by disguise. Disguise appears so often in Defoe's novels that it finally occupies some shadowland between symbol and metaphysic. Through disguise Defoe and his characters can simultaneously escape the world of facts, lists, and documentary realism, and manipulate it at a distance. By changing names, they assert that finally there is something unspecifiable about human nature, a fact that cannot be pinned down.

Defoe's own life provides many intriguing instances of the pitfalls and benefits of disguise and assumed identity. In 1702 he was arrested, pilloried, fined, and given an indefinite prison term for too successfully imitating a High Church point of view in *The Shortest Way with the Dissenters*. Biographers of Defoe, like James Sutherland, do not speak of any attempt at recantation or explanation, as if Defoe were willing to take the consequences of either the inability of his plain-listening audience to understand his ironies or his own inability to project it. Three of his anti-Jacobite pamphlets in 1712–13 tried the ironic approach by setting forth an exaggerated pro-Jacobite case. In the early 1700s, Defoe travelled about the countryside, acting as a kind of political spy for Robert Harley and later went to Scotland to report on the political climate preceding the Act of Union in 1707. From 1704 to 1713 he published the *Review*, professing an independent political point of view, although in fact he conferred with Harley regularly and was paid with government secret-service money "rather irregularly." From 1715 to 1724, after the Hanoverian Succession had brought the Whigs into power and Harley and Bolingbroke were out, Defoe made some kind of deal with the Whig government by which he would write most of *Dormer's News-Letter* and later *Mist's Weekly Journal* as if they were continuing their previously pro-Tory point of view, when in fact he was supporting Whig policies. James Sutherland has noted that "the extension of Defoe's habit of playing a part in real life to playing one in such ironical pamphlets as *The Shortest Way with the Dissenters* is sufficiently obvious. But deception and make-believe are also prominent features in the stuff of his fiction" (*Daniel Defoe, A Critical Study*, Cambridge, Mass., 1971). One may argue, as Sutherland has, that Defoe's main interest was the support of the Protestant Succession and that he had the ability to write as he wanted to, trimming his Whig or Tory sails to suit himself when the issue was particularly important to him. But the second- and third-guessing involved in such long-term projects as *Dormer's* and *Mist's*, the political spying, and the attempts at plainspeaking irony could not help but breed many minds in Defoe. Conscious deception may be in part a restitution for being previously misunderstood. Typically in Defoe's novels we find characters who are simultaneously trying to explain themselves and conceal themselves. Perhaps through his experience in political deception, Defoe was able to strike a chord in an anxiety about identity more general than he knew.

Defoe's own experiences with disguise seem to permeate his characters, and in the light of his sometimes unsuccessful experiments with irony, it is appropriate that his characters tend to consider disguise a liberation from more confining conceptions of their identities. Ironically enough, Defoe may have gotten the cue to draw upon this shifting side of his literary personality when Charles Gildon attacked *Robinson Crusoe* as an impersonation in which Defoe was actually talking about himself in the fantastical guise of Crusoe and Friday. In *Serious Reflections of Robinson Crusoe*, Defoe picks up and elaborates the allegorical suggestion beyond anything Gildon anticipated. He was obviously intrigued by it and, better than Gildon, perceived that it was a way of vindicating himself from charges of entertainment by showing the more metaphysical uses of *Crusoe*. But Defoe also turned another of Gildon's charges to his benefit, less obviously than the moral allegory. Gildon began his attack by calling Defoe a "Proteus" for his constant changes of political allegiance and writing voice, for his disguises of himself under the name and nature of others. It is difficult to say that Defoe immediately saw the validity and importance of this attack; but in *Singleton* and the novels that follow, disguise assumes an importance far greater than it had in *Crusoe*, and the relation between providential order and personal identity becomes correspondingly less important. Moll Flanders first describes a theft she made without special disguise and then continues, "but generally I took up new figures, and contriv'd to appear in new shapes every time I went abroad." Colonel Jacque may complain that his second wife "was a mere posture mistress in love, and could put herself into what shapes she pleased" and call her a "chameleon," but he himself changes names and disguises with frequency, at one point living in Canterbury and passing among the English as a Frenchman and among the French as an Englishman, with the alternate names of Mr. Charnock and Monsieur Charnot.

Being able to impose on others through disguise brings a joy and elation to Defoe's characters far beyond any pragmatic gains the disguise may bring;

it seems to assure them that they are real. Such situations might be compared with Defoe's description to Harley of his travels in Scotland before the Act of Union:

> I Converse with Presbyterian, Episcopall-Dissenter, papist and Non Juror, and I hope with Equall Circumspection. I flatter my Self you will have no Complaints of my Conduct. I have faithfull Emissaries in Every Company and I Talk to Everybody in Their Own way. To the Merchants I am about to Settle here in Trade, Building ships &c. With the Lawyers I want to purchase a House and Land to bring my family and live Upon it (God knows where the Money is to pay for it). To day I am Goeing into Partnership with a Membr of parliamt in a Glass house, to morrow with Another in a Salt work. With the Glasgow Mutineers I am to be a Fish Merchant, with the Aberdeen Men a woollen and with the Perth and western men a Linen Manufacturer, and still at the End of all Discourse the Union is the Essentiall and I am all to Every one that I may Gain some.

Sutherland wonders why Defoe had to tell so many lies, since a sceptical Scot could always collate the stories. But Defoe seems to exult in the ability to change, assuming and discarding identity. "Converse" and "Union" define the poles of his identity. Defoe in Scotland resembles Colonel Jacque, with his two names and two nationalities within the narrow confines of Canterbury, or Moll Flanders, who steals a watch from a woman after pretending to be a friend of the family and then toys with the idea of getting into the woman's coach when the theft is noticed to help catch the thief; all three manipulate disguise on the edge of exposure and even move closer to exposure in order to savor the preserved self more keenly.

As part of their natural progress through the world, Defoe's narrators take on new names and shed old ones, and another indication of the distance between *Crusoe* and the later novels is the way Crusoe is solaced by the parrot who continually calls him by name, a recognition characters like Moll, Jack, and Roxana often live in fear of. *Memoirs of a Cavalier*, written between *Crusoe* (1719) and *Singleton* (1720), spends most of its time presenting the main character within the framework of military engagements and public history. But it begins with a taste of the kind of mystification about names that will become more prevalent in the later novels:

> It may suffice the reader, without being very inquisitive after my name, that I was born in the country of Salop, in the year 1608,

under the government of what star I was never astrologer enough
to examine; but the consequences of my life may allow me to
suppose some extraordinary influence affected my birth.

Whatever Defoe's motives at this point in his novel-writing career, this
introduction contains the same combination of revelation and reticence that
he exploits more elaborately in other works: specificity about date, vagueness
about name, and assurance about self-importance.

A name you are born with can relate you to a past history, especially
to a genealogy; a name you choose yourself can help you to disengage yourself
from your past and family. Even in *Crusoe*, the novel most preoccupied with
the pressure of authority and the past on the individual, one of the first
things we learn about Robinson Crusoe is that his last name is really Kreutz-
naer, "but by the usual corruption of words in England, we are now called,
nay, we call our selves, and write our name *Crusoe*, and so my companions
always call'd me." Names connect an individual to a world of verifiable facts:
baptismal records, prison records, newspapers, rate rolls—all of the legal
ways Locke defines personal identity as a social term. But Defoe's characters
slip their moorings to this world of human facts and steer carefully between
it and total anonymity. Both Singleton and Moll, for example, are presented
as widely known figures now finally telling their own stories: *The Life, Adventures, and Piracies of the Famous Captain Singleton* and *The Fortunes and
Misfortunes of the Famous Moll Flanders*. Yet their "fame" contrasts strangely
with the elusiveness of their "real" selves. Singleton gets the name "Captain
Bob" only when he asserts and separates himself from the anonymous crowd
of pirates: "Before I go any farther, I must hint to the Reader, that from
this time forward I began to enter a little more seriously into the Circumstances I was in, and concern'd my self more in the Conduct of our Affairs."
Both he and Crusoe brag that they have been in places no other man has
ever ventured into before. (I'll forego any allegorical speculation about Singleton's name.) But at the end of *Singleton*, he and William are sworn to
disguise and anonymity. Moll too is "famous," yet changes her name and
guise with the speed and opportunism of the Proteus Gildon accused Defoe
of being. She is called Betty early in the novel and takes the name Mrs.
Flanders while living in the Mint; "Here, however, I conceal'd my self, and
tho' my new acquaintance knew nothing of me, yet I soon got a good deal
of company about me." When she is called Moll Flanders later, she is puzzled:

It was no more of affinity with my real name, or with any of the
names I had ever gone by, than black is kin to white, except that
once, as before, I call'd my self Mrs. Flanders, when I sheltered

my self in the Mint; but that these rogues [other thieves who
were jealous because she was so rarely caught] never knew, nor
could I ever learn how they came to give me the name, or what
the occasion of it was.

Later she gives the name "Mary Flanders" when she is arrested for something
she did not do, and at the one point is even disguised as a man, named
Gabriel Spencer, the name of one of the actors in Shakespeare's Globe
company, although how strongly Defoe meant us to feel the force of this
allusion, a piece of rhetoric he rarely uses, is questionable. Moll preserves
her name from her companions in the same way that she preserves her money;
no matter how open with them she may be, no matter how much she trusts
and loves them, there is always something withheld, some mystery to keep
for herself. By a quick switch of her apron she changes disguise and disappears. But the most remarkable part of this mystification is that it does
not stop at her companions in crime. The reader is told when she holds back
money, but we never learn her true name. The freedom to establish a new
identity in America may make her less apprehensive about this final revelation, and we do learn that she sends goods "consign'd to my real name in
Virginia." But the phrase is ambiguous, and in any case we never hear what
this "real name" is.

     Colonel Jacque changes disguise with as much glee as Moll; I have
already mentioned the way he passes as a Frenchman among the English
and an Englishman among the French. In some basic way he does not feel
comfortable among his native society, and he uses the possibilities of freedom
in America and stylization in France to purge the anxieties of being born
poor and English. Like Moll, Colonel Jacque considers that money and name
are inextricably bound in the validation of identity. At the beginning of the
novel, he is only one of three orphan boys named Jack who live among the
ashes at the glassworks. There seems to be little reason to have the other
Jacks around—they hardly play any part in his later adventures—except to
heighten the way he emerges as the most important Jack, who can easily
change himself into a Jacque when necesssary, even to the extent of being
"Colonel Jacque" in the book's title. Jack believes that his mother "by oral
tradition" was a gentlewoman and his father a man of quality; his actions in
life are predicated on that belief. When he assumes the clothes of a gentleman,
he becomes what he has been innately all along. Like Roxana, he uses French
culture as a means of assuming and changing identity. Roxana's own name
is given her at a fancy dress ball because she is wearing a Turkish costume;
the ability to change clothes is directly related to the ability to change

identity. Roxana's daughter pursues her in order to verify that this older woman is the same who appeared in Turkish clothes at that ball long ago. Amy, Roxana's maid and alter ego, kills Roxana's daughter because she threatens to link the various identities in Roxana's life; she presents little threat to Roxana beyond the fact that she is *someone who knows*. The hasty ending of *Roxana*, in which the final sentence hurriedly hints of some "Blast of Heaven" that many years later seems to punish her and Amy for their crime, preserves the ambiguous status of the murder, part mortal sin and part psychological necessity. Unlike the titles of the earlier novels, which detailed adventures (*Robinson Crusoe, Singleton, Colonel Jacque*) or social roles (*Moll Flanders*), *Roxana* speaks of its subject in terms of her many names, "Mademoiselle de Beleau, afterwards called the Countess of Wintselsheim in Germany, Being the Person known by the Name of the Lady Roxana in the time of Charles II." And once again the reader is never quite told what her real name is. For people writing about themselves, Singleton, Moll, Jack, and Roxana seem singularly hostile to the idea that anyone might want to meet them in person; no matter how much she may reveal, Roxana does not drop the final veil, even for the reader.

Defoe therefore seems to define personal identity simultaneously as a structuring and merchandising of the self in a public form (your talent sold to politicians, your adventures to sensation-hungry readers), and a final reticence about the depths of the private self. Balanced between seventeenth-century and earlier "patterned" autobiographies and the idiosyncratic confessions of the later eighteenth century, his characters use disguise to preserve the final secret. In the world of Defoe's characters everything that preexists the individual—family, society, culture, and Providence—threatens his or her identity. These orders can be accepted, if at all (e.g., *Crusoe*), after the individual has become secure in his sense of self. Throughout his first-person novels, Defoe searches for the source of self-knowledge and self-realization, through the constant movement of Singleton, Moll, and Roxana, or the stasis of H. F. in London and Crusoe on the island. In some cases, his main characters spawn partners, so that the problem of individuality might be studied in more detail: Crusoe has Friday, Singleton has William, Moll has the "governess," Roxana has Amy. These "doubles" emphasize the inner complexity of human character in opposition to any unitary view, which believes evil, for example, to come from the outside. Friday allows Crusoe to discover things about himself he never knew before; and the pairing of the philosophical William with the adventuring Singleton, or the pragmatic Amy with the romantic Roxana, makes their individual stories larger comments on human personality in general.

Defoe's characters use disguise to facilitate the search outside themselves for ways of proving their separate being. Moll's "governess" joins Friday, William, and Amy as part of a new "family of the self" that Moll, Crusoe, Singleton, and Roxana seek to create. But the most important means of self-definition and self-justification for Defoe's narrators is the act of telling their own stories. Throughout the novels there are points when each narrator decides the limits of his or her story. They use the formula "that's another story" to define what their story is and what their world contains to the exclusion of anyone else's. By this literary formula each establishes his own uniqueness, his separability from others. By this means, Moll separates her story from those of her many husbands, and Jack even more explicitly separates his from the stories of the two other boys named Jack who lived with him in the glasshouse ashes. Within each narrator's story, there are other stories that further enhance the separate importance of his own: Singleton tells about Captain Knox; H. F. tells of the biscuit baker, the sail-maker, and the joiner; and when Colonel Jacque meets his second wife again in Virginia, she won't tell him her story in full because "it would take a great many days to give me a history of it." The book, or the story, instead of being an external form to which the self subordinates its uniqueness for the edification of an audience in search of general truths, becomes a vehicle for a kind of guarded self-expression, in which the reader may explore his own rudimentary and changing sense of himself.

Defoe's narrators gradually realize that the creation of a book can be a source of identity for themselves, as well as self-justification before the world. In proving to a buyer that one's self is worth something, one proves it to oneself. In July 1711, Defoe proposed to Harley a plan to colonize Patagonia and southern Chile; it was shelved. But, as James Sutherland points out, Defoe did not rest there. In 1724 he includes such a venture, successful but fictional, in *A New Voyage round the World*. The reality of the book can restore some failed reality in life. In *Moll Flanders* the life of "infinite variety" and the book of "infinite variety" are already identified. H. F. writes *Journal of the Plague Year* because he believes that he has been spared from the plague specifically to write. By *Roxana* the identification between narrator and book has been made explicit: "The History of this *Beautiful Lady*, is to speak for itself: If it is not as beautiful as the Lady herself is reported to be . . . the *Relator says*, it must be from the Defect of his Performance; dressing up the Story in worse Cloaths than the *Lady*, whose Words he speaks, prepar'd it for the World." We remember here how important Roxana's clothes are for the definition of her identity (and recall the similar importance of clothes in *Colonel Jacque*), at the same time that we note that Roxana hides behind a

"Relator," who doesn't even say he has ever seen her, her beauty only "reported" to him. Without arguing influence, one could say that Defoe brings Montaigne's identification of book and self into English literature. But, unlike Montaigne, Defoe also concentrates on that sense of self the book preserves only because its inner nature remains inaccessible.

Diana Trilling once wrote of Norman Mailer, "Where the novelists of an earlier day helped us to undertand and master a mysterious or recalcitrant environment, the present-day novelist undertakes only to help us to define the self in relation to the world that surrounds and threatens to overwhelm it" ("The Radical Moralism of Norman Mailer," *Claremont Essays*, New York, 1964). Diana Trilling is here obviously defining Mailer against the earlier novelists of society. But it is fascinating to see how easily Defoe can sit beside Mailer in her definition. Society in Defoe is never an object of exploration. It is precisely that threatening world of others that Diana Trilling says Mailer tries to deal with. The world is not to be understood; it is to be gotten through with the least damage to skin or psyche, as Moll Flanders or Colonel Jacque or Roxana speed through the labyrinth of London streets. Defoe's first-person novels move further and further away from older definitions of human character, based so much on the position of an individual soul in the providential order. His works deal basically with the difficulty of knowing and being yourself, amid the bankruptcy of previous psychological and autobiographical forms. Defoe is fascinated by the rigid orders to which human beings so often appeal when they try to explain themselves, and he sees the potential of such orders—genealogy, society, Providence— to help avoid explanation. The form of autobiography, which his narrators manipulate to expose and hide themselves is another such form. But it is self-created, through an isolation and retrospect that becomes an important part of its meaning. Through the isolation of his characters, Defoe examines the epistemological and ontological basis of his own detached narrative voice and discovers its inadequacies. In a narrator like H. F., in *Journal of the Plague Year*, we sense Defoe's engagement with the wellsprings of such detachment: the fear of others, and the implication that sociability automatically means sickness and death. Such a fear is constant in Defoe's narrators, even if they are not on a desert island or in the middle of a plague-stricken city. It is basically a fear of discovery, not the discovery of something tangible, but the discovery and therefore the violation of a sense of personal identity, a sense of self.

Defoe, therefore, has no real answer to the anxieties of self-definition he explores with such power. The closest he comes to one lies in his exploration of the possibilities of retreat, a concept from which the inadequacies of detachment have been distilled. One fascinating characteristic shared by many of Defoe's narrators is a sympathy with Catholicism; Charles Gildon even called Defoe pro-French and pro-papist. But I think that the real lure of Catholicism for Defoe was in the combination of society and refuge encompassed by the concept of "retreat." In *The Memoirs of an English Officer* (1728), the narrator, Captain Carleton, visits a monastery in Spain. He envies the lives of the monks, the mingling of nature and art in their work, and the unique beauty of each cell, with its individual rill from a common spring. This is not the cave in which the fearful Crusoe finds a sick goat, but an image of fruitful isolation, the "most happy and comfortable retreat, though it was a kind of an exile" in which Colonel Jacque tells us he wrote his memoirs. Money is an anchor for the identity of those who wish to stay within society, manipulating disguises and names so that the core of self is never revealed. But "retreat" has no need of money, and Defoe's final ideal seems to be an introspection without society, a replenishing of human insides that, although it takes its image from a religious situation, is basically pastoral and pagan in impulse. Through their compelling delineation of the mystery at the heart of human personality, Defoe's first-person novels change the basic nature of autobiography and announce one of the most important preoccupations of eighteenth-century literature.

GEORGE STARR

Defoe's Prose Style:
The Language of Interpretation

CAIN: Have you then seen the venerable Tents
    Where dwell the Heaven born, the Angelic Pair,
    To whom all human Reverence highly due,
    Is and ought always to be humbly paid?
DEVIL: We have.
CAIN: Did you, together with my grand Request,
    A just, a humble Homage for me pay
    To the great Sire and Mother of Mankind?
DEVIL: We did.
CAIN: Did you in humble Language represent
    The Griefs and Anguish which oppress my Soul?
DEVIL: We did, and back their Blessing to thee bring.
CAIN: I hope with humblest Signs of filial Duty
    You took it for me on your bending Knees?
DEVIL: We did, and had our Share; the Patriarch
    Lifting his Hands to Heaven express'd his Joy
    To see his spreading Race, and bless'd us all.
CAIN: Did you my solemn Message too deliver,
    My Injuries impartially lay down,
    And due Assistance and Direction crave?
DEVIL: We did.
CAIN: What spoke the Oracle? he's God to me;
    What just Command d'ye bring, what's to be done?

From *Modern Philology* 71, no. 3 (February 1974). © 1974 by the University of Chicago.

Why this lumbering blank verse at the head of an essay on Defoe's prose style? To make the preliminary point that we should probably begin by enumerating styles, not generalizing about a style. That fact is that these lines appear here as verse for the first time; until now they have always been printed as prose. Whether or not I am correct in surmising that they originated as blank verse, previous commentators have noticed nothing anomalous about them. They have always passed as normal Defoean prose, yet they are clearly at odds with the prevailing view of his style. Critics are unanimous in stressing the plainness of Defoe's language, but this passage aspires to elevation through epithet and periphrasis; his syntax is usually characterized as loose and sprawling, and thus as structurally equivalent (or at least appropriate) to the homely naturalness of his vocabulary, but this passage strives for formality through metrical regularity, and through various figures of speech and thought.

Nor is this passage altogether idiosyncratic: although its inversions of normal word order are rarely found elsewhere in Defoe's prose, some of its other schemes of construction recur both in the fictional and nonfictional writings. They are less frequent in narrating action than in expounding ideas, but even in the tales of adventure there is more exploring of states of mind, and more deliberate, balanced prose, than criticism has yet recognized. One notable specimen is the slave-tutor's elaborate speech to Colonel Jack, comparing the prosperous wickedness and guilty anxiety of his former life in England with the physical hardships and virtuous calm he now experiences in Virginia. Toward the end of *The Farther Adventures of Robinson Crusoe*, when a Russian grandee explains his decision to remain in Siberian exile, Defoe exploits the oxymorons of "miserable greatness" and "blessed confinement" in a similar series of carefully turned paradoxes. With their sustained antitheses and parallelisms, such passages smack too much of artifice to represent Defoe's prose at its best. Used on a more limited scale, these schemes of balance can seem impressively artless, especially when they bring to an aphoristic point a loosely strung series of thoughts or events: one celebrated example is Moll's summary of the joint career of two fellow criminals: "In short, they robb'd together, lay together, were taken together, and at last were hang'd together." My object, however, is not to vindicate Defoe's endeavors toward stylistic balance and formality, let alone to maintain that they are the most common or distinctive feature of his prose, but simply to suggest, by calling attention to their existence, that immethodical homespun garrulity is not Defoe's only style.

A second preliminary point is that no valid stylistic comments can be based on nuances of punctuation, capitalization, italicization, or spelling in the texts of Defoe's novels. His only major work of which a manuscript survives is *The Compleat English Gentleman:* its editor [Karl Bülbring] observes that "the close and hurried writing, the indistinct characters, which may very often mean different letters, the great number of emendations, additions, and deleted passages, the extensive use of contractions and of shorthand and other abbreviations, and the uncommon, irregular, and often curious and faulty spelling make it difficult and sometimes perplexing to read . . . Defoe scarcely puts any commas, and only very rarely puts a full stop or other mark; . . . he puts [capitals] quite at random." There is no reason to suppose that this manuscript differs from those of the fictional writings of the half-decade between *Robinson Crusoe* (1719) and *Roxana* (1724). As occasional critic, Defoe was aware of the importance of correct "pointing," but as practicing novelist he seems to have disregarded the matter entirely. Analysis of the early printings of *Moll Flanders* indicates that he had little to do with the accidentals in this typical text. We can assume that every word in a Defoean first edition corresponds (however erroneously) with some mark in his manuscript, but no such assumption can be made about the accidentals; in *Moll Flanders*, at any rate, they largely represent compositorial guesses at Defoe's intended meaning. If this is generally true of the novels, then such features of the texts can provide no firm basis for further interpretations.

This point can be clarified by a glance at critical commentary on the famous passage in *Robinson Crusoe* where the hero finds some money in the cabin of the wrecked ship: "I smil'd to my self at the Sight of this Money, O Drug! Said I aloud, what are thou good for, Thou are not worth to me, no not the taking off of the Ground, one of those Knives is worth all this Heap, I have no manner of use for thee, e'en remain where thou art, and go to the Bottom as a Creature whose Life is not worth saving. However, upon Second Thoughts, I took it away; and wrapping all this in a Piece of Canvas." The penultimate clause, Coleridge observes, is "Worthy of Shakespeare;—and yet the simple semi-colon after it, the instant passing on without the least pause of reflex consciousness is more exquisite and masterlike than the touch itself. A meaner writer . . . would have put an '!' after 'away,' and have commenced a new paragraph." In *The Rise of the Novel*, Ian Watt quotes these passages and questions the validity of Coleridge's praise: he faults Coleridge for using the 1812 edition of the book, which "had put a good deal of order into Defoe's haphazard punctuation," whereas "the early editions actually give a comma, not a semi-colon, after 'I took it away.' " But whatever punctuation the early editions "actually give" has little foundation in what Defoe wrote; rather, it constitutes an attempt to put order, not into Defoe's own virtually nonexistent punctuation, but into his narratives by means of punctuation, supplied zealously but often inconsistently and uncomprehendingly by the compositors. In short, Watt's comma probably has no more authorial sanction than Coleridge's semicolon; neither his reading, Coleridge's, nor anyone else's can be sustained or refuted by an appeal to the accidentals of Defoe's texts.

A third and final preliminary point is that historical evidence can sometimes help to illuminate Defoe's prose style. The *Crusoe* passage just quoted, for instance, has an allusive resonance missed by past commentators. Crusoe's apostrophe to the gold may be typical, as Watt maintains, "of Defoe the economic publicist ever on the alert to enforce the useful truth that goods alone constitute real wealth"; but it does not follow that the monologue is not "really suited to Crusoe's character or his present situation," for Defoe is using a classical *topos* to characterize the hero and his predicament. Elsewhere in the book similarities or direct references to the Prodigal Son, Elijah, Balaam, Adam, etc., help to define, evaluate, or intensify Crusoe's situation; in the background of the present scene stands the cock in Aesop's first fable:

> As a *Cock* was turning up a Dunghill, he spy'd a *Diamond*. Well (says he to himself) this sparkling Foolery now to a Lapidary in my place, would have been the Making of him; but as to any Use or Purpose of mine, a *Barley Corn* had been worth Forty on't.

What matters here is not the role of Aesop's fable as possible source or influence, but its usefulness in highlighting certain stylistic features of Crusoe's language when the two passages are juxtaposed. For one thing, the effect of Crusoe's apostrophe to the gold—his "sudden removing from the third person to the second," the "turning of [his] speech to some new . . . thing, that [he himself] gives show of life to" (L. Sonnino, *A Handbook to Sixteenth-Century Rhetoric*, London, 1968)—becomes clearer when compared with the Aesopic cock's monologue: from wry amusement ("I smil'd") analogous to the cock's facetious detachment ("this sparkling Foolery"), Crusoe shifts to vigorous denunciation, and eventually condemns the money, by now exalted to the status of a human adversary, "to the Bottom as a Creature whose Life is not worth saving." The cock had made his paradoxical point through simple contrast ("a *Barley-Corn* had been worth Forty on't"), as does Crusoe ("one of those Knives is worth all this Heap"); and the cock had made explicit the linking quality of his contrast ("Use or Purpose of mine") as does Crusoe ("I have no Manner of use for thee"). But Crusoe submerges this crux of his argument in the surrounding reiteration of "not worth . . . no not [worth] the taking . . . not worth saving," and although these purport to be answers to the rhetorical question "what are thou good for," they actually answer no question, nor do they qualify or extend an argument, for example, "the useful truth that goods alone constitute real wealth." Instead, they serve chiefly to do what Watt says the passage fails to do—that is, they give a "useful truth" rhetorical substance by projecting human qualities onto the money, by making it and Crusoe momentary antagonists, and thus by dramatizing an economic paradox as a clash of personalities.

So much for preliminaries: we should beware of generalizing prematurely about Defoe's prose, of basing our arguments on the shaky evidence of accidentals, and of neglecting the relevance of literary history to discussions of style. Here now is my thesis. Defoe's prose is indeed "realistic," but in a special and limited sense: his characters tell us directly rather little about themselves or their external world, but they create an illusion of both by projecting themselves upon their world in the act of perceiving it. This is to say that the monologue just considered is not only "suited to Crusoe's character [and] his present situation," but epitomizes in a crude yet striking way Defoe's main technique for rendering both character and situation. Character is revealed through response to the other, the external thing or event encountered; at the same time, the external thing or event is described less in objective terms, as it is in itself, than in subjective terms, as it is perceived by the narrator. Nor is the very act of perception a passive state but an outgoing process, in which Defoe's narrators imprint their own nature on the world around them, by imputing to it human qualities not inherently "in" it at all.

I agree with all the commentators, for instance, that *A Journal of the Plague Year* seems impressively realistic in its evocation of what life must have been like in the stricken city. Yet when we come to examine the sources of its lifelikeness, we find that this effect depends less on a vivid or precise rendering of the grim spectacle surrounding the narrator than on his interpretative responses to it. "We hear again," says J. H. Plumb, "the shrieks of the dying and the lamentations of the living" (Foreward to *A Journal of the Plague Year*, New York, 1960), but in what sense do we "hear" them? The narrator repeatedly mentions the "dismal Shrieks and Out-cries of the poor People"; the "terrible Shrieks and Skreekings of Women, who in their Agonies would throw open their Chamber Windows, and cry out in a dismal Surprising Manner"; the "most grievous and piercing Cries and Lamentations"; "the most horrible Cries and Noise the poor People would make"; and so on. Perhaps words like "Shrieks" and "Skreekings" do convey through onomatopoeia some sense of the sounds the narrator tells us he heard, but for the most part these are not auditory descriptions at all: they specify nothing about the sounds themselves, but refer instead either to the impact they made on the narrator, or to the circumstances under which he infers they were uttered. Defoe represents a given cry as expressing emotion A in the crier, or generating emotion B in the hearer; by predicating either A or B of the sound itself, he is "reading into it" human values, interpreting its significance in the very act of recording it.

Since the emphasis is more on how things are perceived than on what they are in themselves, Defoe's narrative style tends to be more adverbial than adjectival, and many words classifiable grammatically as adjectives are in effect functioning as adverbs. Thus "terrible," "grievous," "horrible," etc., appear to modify the shrieks and cries, but refer to these sounds only indirectly; what they primarily tell us is how H. F. the saddler was affected, for the terror, grief, and horror are his. By this I do not mean that Defoe fails to make us "hear again the shrieks of the dying and the lamentations of the living"; my point is that things and events are rendered *as* perceived, as in some sense transformed and recreated in the image of the narrator.

Defoe's rendering of visual experience furnishes abundant evidence of this procedure. The following passage is Robinson Crusoe's initial description of Friday:

> He was a comely, handsome fellow, perfectly well made, with straight strong limbs, not too large, tall, and well-shaped, and, as I reckon, about twenty-six years of age. He had a very good countenance, not a fierce and surly aspect, but seemed to have something very manly in his face; and yet he had all the sweetness and softness of an European in his countenance too, especially when he smiled. His hair was long and black, not curled like wool; his forehead very high and large; and a great vivacity and sparkling sharpness in his eyes. The colour of his skin was not quite black, but very tawny; and yet not of an ugly, yellow, nauseous tawny, as the Brazilians and Virginians, and other natives of America are, but of a bright kind of a dun olive colour, that had in it something very agreeable, though not very easy to describe. His face was round and plump; his nose small, not flat like the negroes; a very good mouth, thin lips, and his fine teeth well set, and white as ivory.

In *The Rise of Modern Prose Style*, Robert Adolph analyzes this passage as a specimen of "The New Prose of Utility." In the older prose of Nashe and Overbury, Adolph argues, "the details reflect the narrator's own attitudes," whereas "Defoe's emphasis is all . . . on the difficulty of exact, objective description, . . . not on the author's momentary feelings toward the subject.

. . . Defoe seems to aspire toward an objective report on a laboratory specimen." In earlier chapters Adolph had maintained that both in theory and practice, the chief aim of the new prose that emerged after the Restoration is "utility," and that "the escape from subjectivity is universal." However valid these contentions may be with respect to the evolution of seventeenth-century prose as a whole, their applicability to the present passage is questionable. Nor does this passage seem to bear out Adolph's further contention that "Crusoe's only important interest in Friday is utilitarian": Crusoe's language is heavily evaluative, but his values here are not primarily, let alone exclusively, utilitarian. Up to this point the "savage wretches" have posed a mortal threat to Crusoe, and their "inhuman, hellish brutality" has been labeled the worst "degeneracy of human nature," so that we have been led to expect an individual savage to present a "horrid spectacle," a countenance expressive of the "abominable and vitiated passions" of these "monsters." But Crusoe's description of Friday is clearly designed to counter these expectations, for this alien creature is rapidly made to appear attractive. This is not achieved through "an objective report on a laboratory specimen," by avoiding the author's or narrator's "feelings toward the subject," but the reverse: what is rendered is the narrator's interpretative response to the external object, and particularly certain character traits which Crusoe infers from (or imputes to) Friday's physiognomy. The presence of such qualities as manliness, sweetness, and softness—and the absence of fierceness and surliness—is not, strictly speaking, observed on but read into Friday's face. Tawny skin is no more "ugly" or "nauseous" to a scientist reporting on a laboratory specimen than it is, presumably, to a Brazilian or Virginian endowed with it; to Crusoe it is disagreeable aesthetically and emotionally, just as to him there is "something very agreeable" in skin "of a bright kind of dun olive colour"—whatever shade that may be. The entire passage is ethnocentric (which is to say subjective) in its intimation that Friday embodies the virtues of Indians and Negroes without their moral, temperamental, or aesthetic drawbacks; its recurrent pattern is to assign Friday mildly exotic features, but to associate them with the grace and delicacy of civilized Europeans rather than the gross animality of African or American natives. Of course this effect is not created by language alone; syntax plays an equally important part, but consideration of the structural aspects of Defoe's prose must be reserved for a separate study.

It would be a mistake to overstate the case against Defoe's concern with utility, or with describing things exactly; my point is that in this passage, the expression of both concerns is to a striking extent personal and subjective rather than scientific or objective. In Defoe's novels utility is not the mere shibboleth of a moral, social, or economic theorist; the question is commonly one of usefulness to a specific person in specific circumstances. As we have seen, the gold-finding passage in *Robinson Crusoe* poses not only the abstract thesis that economic value is determined by utility, but also the dramatic paradox that the very thing most prized by one person may be of no use to another (the lapidary and Defoe's reader versus the cock and Defoe's hero), or to the same person in a different situation (Crusoe in civilization versus Crusoe insulated). In the present passage Crusoe may in part be "sizing up Friday as a slave," as Adolph asserts, but he also seems to be doing something more interesting and less sinister. Crusoe is here seeing for the first time an individual fellow man where he had hitherto thought to find only monsters. His very "seeing" involves the projection of his own feelings and values onto Friday, so that through this initial act of perception, Crusoe in a sense endows Friday with his own humanity. It is not, in other words, a matter of scientific observation, though, as we shall see in a moment, scientific prose of the period was itself often far less impersonal and objective than Adolph's account of it indicates.

At all events, it is curious that Adolph should regard *Robinson Crusoe* or any other novel as the "logical culmination" of the post-Restoration development of an impersonal, objective prose; there would seem to be stronger grounds for regarding the novel as proceeding in an opposite direction—toward rather than away from subjective consciousness and personal interpretation—with regard both to its content and its prose style. In view of what the novel was subsequently to become, it cannot be claimed that Defoe carries this process very far; but if the present argument is correct, his prose does considerably more subjective interpreting of the external world than critics have recognized. By the mid-nineteenth century, according to J. Hillis Miller, "everything is changed from its natural state into something useful or meaningful to man. Everywhere the world mirrors back to man his own image, and nowhere can he make vivifying contact with what is not human." (*The Disappearance of God: Five 19th-Century Writers*, New York, 1965). It is perhaps debatable whether man can ever perceive the external world—or at any rate can communicate his perceptions—without transforming it from its natural state into something meaningful to him, and thus in some measure imposing upon it his own image; but in any case, Defoe's narrators often make contact with what is not human precisely *by* vivifying it, by discovering in it values and meanings which are not its own but theirs.

Does Defoe's style show an indebtedness, or even a resemblance, to "scientific" prose? The Royal Society is sometimes cited as having supplied a model or precedent for Defoe's factual plainness. Without claiming that there was any direct influence, Ian Watt observes that "certainly Defoe's prose fully exemplifies the celebrated programme of Bishop Sprat: 'a close, naked, natural way of speaking; positive expressions; clear sense; a native easiness; bringing all things as near the mathematical plainness as they can; and preferring the language of artisans, countrymen, and merchants before that of wits and scholars.' " But it is usually Sprat's description (or prescription) of the Royal Society's ideal, not an actual specimen of scientific prose by one of the "Royal So-So's," that is compared with Defoe's literary practice; and this prose sometimes turns out to be stylistically different from what Bishop Sprat's formula might lead us to expect. The following passage, for instance, is on a down-to-earth subject—clay—yet the clarity and plainness which it achieves is anything but mathematical, for its crucial device is *prosopopoeia*, an insistent humanizing of the inanimate. Although its style is typical of the scientific prose of John Evelyn (1620–1706), who in turn is an unusually distinguished but quite representative Restoration virtuoso, I quote the passage here because it exhibits, in a charmingly extreme form, the anthropomorphizing tendency already noted in Defoe. There is a kind of clay, writes Evelyn in *Terra*, which is

> so obstinate and ill-natured, as almost nothing will subdue; and another so voracious and greedy, as nothing will satiate, without exceeding industry, because it ungratefully devours all that is applied to it, turning it into as arrant clay as itself. Some clays are . . . in dry seasons costive, and . . . most of them pernicious and untractable. . . . Clay is, of all other [soils], a cursed step-dame to almost all vegetation . . . whether it be the voracious, hungry, weeping, or cold sort. In these cases, laxatives are to be prescribed.

No doubt Evelyn's values here can be described as utilitarian. But to do so is not very illuminating stylistically unless one goes on to observe that man, not utility, is Evelyn's ultimate norm; that it is not only *to* man that Evelyn deems clay useful or worthless, but *from* man that he draws these and other categories for meaningfully perceiving it; and that his main descriptive and evaluative strategy, like Defoe's in the gold-finding episode, is to project human (and specifically moral) qualities onto an inanimate thing, so that it becomes a dramatic adversary rather than an object of detached, impersonal, "scientific" scrutiny. Marjorie Nicolson and others have made us aware of the importance to belles lettres of imagery drawn from science in the late seventeenth and eighteenth centuries; less widely recognized is the extent to which scientific prose of the period was itself metaphorical and poetic—qualities conspicuous in Evelyn's treatment of clay. More generally, this passage points to what may be a fallacy in Adolph's conception of post-Restoration prose, for it reminds us that the more an author of this period is preoccupied with the utility of a thing, the less his account of it is likely to resemble "an objective report on a laboratory specimen"; in other words, the two tendencies may often be inversely proportional, not directly proportional as Adolph maintains.

But let us suppose that Evelyn is attempting to treat his subject according to Sprat's program: if we were to set aside the adjective "mathematical," might we not conclude that he has succeeded? When the phenomena to be described are unfamiliar, or when there is as yet no settled vocabulary with which to describe them, then the writer would seem faced with a choice between inventing new terms or applying existing terms in a more or less metaphorical fashion to the new subject matter. The problem is more complex than this, both theoretically and historically, but such a scheme may help to clarify Evelyn's position (and ultimately Defoe's) relative to the stylistic ideals of the Royal Society. A preference for "the language of artisans, countrymen and merchants before that of wits and scholars" might authorize the use of specialized terms of art, were they available; but when they are not, the ideals of the Royal Society may best be served by representing the unfamiliar metaphorically, in terms of the familiar. The question then becomes, How far can prose go in this direction without falling into the proscribed language of "wits"? To this, the answer appears to have been that when metaphor attracts attention to itself or is pursued for its own sake, when it leads to "amplifications, digressions, and swellings of style," when it is a source of "luxury and redundance of speech" or a "superfluity of talking"—in short, when metaphor is a mere ornament, tending to obscure rather than clarify—it constitutes a stylistic vice, and by the same token a philosophical and moral vice. These phrases are from the two paragraphs in Sprat's *History* immediately preceding the positive program cited earlier, and indicate that Sprat's real target of attack is not metaphor per se but the verbose "extravagance" and "excesses" of traditional eloquence—as is also evident from his one specific reference to metaphor in the series: "this vicious abundance of phrase, this trick of metaphors, this volubility of tongue." That his rejection of metaphor is not complete is shown further at the end of the *History*, when Sprat comes to defend—quite consistently, in my opinion— a kind of metaphor "founded on such images which are generally known, and are able to bring a strong, and a sensible Impression on the *mind*." In other words, Sprat himself, though generally regarded as a staunch enemy to metaphor, recognizes that it may be legitimate as well as necessary insofar as it makes for clarity, ease, and naturalness. It can therefore be maintained that Evelyn's lines on clay carry out in their own peculiar way the essential spirit of Sprat's program—assuming (as I think we must) that Evelyn introduced his anthropomorphic imagery not as a sustained conceit, to be relished for its own sake, but as a body of "images which are generally known" by means of which he could make his observations intelligible to his contemporaries.

Returning to the language of Defoe, we may now be in a better position to assess both Watt's contention that it has "a certain 'mathematical plainness,' a positive and wholly referential quality," and the relation he sees between it and "the attempt of the Royal Society to develop a more factual prose." On the latter question, Defoe may be said to share the stylistic ideals of the Royal Society, with the caveat that neither he nor Sprat is as radically opposed to figurative language as is usually supposed. Defoe may seek to put things simply and exactly, but is evidently aware that the dry impersonality we now associate with scientific prose is not necessarily the best way to achieve this, and that the more Crusoe and H. F. the saddler project themselves into their descriptions, the better we will understand not only their subjective states but the objects and events they encounter. As to Watt's general description of Defoe's prose, a necessary qualification would seem to be that much of Defoe's rendering of things is not "factual" or "referential" at all, but creates this illusion by ascribing to the object qualities which the narrator comes upon, not through simple observation, but through processes of ego-, ethno-, or anthropocentric interpretation. In his fictional prose, to be sure, Defoe cannot afford to call attention to such devices. The illusion that the things and events he is describing are real depends to some extent on our not noticing the fundamental artificiality—the "fictiveness" if not arbitrariness—of his humanizing the external world in this way. Nevertheless this illusion is created in part by an essentially symbolic activity, the metaphoric ascription of human traits to external objects.

This is by no means the sole source of Defoe's realism, and if its role had not been overlooked or denied by most previous commentators, there would be less need to insist here on its importance. It will be useful to examine at this point some features of Defoe's writing which are more commonly regarded as contributing to its realism. I shall continue to confine my attention to language, and to base most of my remarks on passages which other critics have chosen to discuss, not only to avoid culling evidence which happens to fit my views, but to make clear how these views differ from existing accounts of Defoe's prose style.

It is often said that Defoe's realism owes a great deal to the sheer abundance of *things*. One modification of this thesis has already been proposed: namely, that Defoe often presents not things but people perceiving things, so that both the existence and the nature of the things are established by indirection, by showing us people in the act of perceiving them. A second modification might be introduced here in the form of a rhetorical question: how many of Defoe's things are *un*familiar? As soon as representation calls for more than simple naming, there comes into play some such technique as I have been describing. What should be stressed at once, though, is that much of Defoe's realism is on the elementary level of naming: many objects and places take on whatever fictional reality they possess, and make whatever contribution they do to the realism of their narrative contexts, simply because we happen to know what their names stand for.

In Lancashire, Moll Flanders is courted by an Irish fortune hunter who

> talk'd as naturally of his Park, and his Stables; of his Horses, his
> Game-Keepers, his Woods, his Tenants, and his Servants, as if
> we had been in the Mansion-House, and I had seen them all about
> me.

Jemmy actually owns these things no more than Moll does, but he beguiles her in the same way that she and Defoe's other narrators often beguile us, for the passage epitomizes Defoe's realism at its simplest. The naming of a great many commonplace objects creates the illusion that we are amidst them; or to speak more accurately, our own imaginations, fastening on the familiar names, create such an illusion. In this context the scope of "imagination," of "illusion," and ultimately of "realism" itself, is quite limited. Here as elsewhere Defoe's chief concern is with objects not in themselves but in relation to human actions and values—in relation to the person perceiving them or, in this case, alluding to them "as naturally . . . as if" they were there to be perceived. The real point of the passage, after all, is that these things are *his*: note the cumulative force of "*his* Park, and *his* Stables; of *his* Horses, *his* Game-Keepers, *his* Woods, *his* Tenants, and *his* Servants." That they exist follows a fortiori from the "fact" that he owns them, and this order of priorities is very characteristic of Defoe's realism. It is usually a significant relationship to the narrator that confers imaginary existence on external people, places, and things, rather than a rendering of the kind of inherent, individual qualities which would give them an existence independent of the narrator. Needless to say, Defoe regards the relationship of owner to property as a particularly meaningful one; but it does not follow that this is the only one he is capable of conceiving, as some of his critics have maintained.

In Defoe's novels, God and the Adam of Genesis 1:19–20 tend to become one: things are not called into being and then named, but often called into being *by* being named. Certainly this is what Jemmy does here; the bulk of the passage consists of his catalogue of squirely appurtenances, and it deserves emphasis that these things are only said, not "shown," to exist. Moll's imagination is not aided, so far as we are told, by his vivid or detailed descriptions. That Moll can imagine Things when she hears bare Names is owing rather to her own experience—not only of language but of life. For the modern reader, in turn, much of Defoe's realism depends on the historical accident that so many objects named in the stories, which were commonplace at the time, happen to remain familiar today. When Moll speaks elsewhere of pieces of "Holland," or of "Lac'd-heads," or of a "Suit of Knots," the latter condition is not met: lacking special knowledge of the history of English dress, the modern reader is likely to find such details *un*realistic, in the sense that the names evoke no memory of corresponding objects in his own experience. True, a book might be filled with casual naming of vanished customs, objects, and locales, and still have a valid title to be called realistic in some genetic or mimetic sense, as a document of social history; but in affective terms such materials do not make for realism, and may in extreme cases (e.g., some of the *hapax logomena* in Old English) result instead in impenetrable obscurity.

To put it another way, there are no cassowaries in Jemmy's park. I am not maintaining that the scene would have been ipso facto less realistic had he chosen to put them there, although the very ordinariness of Jemmy's inventory—just what we would expect of a country gentleman, and nothing more—no doubt helps to prevent suspicion on Moll's part or ours. What I am suggesting is that if he had fancied laying claim to an aviary, merely naming his exotic birds would not have sufficed. Some indications of what they were like, and particularly of why he had them, would also be called for; and it is information of the latter kind—about their meaning and value to Jemmy himself—which Defoe would be most likely to marshal to make them realistic. At all events, unless Moll and the reader were already acquainted with them, simply naming them would not increase but reduce the realism of the passage.

As to Defoe's presentation of things beyond merely naming them, the following two statements sum up—and were influential in establishing— what has come to be the prevailing view on this matter. Dorothy Van Ghent observes:

> What is important in Moll's world of things is the counting, measuring, pricing, weighing, and evaluating of things in terms of the wealth they represent and the social status they imply for

the possessor. What is unimportant (and we learn as much by
what is unimportant as by what is important) is sensuous life,
the concrete experience of things as they have individual texture.
              (*The English Novel: Form and Function*, New York, 1961)

Ian Watt also regards these socioeconomic indicators as more crucial to
Defoe's rendering of the "world of things" than the "individual texture" of
objects as the narrators "concretely experience" them. But he sees Defoe's
bias as having a distinctive epistemological foundation as well. "Defoe's
style," he says

> reflects the Lockean philosophy in one very significant detail: he
> is usually content with denoting only the primary qualities of the
> objects he describes—their solidity, extension, figure, motion,
> and number—especially number: there is very little attention to
> the secondary qualities of objects, to their colours, sounds, or
> tastes.

Neither formulation is entirely at odds with the thesis which has been
advanced here. In calling attention to an element of constant interpretation—
Defoe's habit of treating things "in terms of" what they "represent" or
"imply"—Van Ghent makes a valid and important point; but just as Adolph
narrows Defoe's interpretative range unduly by regarding utility as his sole
evaluative category, so Van Ghent distorts Defoean evaluation by reducing
it to a question of wealth or social status. It is clear, from the *Journal of the
Plague Year* and *Robinson Crusoe* passages already considered, that psychological, aesthetic, and moral as well as socioeconomic values enter into the
language with which Defoe renders the "world of things"; considerations of
utility are often uppermost in Crusoe's mind, and of wealth and social status
in Moll's, but what is stylistically significant is the process by which these
and other values are ascribed *to* a world of external things *by* Defoe's narrators.
To the extent that Defoe describes things at all (rather than merely naming
them), it is their significance—in the widest sense, their position in relation
to the narrator—that he is chiefly concerned to establish.

Watt has chosen for analysis the following passage in *Moll Flanders*:

> The next thing of moment was an attempt at a gentlewoman's
> gold watch. It happened in a crowd, at a meeting-house, where
> I was in very great danger of being taken. I had full hold of her
> watch, but giving a great jostle as if somebody had thrust me
> against her, and in the juncture giving the watch a fair pull, I
> found it would not come, so I let it go that moment, and cried

as if I had been killed, that somebody had trod upon my foot, and that there was certainly pickpockets there, for somebody or other had given a pull at my watch.

Watt quotes more, but his comment on these lines is most relevant here:

> It is very convincing. The gold watch is a real object, and it won't come, even with "a fair pull." The crowd is composed of solid bodies, pushing forwards and backwards. . . . All this happens in a real, particular place. It is true that, as is his custom, Defoe makes no attempt to describe it in detail, but the little glimpses that emerge win us over completely to its reality.

What seems to me most important in this passage is the element that Van Ghent would deny—Moll's "sensuous life." This consists largely of active contact with things: having hold, giving a jostle, giving a pull, being balked, letting go. Moll cannot afford to linger over the "individual texture" of external objects, but she does convey the sensations of a body and mind energetically in touch with them. People, places, and things concern her less in themselves than in their bearing on what she does and undergoes. This attempt happened, Moll tells us, "*in* a crowd, *at* a meeting house." Watt speaks of "a real, particular place," but these adverbial and prepositional phrases scarcely realize or particularize the place itself: they modify Moll's experience, which they situate less in actual time and space than in its own patterns of spatial movement and temporal sequence. What matters most to Moll about these surroundings is that they are "where [she] was in very great danger of being taken," and I am not sure her sense of danger would have seemed more convincing if she had indeed specified "a real, particular place" (e.g., St. Anne's Church, Soho) as the setting. Similarly, such phrases as "in the juncture" or "that moment" locate fresh developments in relation to other fragments of Moll's experience, not according to an objective chronology of clocks or calendars.

As to the focal object in the episode, it does not seem to me that its reality (such as it is) can be accounted for adequately in terms of Defoe's concentration on Lockean "primary qualities." The watch is gold; it is a gentlewoman's (though only accidentally, not essentially, according to Moll's traditional philosophy); and Moll wants it. The lines quoted are about Moll's strenuous efforts first to get it, then to avoid being caught; and neither the watch nor the other external things—gentlewoman, crowd, meeting house—have any independent reality worth speaking of. Eventually an illusion of solidity may be imparted indirectly to the watch by the unavailing "fair

pull," but once again it is an act or perception of the narrator's, not the
external object, which is rendered directly. In this connection it is worth
noting that in Moll's long third sentence, the phrases "*as if* somebody had
thrust me against her" and "*as if* I had been killed" furnish not facts but
Moll's commentary on the facts. Unobtrusive as they may be, such metaphorical devices are important: they contribute not to what Watt calls the
"immediate presentation" of the scene, but to a presentation constantly mediated by Moll's imagination.

It was suggested earlier that Defoe's presentation of any given thing
depends a good deal on whether it is already familiar to readers; that when
it is, simple naming often suffices, and that when it is not, Defoe relies more
on a metaphorical approach to the unknown via the known than on an
objective specification, Lockean or scientific, of its distinguishing qualities.
These contentions are borne out interestingly by Defoe's handling of Captain
Singleton's trek across Africa. Here Defoe had a splendid opportunity to
invest exotic objects with solidity and particularity, and ample factual information was available to him, had he wished to make the African settings
convincing in Watt's terms. But as Gary J. Scrimgeour points out, Defoe
makes very limited use of such material:

> Those elements which are specifically African were matters of
> common knowledge and were often handled with equal or greater
> concreteness by other writers on Africa. . . . Much of the realistic
> atmosphere is in fact not African, but English. One of Defoe's
> favorite tricks is to compare an African bird, animal, or river
> with its English equivalent—a device which, in the mouth of
> the unlettered Singleton, often does produce an illusion of
> verisimilitude.
> ("The Problem of Realism in Defoe's *Captain Singleton*,"
> *Huntington Library Quarterly* 27, p. 29).

Yet what Scrimgeour regards as a limitation on the realism of *Captain Singleton*, and the "trick" with which he sees Defoe as disguising this inadequacy,
are characteristic of Defoe's narratives whenever more than mere naming of
familiar objects is called for, and it is not only in the hands of "unlettered"
narrators that they "produce an illusion of verisimilitude." Nevertheless,
Scrimgeour's illustrations of the device are pertinent here:

> Vegetables of various kinds are brought to the Europeans by the
> natives, but they are then described either by reference to the
> nearest English equivalent or in the vaguest terms: "a great heap

of roots and plants for our bread, such as the Indians gave us"
or "we met with a little negro town, where they had growing a
sort of corn like rice, which ate very sweet." The beasts of burden
consume a plant "like thistles" in place of water and a root "not
much unlike a parsnip, very moist and nourishing." . . . [Defoe's]
sole monster "seemed to be an ill-gendered kind, between a tiger
and a leopard." . . . The only serpent in *Captain Singleton* is the
one of "a hellish ugly deformed look and voice" that the men
mistake for Satan.

Scrimgeour contends that Defoe's attempt at realism "was totally subordinated to other interests"—namely, a demonstration of the opportunities open
to "The Compleat English Tradesman" in Africa—and concludes that "both
aesthetics and reality bow their heads before commerce." This seems to me
an exaggeration, analogous to Adolph's narrowing of Defoe's values and
purposes to the purely utilitarian. Profit and utility are important themes in
Captain Singleton, but they are not the only considerations that affect Defoe's
rendering of the African scene: as the serpent description indicates, other
values are clearly present.

Scrimgeour is a sensitive reader, and it is instructive that he should
equivocate on the question of whether *Captain Singleton* is realistic. On the
one hand, he suggests that the book is considerably less realistic than it might
have been, had Defoe stocked it more abundantly with African *realia*. In
other words, he shares Watt's view that particularized things make for realism, but holds that Defoe's achievements in this line are not at all "im-
pressive" in *Captain Singleton*, and finds the vagueness and paucity of Defoe's
Africana somewhat "surprising." On the other hand, he recognizes that the
narrative does achieve a "necessary though meretricious authenticity,"
through what I have called the projection of familiar English categories and
values onto the alien landscape; yet he regards this aspect of realism with
suspicion, twice labeling it "simply a device, almost a trick," denying that
it is "in any sense created by an artistic or ethical ideal," and finding it
"necessary" only because of Defoe's "preoccupation with certain attitudes
unrelated to literature"—that is, as a vehicle for economic propaganda. But
by now it should be clear that this "trick" is characteristic of Defoe's imaginative writings in general, and that it is "necessary" not only to the pro-
pounding of ideological theses, but to the meaningful experiencing and
communicating of all kinds of "strange surprising adventures," which is made
possible by interpreting the strange in terms of the familiar.

We praise *Robinson Crusoe* for its hero's demonstration that thrust into a "waste, howling wilderness," man can create order. This is usually put in economic terms: we are fascinated (and perhaps reassured) by Crusoe's capacity to conquer and regulate his physical environment. A similar process takes place within the soul of the hero: in religious terms, divine grace subdues and redeems errant human nature, and several recent critics have found Crusoe's spiritual progress as striking as his mastery over external nature. A Freudian critic might admire *Robinson Crusoe* for tracing an attainment of psychological order as well: initially torn between the anarchical demands of a powerful id and the constraints of superego, Crusoe eventually pieces together not only an economic utopia, not only a spiritual salvation, but an ego. The implication of the present argument is that all these processes are reflected in, and in some sense dependent on, the nature of Crusoe's language, for it is on this level that the ordering of experience most fundamentally takes place. Externally, wild animals are domesticated, the wilderness is enclosed, Friday is Europeanized, and so on; internally, the hero's own chaotic, wasteful, and sinful impulses are sublimated, disciplined, or converted into methodical, productive, and virtuous industry: my point is that Crusoe's language not only describes these processes, but enacts or embodies them. By animating, humanizing, and Anglicizing the alien things he encounters, Crusoe as narrator achieves verbally exactly what Crusoe as hero achieves physically, spiritually, and psychically. In the poetry of the period, personification constantly implies a relation between man and the external world; in *Robinson Crusoe*, the hero not only makes contact in this way with what is foreign and threatening to him, but by imposing on it his own values, he attains through the act of narration a mastery over it. In the same way, Captain Singleton may be said to conquer Africa, and H. F. to overcome the Plague. It is in this general sense that it seems to me most meaningful to speak of the "functional" quality of Defoe's prose. His characters are not secure, detached observers of the world, but actors in it, vulnerable to it and intent on triumph over it; even at the supposed time of writing, in affluent retirement, they remain somewhat unsure of themselves. As a consequence, the act of recounting their lives, no less than the struggles they narrate, represents an effort to achieve control over experience, to formulate a conception of themselves as stable and respectable as the place they have outwardly attained in the world.

There are other ways, of course, of approaching Defoe's language. One can calculate statistically the relative frequency of different parts of speech, or of words derived from Romance or Germanic stock. One can examine the social, political, economic, and religious milieux reflected in Defoe's vocabulary; or one can analyze this element rhetorically rather than genetically, in terms of the class, party, occupational, and denominational interests which his vocabulary serves to articulate or advance. Formally, one can weigh the fitness of Defoe's language to the personalities and situations of his various fictional narrators; or one can attempt to isolate certain terms or clusters of words which Defoe habitually uses in an insistent or unusual way. The present essay has dwelt instead on certain interpretative and figurative qualities which Defoe's language shares with most poetry and much other prose; it has deferred the task of defining Defoe's stylistic individuality until the structural aspects of his prose have also been considered. In the meantime, examination of his language has indicated that Defoe's realism has to do primarily with his narrators' perceptions, only secondarily with the "world of things" on which most previous criticism has focused; that apart from simple naming, Defoe is less concerned with rendering external things directly than with presenting them as experienced by or related to his narrators, and less concerned with rendering them objectively than with assigning them human significance; and that this significance is broader, in some respects, than most commentators on Defoe have acknowledged.

In other respects, however, it is curiously narrow. In a Defoe novel, everything and everyone mentioned matters to the narrator, and it makes for a certain kind of realism that all should be so plausibly filtered through the narrator's consciousness—or at any rate that so little should seem interpolated by an authorial consciousness independent of the narrator's. Whatever contradictions there may be in the characterization of Defoe's heroes and heroines, most critics do not seem to feel that these inconsistencies make his characters less lifelike. On the contrary, modern readers are more likely to balk at the opposite aspect of Defoe's characters—to feel that individually and collectively their personalities embrace not too much but too little to be entirely realistic. They share an anxious egoism which tends to give unity and meaning to the episodic materials of adventure stories, but which at the same time confines them and their capacity for experience. If it helps them to see life steadily, it prevents them from seeing life whole. Important dimensions of both human and nonhuman nature are closed to them. Such mastery as the Defoean hero achieves over himself and his world is quite precarious: it involves insulation and repression rather than openness and liberation, an imposing of order on everything alien and threatening rather than that benign acceptance of the facts of otherness and disorder (or order beyond man's contriving) which we find at the conclusion of a Sophoclean or Shakespearean tragedy. We may regard man as capable of more expansiveness and love than Defoe's heroes and heroines ever attain—our classic drama offers a vision of what man can potentially become, alongside which they seem somewhat stunted figures—but the fact that they are limited people, according to various poets', moralists', and psychoanalysts' ideals of human development, does not limit their reality or interest. What it does mean is that there are some things Defoe's characters can encompass and some things they cannot, and the same is true of Defoe's style. His prose cannot render other people and things as they are in themselves, since his narrators must recast the world in their own images in the very act of perceiving it. They may scrutinize their surroundings as attentively as one of Robbe-Grillet's narrators, but their gaze is obsessively purposeful, seldom coolly contemplative: in a sense they see only what they want to see, and what they want to see is chiefly how things stand in relation to themselves. Nor do we in turn see as much through their eyes as through their busily analyzing and combining, imagining and judging minds. "In my dear self I center everything": this line of Rochester's may not exhaust Defoe's theories about human motivation, but it does sum up accurately his narrators' habitual mode of experiencing and describing their world.

ARNOLD WEINSTEIN

The Self-Made Woman: Moll Flanders

En un si grand revers que vous reste-t-il?—Moi;
Moi, dis-je, et c'est assez . . .
                    —CORNEILLE, *Médée*

Defoe has not had an easy time with critics. The excellences of his book
seem too haphazard, the ironies too unintended. The finer the critical nets,
the more rewarding, but also the more ambiguous, Defoe's novels appear.
Surely, *Moll Flanders* is the richest of his fictions. But, to claim, as I shall
be doing, that Moll is one of the most fully realized individuals in literature
is to face the immediate charge: who is Moll Flanders? Does the reader
know? On the first page of her story, she hedges radically:

> It is enough to tell you, that as some of my worst Comrades,
> who are out of the Way of doing me Harm, having gone out of
> the World by the Steps and the String, as I often expected to go,
> knew me by the name of *Moll Flanders*; so you may give me leave
> to speak of myself under that name till I dare own who I have
> been, as well as who I am.

Moll is, from the outset and definitively, for her world and also for ours,
incognito. With so much withheld, what can be given? Even the appellation
Moll Flanders seems to be grudgingly meted out to the reader ("It is enough
to tell you"). Moreover, names count in this novel. It is important to know
with whom one is dealing, to see clear; and Moll herself, as narrator, takes
considerable pains to orient the reader, to qualify words, to distinguish
between apparent usage and reality. "In plain English," "my Brother, *as I*

From *Fictions of the Self: 1550–1800.* © 1981 by Princeton University Press.

now call him," and a host of other qualifications indicate Moll's sharp awareness of reliable and unreliable language.

Moll's initial statement may equally be construed as a forthright offering to the reader: this much, and no further. How much? At a crucial moment, Moll, in her fifties, at Newgate at last, is reunited with her Lancashire husband, and her poignant question rings throughout the novel: "*My dear,* says I, do you not know *me?*" Even, we may recall, during their passionate youthful encounter, Moll still "reserv'd the grand Secret, and never broke my Resolution, which was not to let him ever know my true Name, who I was, or where to be found." Again, can there be knowledge or intimacy, where there is such holding back?

To sketch an answer to that question, let us consider the double nature of disguise, what it hides and what it enables. Moll has wanted, from childhood on, to be a gentlewoman. At best, however, she can only appear to be one; hence those carefully plotted marriages wherein Moll artfully parades as a woman of means, thereby ensnaring a husband but remaining technically honest by avoiding outright verbal deception. In these cases the feint is marginal, and Moll is easily forgiven by her husbands once they find out the truth. In other instances, however, the deceit is more fulsome. One of the most radical deceptions occurs when Moll "transforms" her sex, i.e., she steals as a man. Defoe offers us here a very concise business vs. pleasure image, as Moll successfully keeps her affairs separate:

> And as we kept always together, so we grew very intimate, yet he never knew that I was not a Man; nay, tho' I several times went home with him to his lodgings, according as our business directed, and four or five times lay with him all Night: But our Design lay another way, and it was absolutely necessary to me to conceal my sex from him, as appear'd afterwards.

Here again we see the bewildering double claim: "we grew very intimate," but "our Design lay another way." On the surface, Moll reneges drastically. Yet, the book bears her out, since, in this particular case, she escapes the gallows precisely because a male accomplice is being sought. To be known, either by one's true name, perhaps even in one's sex, is manifestly dangerous business. In light of these maneuvers and disguises, how can one talk of authenticity or identity?

Although Moll did not invent the mercantile, barter code of her time, she demonstrates a ready willingness to cope with it. It is hard not to view both the marrying and the thieving as dehumanized, impersonal exchanges, devoid of all ethical content. Much time is spent in the novel counting money and describing the plate, cloth, and watches that Moll steals. We seem to be close to the exclusively materialist world encountered in the *Lazarillo*. Even the vocabulary used for affective matters is a mercantile one: in describing her first, least "seasoned" love affair, Moll consistently refers to lovemaking as work (e.g., "he comes up again in half an Hour or thereabouts, and falls to Work with me again as before"); equally telling is the ubiquitous word "offer" (e.g., "but he had no more to do with me, or offer'd anything to me other than embracing me"). The most brazen, paradigmatic instance of sexual activity depicted as exchange-work-offer occurs in the anecdote that Moll recalls:

> I knew a Woman that was so dexterous with a Fellow, who indeed deserv'd no better usage, that while he was busie with her another way, convey'd his Purse with twenty Guineas in it out of his Fob Pocket, where he had put it for fear of her, and put another Purse with guilded Counters in it into the room of it: After he had done, he says to her, now han't you pick'd my Pocket? she jested with him, and told him she suppos'd he had not much to lose, he put his Hand to his Fob, and with his Fingers felt that his Purse was there, which fully satisfy'd him, and so she brought off his Money.

This scene epitomizes the business exchange, and it has the extra spice of being, in all senses, a counterfeit exchange.

Moll has been judged by many to be equally callous and mechanical, and that is the parallel I would now like to test. My thesis is that Moll's exchanges and deceptions—even the most blatant ones—usually become acts of communication and even commitment; enrichment there may be, but it is more than monetary. As Faulkner would say, there is nothing "fault nor false." One of the finest such sequences involves Moll's efforts to remain demure while accepting money from a wealthy suitor. Let us then keep in mind the episode of the whore and the false coin as we see how Moll gets hers. Asked to show her suitor all her money, Moll fetches "a little private Drawer" containing some six guineas and a little silver, and she throws it all on the bed:

> He look'd a little at it, but did not tell it, and Huddled it all into the Drawer again, and reaching his Pocket, pull'd out a Key, and then bade me open a little Walnut-tree box, he had upon the Table, and bring him such a Drawer, which I did, in which Drawer there was a great deal of Money in Gold, I believe near

> 200 Guineas, but I knew not how much: He took the Drawer,
> and taking my Hand, made me put it in and take a whole handful;
> I was backward at that, but he held my Hand hard in his Hand,
> and put it into the Drawer, and made me take out as many
> Guineas almost as I could well take up at once.
>
> When I had done so, he made me put them into my Lap, and
> took my little Drawer, and pour'd out all my own Money among
> his, and bade me get me gone, and carry it all Home into my
> own Chamber.

Parallels are not lacking between this scene and the whore's theft. But the
insistence on hands being placed in and out of drawers, money in and out
of laps, lends a powerful erotic interest to these gestures. Defoe has drawn
this scene with considerable fineness, and it wholly merges the economic
and the affective into a fusion of motives, a rather touching and surprising
intimacy. In this light, it is a moment of tenderness, and the language of
hands and coins achieves a delicacy rarely found orally in the novel. Above
all, this is a felt, realized exchange between two human beings, not a fraudulent deception as in the whore's trick. And this leads me to the central
argument in my reading of Defoe: Moll authenticates the exchange, just as
she personalizes the masks and makes good on the deceptions. Herein she
differs radically from Lazarillo and Pablos, because all that would be sham
or dehumanizing in her conduct is ultimately *assumed* by Moll, yoked into
the service of an integral self.

Let me now reconsider the question of Moll Flander's identity. Her
childhood ambition remains with her throughout: to be a Gentlewoman.
When she first states this goal as a helpless orphan, she is roundly ridiculed;
but her definition of the term is most illuminating: "all I understood by
being a Gentlewoman, was to be able to Work for myself, and get enough
to keep me without that terrible Bug-bear *going to Service*, whereas they
meant to live Great, Rich and High, and I know not what." This is really
no less than a declaration of independence, a desire for being one's own
person, which ultimately has little to do with societal codes. Two routes,
taken sequentially, seem to be open to Moll: marriage and then thieving.
Many novelists would have doubtless abandoned Moll after her last erotic
affair. Defoe somewhat hugely stops her love(s) story midway in the book,
so that the second life (in the fullest sense of the term) of thieving may begin.
In so doing, he reminds us how far life exceeds the boundaries of romance,
how limited the erotic interest must be in a life that goes from infancy to
three score and ten. Life does not stop with marriage (although literature

often does), and Defoe achieves something rather enormous in his portrayal of a vigorous old lady bent on affirmation at all costs. Thieving, we realize, is, like marrying, essentially an arena for deploying talents and resources. The body may no longer seduce, but the fingers remain nimble, the eyes keen, the feet agile. There is a powerful and lithe intelligence at play in Moll's exploits. As she dons disguise after disguise, walking about the city, "peering, and peeping into every Door and Window I came near," she becomes a veritable allegory of urban intelligence and consciousness. Powers of intellect and perspicacity are needed for successful thieving:

> a Thief being a Creature that Watches the Advantages of other People's mistakes, 'tis impossible but to one that is vigilant and industrious many Opportunities must happen, and therefore she [Mother Midnight] thought that one so exquisitely keen in the Trade as I was, would scarce fail of something extraordinary where ever I went.

Moll's prowess along these lines is so remarkable that she becomes, in words that will resonate throughout this study, "the greatest artist of my time."

Moll's triumphs are those of cunning and creativity (disguise is, by definition, creative), but her goal is essentially that of pleasure rather than material benefit, the pleasure of self-assertion, the supremely human pleasure of technique. If she cannot be a "gentlewoman" in the accepted social manner, then she will be one *à sa façon*. In one of the most stunning sequences of the novel, Moll splendidly demonstrates her mastery over circumstances, her ability to make the two gentlewoman-definitions merge: independence *and* social stature. Falsely (!) accused of theft in a mercer's store, Moll enacts an elaborate drama of offended dignity. She demands and receives reparation, and the entire episode is a tribute to the power of art over life, the orphan's resources over society's standards. Decked out in all her stolen finery, accompanied by an entourage of dignified impostors, Moll has her day of victory. Even the Law proclaims Moll's legitimacy, and we witness her imposing on the world her private show. Here is a special victory of individualism, admittedly less exotic than Crusoe's mastery over the elements, overtly immoral in its con-game dimension, but authoritative and arresting for those who are concerned with avenues of self-realization.

At times Moll's talent is so compelling as to be demonic, and there is more than a little obsession in Defoe's novel. Donning disguises at a frenetic pace, exponentially expanding her "identity," Moll often appears overwound, addicted to the challenge of thieving and deceiving. When she actually steals a *horse*, essentially just to show that it can be done, her behavior verges on the pathological. She clearly plies her art far beyond the realm of need; her performances are strangely disinterested. How does one assess this behavior ethically? To be sure, there is talk about repentance, shame, and wickedness, but Moll's technical prowess seems to belong to another realm. False to morality, she is true to her gifts. Many therefore see in her the consummate hypocrite, mouthing pieties and committing felonies. But I suggest that she affirms her particular brand of excellence over and above morality, because she cannot deny what is richest and fullest in her. And, in this regard, she is astonishingly honest. Moll *knows* what virtue is, and she knows it to be largely a tangential rather than a central truth, a reminder rather than a stimulus. After robbing a family in distress, Moll acknowledges brief pangs of conscience:

> I say I confess the inhumanity of this Action mov'd me very much, and made me relent exceedingly, and Tears stood in my Eyes upon that Subject: But with all my sense of its being cruel and Inhuman, I could never find it in my Heart to make any Restitution. The Reflection wore off, and I began quickly to forget the Circumstances that attended the taking them.

Morality and conscience exist, but not for very long at a time. One cannot imagine Richardson achieving such a truth. Perhaps her most impudent slap in the face to piety is her avowal, when Fortune is again smiling in America, that it might have been better not to bring her Lancashire husband with her. Those readers who are resurrecting a last-minute Romance will find such incorrigible egoism hard to take. Moll cannot be absolved of her self-interest.

In fact, Defoe seems to be demonstrating that only one with such a powerful sense of self truly has something to "offer." Moll's fleeting desire to be free of her husband—which only the reader is privy to—is followed by a second movement of conscience and commitment: "However, that wish was not hearty neither, for I lov'd my *Lancashire* Husband entirely, as indeed I had ever done from the beginning." Relationship is always beyond, rather than instead of, self-interest. You cannot exchange what you do not have, and Moll becomes a gentlewoman in just that sense: she is her own person.

That education began early. The first marriage with the younger brother, Robin, is unpalatable not only because she loves the elder brother, but also because *her* will is counted for nothing: "Ay! *said I*, does he think I can not Deny him? but he shall find I can Deny him, for all that." A moment later, she adds, "Yes, yes, *says I*, you shall see I can Oppose him; I have learnt to say NO now, tho' I had not learnt it before; if the best Lord in the Land offer'd me Marriage now, I could very chearfully say NO to him." The marriage with Robin will take place, but the lesson, the first lesson of selfhood, has been learned. To say NO means to recognize one's own will, to go one's own way. Moll becomes a quasi-spokesperson for women's right to deny: "as the Market run very Unhappily on the Mens side, I found the Women had lost the Privilege of saying No." In remarkably modern words, Moll exclaims that marriage need not be a master-servant affair:

> I cannot but remind the Ladies here how much they place them-
> selves below the common Station of a Wife, which if I may be
> allow'd not to be partial is low enough already; *I say* they place
> themselves below their common Station, and prepare their own
> Mortifications, by their submitting so as to be insulted by the
> Men before-hand, which I confess I see no Necessity of.

Yet, if Moll were merely a prefiguration of women's lib, she would hardly be an enduring character in fiction. What is most noteworthy about her is the inner strength and, even, generosity which attend her ability to say NO. Because Moll can say No, she can, more importantly, also say Yes, Yes to herself, to others, to life in general. If Goethe's Mephisto is *"der Geist der stets verneint,"* then Moll is the spirit of affirmation. We see this writ both large and small. After the Lancashire fiasco, Moll finds that she is pregnant; once the child is taken care of, she is ready to pick up with her banker-suitor with whom she has been deviously corresponding all this time. At last, fit to be seen again, she meets him in the country. He is prepared to do some "offering" of his own, and he is equipped with ring, license, and still more:

> Why, *says I*, are you Distracted? Why you were fully satisfy'd
> that I would comply and yield at first word, or resolved to take
> no denial; the last is certainly the Case, *said he*; but you may be
> mistaken, *said I*; no, no, *says he*, how can you think so? I must
> not be denied, I can't be denied, and with that he fell to Kissing
> me so violently, I could not get rid of him.
>   There was a Bed in the Room, and we were walking to and
> again, eager in the Discourse, at last he takes me by Surprize in
> his Arms, and threw me on the Bed and himself with me, and
> holding me fast in his Arms, but without the least offer of any
> Undecency, Courted me to Consent with such repeated Entreaties
> and Arguments; protesting his Affection and vowing he would
> not let me go, till I had promised him, that at last I said, why
> you resolve not to be deny'd indeed, I think; No, no *says he*, I

> must not be deny'd, I won't be deny'd, I can't be deny'd: Well,
> well, *said I,* and giving him a slight Kiss, then you shan't be
> deny'd, *said I,* let me get up.

This is one of the most charming scenes in the novel, and it is emblematic
of Moll's gift for assent. It matters little that she never considered denying
him; what counts is the poetic truth of the passage, the graceful and gracious
Yes which Moll can say to life and chance.

Moll savors happiness, is able to say, and to mean, in the midst of a
turbulent topsy-turvy life, "I never liv'd four pleasanter Days together in
my life." The reader may have some difficulty keeping track of Moll's husbands, but each one is indeed genuine as long as he lasts. Above all, Moll
keeps her own books straight. When married to her banker, she cannot simply
dismiss her past. The entire picture is recalled:

> Then it occurr'd to me what an abominable Creature am I! and
> how is this innocent Gentleman going to be abus'd by me! How
> little does he think, that having Divorc'd a Whore, he is throwing
> himself into the Arms of another! that he is going to Marry one
> that has lain with two Brothers, and has had three Children by
> her own Brother, one that was born in *Newgate,* whose Mother
> was a Whore, and is now a transported Thief; one that has lain
> with thirteen Men, and has had a Child since he saw me! poor
> Gentleman! *said I,* What is he going to do? After this reproaching
> myself was over, it followed thus: Well, if I must be his Wife,
> if it please God to give me Grace, I'll be a true Wife to him, and
> love him suitably to the strange Excess of his Passion for me; I
> will make him amends, if possible, by what he shall see, for the
> Cheats and Abuses I put upon him, which he does not see.

Here is both the maturity and the novelty of *Moll Flanders.* Moll goes a
quantum leap beyond picaresque fictions and asserts the priority of character
in literature: after all the adventures, the masks and disguises, husbands and
thefts, the self is left to take inventory. The episodic plot, the role-playing,
the hurly-burly past which is conveniently invisible, all those things belong
to a person, and Moll is, in our terms as well as hers, "taking stock" in this
passage, recognizing and assuming her estate. Fiction is indeed the only
literary form for depicting Moll's fundamental doubleness, her recorded
adventures and liaisons, on the one hand, and her insistent homing instinct
on the other hand, her possessive sense that this grocery list is *hers,* that she
must not be dispossessed of it, that she alone safeguards it. Defoe is ad-

umbrating a code of humanism and responsibility here that transcends any moral dicta. Moll is the person to whom her adventures have happened. One's past is not visible, and that has its immediate advantages: "O! What a felicity is it to Mankind, *said I*, to myself, that they cannot see into the Hearts of one another!" Yet, one can, and must, at least sporadically, see into one's own heart. Despite all the hustling, beehive activity, Moll Flanders does carry her full life with her. Often, she focuses exclusively on that measurable, stealable, marriable world before her; often she is opaque to herself: "it was all Fear without, and Dark within." But, there are moments (and moments are the only conceivable unit for such activity) of recognition and sounding, a kind of roll call when all the past avatars are acknowledged as parts of the self. Time makes life episodic, but Moll reclaims her episodes.

Doubtless the most poignant effort to fix the episodic life, to wring stability and value from transience and accident, can be seen in the passionate encounter with the Lancashire husband. Each has deceived the other into marriage, and they part, as they must, each to ply his trade alone. It is the picaresque. But Moll is shattered, and her need cannot be denied: "I eat but little, and after Dinner I fell into a vehement Fit of crying, every now and then, calling him by his Name, which was *James. O Jemy!* said I, *come back, come back*, I'll give you all I have; I'll beg, I'll starve with you." He does come back, drawn irresistibly, responding to Moll's voice which he heard some twelve miles away. It is a moment of transcendence; Moll is "amaz'd and Surpris'd, and indeed frighted" at the power of passion over matter. But matter cannot be ignored; their situation is untenable; each is without funds, and Jemy is wanted by the law as well. All the logic of Moll's education dictates that she go her own way, but, instead, she pleads for permanence and union:

> I told him, I was so compleatly miserable in parting with him,
> that I could not be worse; and that now he was come again, I
> would not go from him, if he would take me with him, let him
> go whither he would, or do what he would.

Such lines, coming from Moll, are nothing less than revolutionary; far from being measured or looking out for number one, Moll throws caution to the winds and accepts her lover *totally*, without reservation or limit ("whither he would or what he would"). There is courage and integrity in this utterance. To be sure, Moll will separate, bear her child, and remarry; but the sincerity of her desire is not undercut simply because life leads her in another direction. Here we are at the heart of Defoe's disturbing achievement: Moll is *willing* to pledge her life to Jemy, to redeem the episodic structure of the novel;

later, she will be equally willing to assume *this* event too as part of her past, and she will then try to make amends to her new husband for the invisible experience she carries within her. She accepts her present and incorporates her past; she refuses to deny.

Defoe is disturbing, because Moll's life continues to unfurl, relentlessly, making each of these pacts a mere episode. In so doing, he tempts us to make easy judgments, to view all as ironic, to count the husbands and to discount Moll's sincerity. We seem to place a special value on permanence and stability in novels. Books themselves are such brief affairs that the shifts and infidelities of a fictional life are glaringly evident to us. The fiction of fiction authorizes a miraculous shorthand whereby a few years are condensed into a few pages, a life into a book. It is possible for readers to be most exacting, despying and decrying change at every turn. Defoe's book is quite vulnerable to such a critique: Moll's marriage to the banker is, *for us*, some twenty pages after her union with her Lancashire Jemy; a year has passed for Moll. Five or six husbands over a seventy-year life seems less crowded than it may in a medium-length novel. I am arguing that Moll is neither a hypocrite nor a passive floater; she engages vigorously in life, but she cannot stop it. Life changes her projects, gives her husbands and careers. She brings integrity to each venture, but life brings her new ventures, brutally. Defoe's novel has the lack of economy, lack of rigor that each of us experiences, over a lifetime. Most human principles and standards are short-lived things. If life makes liars of men, it is essentially because they continue living. Rigor and pattern are particularly desirable and at home in art, because they rarely survive time. And it is time that Defoe has miraculously put into his fiction; Moll's is the fullness of a life-in-time, and that is why it is hard to judge her. Her great strength is that she lives in the present. In this light Defoe's book is the precise opposite of Flaubert's *Education sentimentale:* Frédéric Moreau's life is frittered away and dissolved in front of our eyes, whereas Moll is achieving four days of happiness here and there for a full seventy years.

Again, who is Moll Flanders? It took Defoe a whole book to answer. We cannot provide apt one-line appellations for people who have lived seventy years. It is particularly hard to specify their *character*. Assigning a character is one of the central motifs of *Moll Flanders*. For a suitable marriage, and, indeed for general social success, an unblemished, researchable character is a prerequisite; but, as Moll finds out, "the lives of very few Men now-a-days will bear a Character." Social deterrent though it may be, lack of "character" is the sine qua non, in Defoe, for having character. Defoe's deepest interest goes invariably to those who have led chameleon lives, who have lived out each moment with conviction, who have traveled many routes, who have transgressed but not forgotten consistency. The Lancashire husband is a specimen of such lifemanship, and he appeals to Moll both emotionally and aesthetically: "In this time he let me into the whole Story of his own Life, which was indeed surprizing, and full of an infinite Variety sufficient to fill up a much brighter History for its Adventures and Incidents, than any I ever saw in Print." Mother Midnight, too, has been tested by time and found not wanting. When visiting her later in life, Moll

> found that she drove something of the old Trade still, but that she was not in such flourishing Circumstances as before; for she had been Sued by a certain Gentleman who had had his Daughter stolen from him, and who it seems she had helped to convey away; and it was very narrowly that she escap'd the Gallows; the Expence also had ravag'd her, and she was become very poor; her House was but meanly Furnish'd, and she was not in such repute for her Practice as before; however she stood upon her Legs, as they say, and as she was a stirring bustling Woman, and had some Stock left, she was turn'd a *Pawn Broker*, and *liv'd pretty well*.

There is undisguised admiration in this paragraph for the sheer pluck and resiliency evidenced by this old lady still on her legs. Defoe's heart is in these survivors. Life is a marathon, but the best are those who embrace every phase of it. This novel shows the deep cleft between measuring tools, on the one hand (morality, etc.), and the unchartable, unpredictable and, finally, undeniable goodness of life itself.

Eschewing pattern in favor of fullness, Moll exhibits qualities of resourcefulness, suppleness, and energy that amount to a kind of homely wisdom. In reading Defoe's story, we are reminded how long life is and how static our categories are. The answer to Moll's identity is concisely expressed in the title page; like a series of dramatis personae, all the stages of Moll's career receive their due, superficially discrediting her "character," but flaunting her ultimate success as a "gentlewoman," i.e., an independent self:

> The Fortunes and Misfortunes of the Famous Moll Flanders, etc. Who was Born in Newgate, and during a Life of continu'd Variety for Threescore Years, besides her Childhood, was Twelve Year a *Whore*, five times a *Wife* (whereof once to her own Brother) Twelve Year a *Thief*, Eight Year a Transported *Felon* in Virginia, at last grew *Rich*, and liv'd *Honest*, and died a *Penitent*.

Moll is the entire package, an itinerary that needed husbands, old and new worlds and much time. Defoe's accomplishment is to have depicted the span and variety of her life as that of an integral self. Moll may seek husbands and steal plate, but her truest possession, the one she is most committed to, is her own experience. And that experience is shared. For, beneath and undergirding the motif of disguise and concealment, runs a still deeper vein: confession. Confession equals narration of her authentic life, even when it shames her. Moll is authentic. She refuses to counterfeit money, and she refuses to fake feelings. Her disguises are expressive; concealment for other purposes is distasteful to her. When urged by the elder brother to yield to a relationship that smacks of incest, she desperately tries to fight it; pressed by her mother to accept the incestuous union with her brother, she bolts.

Finally, Moll is a woman who wants to communicate. Her marriages take on a different meaning when seen as the acts of a woman who cannot abide being friendless and alone. Men and women, as Moll well knows, are not always "able to bear the weight of a secret Joy, or of a secret sorrow." There must be expression. Hence, the magnificent repentance scene at Newgate is actually a confession, a secular rather than a religious confession. It is the gesture of a person who sees the shape of a life-in-time. Abhorrence is what Moll claims to feel, but what she in fact "offers" the Minister is the narration of her life:

> This honest friendly way of treating me unlock'd all the Sluices of my Passions: He broke into my very Soul by it; and I unravell'd all the Wickedness of my Life to him: In a word, I gave him an Abridgement of this whole History; I gave him the Picture of my Conduct for 50 Years in Miniature.

All the motifs are powerfully fused here, in what is the poetic climax of the novel: passion, opening up to another, time and narration. What Moll has to confess is not so much her sins as her life. To grasp and then to share the fullness of one's life; this is at once the particular excellence of Moll Flanders and of fiction, and Defoe has "offered" it to his readers.

DAVID DURANT

Roxana's Fictions

Daniel Defoe's *Roxana* dramatizes the inherent tension between two functions of the novel. In accordance with his Dissenting heritage, Defoe justified his fiction as a type of extended allegory which provides Christian instruction. Thus his preface to the novel insists that "The Noble Inferences that are drawn from this one Part, are worth all the rest of the Story; and abundantly justifie (as they are the profess'd Design of) the Publication." But this desire to explain to his readers what they must do to be saved is coupled, for Defoe, with an even greater impulse to explain what they must do to succeed in the world. Here, in place of religious allegory, Defoe argues from the perspective of realism, insisting that "This *Story* differs from most of the Modern Performances of this Kind . . . in this Great and Essential Article, *Namely*, That the Foundation of This is laid in Truth of Fact; and so the Work is not a Story, but a History." The boundaries between religious allegory and worldly realism are not rigid; in earlier novels like *Moll Flanders*, Defoe had insisted that worldly success followed and in many ways symbolized moral goodness. But *Roxana* substitutes for the story of virtue rewarded the tale of *The Fortunate Mistress*. Roxana's worldly success does not demonstrate God's providence, but investigates the more difficult problems arising when the wicked are seen to prosper. The crux of these problems, for Defoe's theory of fiction, lies in the ways in which the realistic "history" of fiction comes to undercut the moral allegory it seems shaped to embody.

Defoe does not simply offer the competing perspectives of allegory and

From *Studies in the Novel* 13, no. 3 (Fall 1981). © 1981 by North Texas State University.

realism as vantage points from which his readers can understand his novel, but dramatizes the conflict in the life of his heroine. Roxana is consistently torn between two judgments of herself. On one hand, her early training and a conversion which follows the action of the novel insist that her life is a moral lesson which follows an archetypal pattern. From this perspective, her career recapitulates the original fall from innocence; it consists of a series of moral losses as she becomes progressively cut off from salvation by her immersion in worldly pursuits. On the other hand, however, Roxana's environment teaches her to view her life as a secular success story. She gains wealth, position, and security and is finally able to retire from a life of undetected crime. In worldly terms, she has experienced a fortunate fall, exchanging a credulous innocence for the experience necessary to survive in a dangerous world. These two standards of self-evaluation vie within Roxana throughout the novel, providing the psychological depth of Defoe's portrait of her. They also provide the necessary and complex measuring rods of Roxana's development.

Defoe dramatizes Roxana's personality development as a slow and agonized accretion gained through multiple repetitions of a complex action. Her existence consists of a series of seductions which follow a pattern established in her first affair with the jeweler. Again and again, Roxana experiences the threat of poverty or financial loss, is discovered by a potential supporter, is seduced by him in repayment for his support, and is finally deserted after a period of prosperity. What makes this fairly typical structural device of repetition unusual and valuable in *Roxana* is that it becomes increasingly the product of the central character's design. As Roxana's wealth, experience, and ability to control herself and others grow, what had seemed at first the operation of providence comes to seem instead her creation of a scenario. Eventually, instead of suffering financial loss, Roxana pretends loss; instead of being seduced she seduces; instead of being deserted she engineers separations. In general, *Roxana* moves from the story of a fall from innocence to the complex tale of a woman inventing that story in her life. Roxana's experience becomes increasingly fictive.

The determinative episode in Roxana's life is her experience after her desertion by her first husband. Looking back over her life, the narrating Roxana spends little time describing her first marriage because it was important primarily in its effect of leaving her a victim. That status she depicts in detail, showing her poverty, inability to keep her children, difficulty in finding productive work, terror at living outside the normal protected status of women, and the emotional strain of her new life as an economic individual. The rest of her life is spent in first escaping from and then protecting herself against returning to this precarious situation outside the scope of conventional social patterns.

It is typical of Roxana's innocence that she does not design an escape from this first crisis, but is rescued by the jeweler. Part of Roxana's education in this episode is learning that the jeweler is not perfectly unselfish; his good actions in the rescue are followed by a clever but nonetheless clear charge in his seduction of her. An even more important lesson comes in the dual perspectives she learns are possible in judging her seduction. As narrator, Roxana is sure that the affair recapitulates the first fall. When her maid advises Roxana to give in to her seducer, the narrator-Roxana knows that she "should have repell'd this *Amy,* however faithful and honest to me in other things, as a Viper, and Engine of the Devil." Understanding the story on an archetypal level, the narrator sees clearly what she should have done: "without question, a Woman ought rather to die, than to prostitute her Virtue and Honour, let the Temptation be what it will." But while the narrator is given, necessarily, the last word, things are not at all so clear to the character Roxana. Her alter ego, Amy, presents the matter in a different light, one that becomes the more tempting because, for all its worldly meaning, it is phrased in religious terms. For Amy, it is poverty instead of sex which is evil; she maintains that the jeweler "had brought me out of the Hands of the Devil, by which she meant the Devil of Poverty and Distress." So Roxana acts as much out of a worldly morality as she does out of mere wickedness when she "ruin'd my Soul from a Principle of Gratitude, and gave myself up to the Devil, to shew myself grateful to my Benefactor." At the very outset, Roxana is tempted not by sin, but by the acceptance of another code. Amy suggests a perfectly amoral perspective posed as religion where the seducer becomes the savior, the fall becomes a rescue, the devil becomes poverty, and the good becomes amassing things of the world. The young Roxana does not accept Amy's version. She is wracked by guilt, but the seed of another morality is sown.

After the jeweler's murder, which terminates Roxana's second "marriage," she is left without a protector again. While his death is anything but a part of Roxana's plan, her life with him has been so safe and loving that it prompts her to plan. As a relative innocent, she had been deserted, befriended, and seduced; as an older and wiser woman, what could make more sense than to plan to seem more innocent than she now is so as to set the stage for a rich man to protect her once again? So Roxana becomes "The pretty Widow of Poictou," even though she had scruples against calling herself wife before the jeweler's death. The poverty which had helped to drive her into the arms of the jeweler is now something of a ruse when it helps her into the arms of the prince: "I reply'd, with some Tears, which, I confess, were a little forc'd, That I believ'd if Mr. —— had liv'd, we shou'd have been out of Danger of Want; but that it was impossible to Estimate the Loss I had sustain'd."

The fictions Roxana engineers in her seduction by the prince are followed by a life as happy and as profitable as her affair with the jeweler, and much more contrived. Roxana seems on stage most of the time she is with the prince. He insists that they go to elaborate lengths to hide their amour, to mask the arrangement from his wife. Roxana has had so much experience by this point that much of what she had done earlier by nature now is done by design. She consistently manipulates the prince so that he gives her what she wants without her having to ask for it. And when a visible symbol of her past shows up in the form of her first husband, Roxana carefully segregates him from her new life. She fears, of course, that her first husband will try to steal some of her new gains, but she knows, too, that the evidence from her past which would tell exactly who and what she is must be hidden from her new lover. Even the narrative, didactic perspective seems to involve something like facade. The older Roxana can see that the moral fictions she had earlier foisted on herself: "the Devil had play'd a new Game with me, and prevail'd with me to satisfie myself with this Amour, as a lawful thing." But the focus of her didactic intrusions lies on the bad example the prince sets: "What valuable Pains were here thrown away upon One, who he was sure, at last, to abandon with Regret! How below himself, did a Man of Quality, and of a thousand Accomplishments, behave in all this!" The technique bears out David Higdon's suggestion that "many of her evaluative comments . . . glibly transfer her own guilt to her victims" ("The Critical Fortunes and Misfortunes of Defoe's *Roxana*," *Bucknell Review* 20, p. 79), but it also suggests a growing emphasis on worldly wisdom. Even as Roxana is becoming more experienced as a character, the narrator is changing too— becoming caught up in the story as an example of prudence rather than of morality.

The prince's conversion after his wife's illness leaves Roxana deserted still a third time. Her earlier two affairs being successful, it is no wonder that she stages a new episode to try to recapitulate them. But her changed circumstances make the replay necessarily fictive. In the first episode, want had driven Roxana to a state of desperation where a protector and ultimate seducer seemed almost a godsend. Now that she is rich, she does not need a protector, but the trauma of her first desertion insists that any desertion equals destitution. So she almost unconsciously creates the insecurity which begins each of her affairs:

I confess it was a Circumstance that it might be reasonably expected shou'd have wrought something also upon me; I that had
so much to reflect upon more, than the Prince; that had now no
more Temptation of Poverty . . . but was grown not only well
supply'd, but Rich, and not only Rich, but was very Rich, in a
word, richer than I knew how to think of; for the Truth of it
was, that thinking of it sometimes, almost distracted me, for want
of knowing how to dispose of it, and for fear of losing it all again
by some Cheat or Trick.

The quotation not only signals Roxana's creativity, but summarizes much
of her progress in the novel. Starting with a moral focus, she begins to see
the material world as a temptation, comes to concentrate on poverty and
wealth, and ends by forgetting the moral dimensions altogether.

Life for Roxana has become an act; like any good actress, she becomes
acutely conscious of her audience. Where she had been, in the first seduction,
the ingenue taken in by an experienced man, she is now the old hand conscious of seeking out a "seducer" more innocent than she. She finds him in
the Dutch merchant, "who being an honest Man himself, believ'd every
thing I said, which indeed, [was] all really and literally true, except the
Deficiency of my Marriage." The statement suggests another element of
fiction in this scenario: Roxana's innocence has been replaced by the fiction
that she is a virtuous widow rather than a rejected mistress. Roxana is not
lured to bed by her thankfulness, but has to make the Dutch merchant think
he has seduced her: "I made a seeming Resistance, but it was no more indeed;
for, *as above*, I resolv'd from the Beginning, he shou'd Lye with me if he
wou'd."

The Dutch merchant's proposal of marriage threatens to break the established patterns of Roxana's life; her resistance is immediate if somewhat
baffling to herself. The first marriage led so quickly and painfully to desertion
that she cannot risk it again, even though she sees the differences between
this new suitor and her first husband. It shows how far Roxana has fallen
from grace and gained in experience that in the discussion of marriage the
merchant has all the moral arguments, while Roxana takes Amy's old place
in speaking all the worldly ones. Roxana insists that she did not really believe
that a woman needs to be independent; nor that marriage is economic slavery;
nor that she is safer unmarried; "if ever Woman in her Senses rejected a
Man of Merit, on so trivial and frivolous a Pretence, *I was the Woman*."
Roxana still believes herself essentially moral and basically conventional; she
cannot see how determinative her past life of freedom has become. But when

the final choice has to be made, she picks freedom, despite her real love for the merchant, despite convention, despite even the child she is carrying. The merchant finally carries out his threat to desert her; this desertion is as much a fiction as the rest of the episode, since it is quite consciously engendered by the deserted party: "Thus blinded by my own Vanity, I threw away the only Opportunity I then had, to have effectually settl'd my Fortunes, and secur'd them for this World; and I am a Memorial to all that shall read my Story." This summary by the narrator suggests again the degree to which prudence has replaced morality as the didactic focus.

Roxana's return to England marks the pinnacle of her fortune as a mistress. Instead of a poor deserted wife she is the wise financier, the hostess to nobility, and even, she hints, the mistress of royalty. She has also reached an almost complete transformation of her life into fiction. The brunt of her narrative focuses on her Turkish dress and dance, the self-conscious symbols of her fabricated personality. She is the self-made woman. Her personality is a disguise, the contacts with others a set of staged appearances, and her past a threat which must always be countered by disguise. She is in control of her life and begins to tidy up its loose ends by taking care of her children, by proxy, so that they will forever disappear from her life; even her kindness to them is a means to further detachment.

Defoe structures the conclusion to the novel against the conventional happy ending, where material rewards symbolize moral regeneration. Thus Roxana is a deliberate replay of *Moll Flanders*, but acted out for reasons which rob Roxana of Moll's final inner peace. The first step toward the happy ending in a criminal story necessitates a change of life; Roxana must leave off her wicked ways as a mistress. She does just that, but the motives for her conversion are those of worldly experience, so that Roxana acts morally for what she sees as amoral reasons:

> I found that my Judgment began to prevail upon me to fix my Delight upon nobler Objects than I had formerly done; and the very beginning of this brought some just Reflections upon me, relating to things past, and to the former Manner of my living; and tho' there was not the least Hint in all this, from what may be call'd Religion or Conscience, and far from anything of Repentance, or any-thing that was a-kin to it, especially at first; yet the Sence of things, and the Knowledge I had of the World, and the Vast Variety of Scenes that I had acted my Part in, began to work upon my Sences, and it came so very strong upon my Mind one Morning, when I had been lying awake some time in

> my Bed, as if somebody had ask'd me the Question, *What was I a Whore for now?*

This comprises the most subtle of temptations: to find that the dictates of the fallen world make one act as if one were rejecting that world. What is crippling about Roxana's conversion is that she cannot evolve a strategy by which to combat the temptations which have led her to sexual immorality. Instead, she simply stops being tempted. She lists Necessity, Poverty, Avarice, Vanity, Pride, and Folly as

> my Baits, . . . the Chains by which the Devil held me bound; and by which I was indeed, too fast held for any Reasoning that I was then Mistress of, to deliver me from. But this was all over now; Avarice cou'd have no Pretence; I was out of the reach of all that Fate could be suppos'd to do to reduce me.

Roxana's summary pinpoints the movement of the novel from an interest in morality to a didacticism expressed in Christian terms which ends up being entirely capitalistic. Since poverty is the devil, making money is true virtue; one can repent almost as easily as businessmen retire.

Because her decision to stop being a whore is more a matter of economics than of repentance, Roxana does not really change her life except in incidentals. She continues to think of herself as a person whose real self is disguised by her long life as a whore, but when she stops whoring she finds there is no hidden self to reveal. Instead, there is simply a new disguise: she replaces the Turkish dress with a Quaker one. She is doomed to living as a chameleon because her experience has taught her too well how to make her life a contrivance. She does not become a Quaker; she perfects her performance as one. The acted role of repentant Christian differs from the reality both in the complexity of character involved in knowing one is playing a role and in the necessity to hide rather than reveal oneself. The essence of her "change of life" is to make Roxana believe, even more fervently than when she was acting wickedly, that she must conceal her real self and past. Her amoral conversion brings her the same sort of worldly rewards that had come to Moll Flanders after her moral one. A true love out of the past reappears and gives her that happy marriage which conventionally marks the comic resolution of a romantic novel. But marriage is exactly the same test for Roxana that her earlier life had been: she must constantly act to hide what she was and has become.

Roxana's compulsion to maintain a fictive life cuts her off from the usual novel's happy ending. One basic element of such comic conclusion is the reunion of all the important characters in a finale which stresses community and justice. For Roxana, such a reunion would necessitate revealing her past, so that it is a temptation she must resist. When her daughter shows up through the coincidence so typical of happy endings, Roxana "thought I must have taken her in my Arms, and kiss'd her again a thousand times, whether I wou'd or no." Instead of experiencing that natural embrace as a happy ending, though, Roxana is forced by her experience to resist it: "But I rous'd up my Judgment, and shook it off . . . I cou'd not conceal my Disorder without the utmost Difficulty; and yet upon my concealing it, depended the whole of my Prosperity." All the forces of the world conspire with the full weight of her experience to insist that truth is far too risky to attempt.

In place of the standard comic ending of most eighteenth-century novels, Defoe constructed a conclusion which is finished only according to misleading criteria. As a rags to riches story, *Roxana* is complete: Roxana has her Dutch merchant, riches, security, and a fair measure of independence within marriage. The penultimate scene shows her party's arrival in Holland "with all the Splendor and Equipage suitable to our new Prospect." As a social commentary, *Roxana* is also finished, but this completion denies the validity of the success story. Defoe makes it obvious that prosperity is not worth the psychological price Roxana pays for it. She is miserable in the guilt she feels for her daughter's death: "she was ever before my Eyes; I saw her by-Night, and by-Day; she haunted my Imagination." But her daughter had to disappear for Roxana to be safe in her new life. Taken together, the tales of Roxana's success and guilt highlight the costs of becoming successful in a wicked society. But in a more important sense, Defoe has deliberately made his conclusion as unsatisfactory to his character as it has come to be to his critics. What makes the novel seem unfinished is that Roxana finally does not believe in her own reality either as success or as sinner. The joint perspectives she has fostered throughout her life ultimately cancel each other out, leaving her no way of believing her life complete.

There are those—the picaresque novel is built around them—whose success in the world blinds them to the price they have had to pay to gain their victory. Amy has been Roxana's chief adviser along these lines, insisting repeatedly that almost any price is proper to pay for success. At times Roxana almost can agree with Amy, but she can never completely accept the peace of such an amoral vision of herself. To take the example upon which the final section of the novel concentrates: Roxana cannot believe that the prudent course of hiding herself from her daughter is right. Aided by what amounts almost to a fetish for secrecy, Roxana can formulate the worldly maxim by which her conduct should be governed: *"That Secrets shou'd never be open'd, without evident Utility."* Unconsciously, Roxana tries to formulate a moral schema by which she can justify this prudent dictum. Susan's desire for a mother makes her seem to Roxana "dangerous," "this *Tormentor*," or "This Hussy . . . [who] haunted me like an Evil Spirit." Her descriptions begin not only to make her daughter seem evil, but her own course moral: her husband's "Ignorance was a Cordial to my Soul; and I curs'd them in my Thoughts, that shou'd ever undeceive him." Several times, Roxana goes as far as to equate her daughter's investigations with the spirit of evil, as when she expresses her surprise at a chance meeting with her daughter, by wondering "Who now cou'd have believ'd the Devil had any Snare at the Bottom of all this?" Again, when Susan seems to know more than Roxana hoped she could, Roxana explains the knowledge as evil: "I durst not ask her what was *Roxana*'s real Name, lest she had really dealt with the Devil." The moral terms in which she couches her arguments to justify her prudence suggest the standard by which she finally rejects the justifications. The whole last third of the novel is given over not only to the efforts that Roxana expends in concealing herself, but to her guilt for doing so. Her moral self knows that the actions of her daughter prove

> What a glorious Testimony it is to the Justice of Providence, and
> to the Concern Providence has in guiding all the Affairs of Men
> . . . that the most Secret Crimes are, by the most unforeseen
> Accidents, brought to light, and discover'd.

But while Roxana's scruples forbid her to accept her story as a success or to act out, without guilt, the role of hardened criminal, they forbid her, too, the role of repentant sinner. The moral qualms which forbid her self-satisfaction as a success do not suffice to convince her that she feels true guilt. The doubts as to the authenticity of her penitence come to her repeatedly. Thus when she is wracked with guilt on board ship before arriving in Holland, she decides first that Amy set a much higher standard of self-castigation for less reason than she, and then that she has only faked the experience: "the Repentance which is brought about by the meer Apprehensions of Death, wears off as those Apprehensions wear off." And just as the pangs accompanying fear of death are diminished to "meer" by her standards, so her later moral actions seem suspect to her. When she leaves off her life as a whore, she cannot believe that the decision lives up to her own standards, albeit the actions are all that could be asked for: "there was not the least Hint in all this, from what may be call'd Religion or Conscience, and far from any-thing of Repentance." Roxana's attempts to be a repentant sinner are as unsuccessful as her ventures at being a hardened criminal. In both cases, she invents a self which seems to her more real than the self which she fails to live up to; she consistently judges herself inauthentic and incomplete.

The novel's inconclusiveness is designed to reflect Roxana's personality. Her moral scruples forbid her to accept her worldly success as a sign of her reformed character; a happy ending seems to her a travesty of her guilty experience. But since her guilt does not ring true to her either, she cannot end the novel simply on the downbeat of her psychological anguish. Instead, she invents a conclusion to another novel she never gets around to narrating except in the most sketchy of terms. There, her prosperity disappears, so that her physical world rightly symbolizes what she feels is her fallen state; there she has been reduced by "the Blast of Heaven." Roxana's state at the conclusion of her novel is one where only the future looks real; where the present affords only false perspectives. In that action which takes place in the world after the novel ends, "my Repentance seem'd to be only the Consequence of my Misery, as my Misery was of my Crime." There the material, psychological, and moral worlds all coincide and Roxana will be content in the surety of her "just" ruin, guilt, and damnation.

Defoe's narrative technique depends upon a Roxana located in the world after her novel, looking back on it. The method aptly symbolizes Roxana's dependence on the future as reality. Since the narrator speaks from a vantage point after the conversion Roxana predicts in the conclusion of her novel, she seems much more trustworthy to herself than any of her guises within the novel. From the perspective of allegory, *Roxana* is a series of losses of reliability for Roxana. As she becomes more evil and false, she becomes less reliable as an instructor of the reader in the real meaning of what occurs. The older, narrating Roxana thus feels complete superiority over her earlier, wicked self. But the readers are not privileged to witness the conversion firsthand; instead, we are shown a process in the novel whereby the narrator slowly loses her strictly moral focus in a growing fascination with the worldly didacticism which can be drawn from the events of her story.

While the narrator is quick to point out the increasing moral unreliability of her earlier self, she is almost necessarily unaware of the growth involved for Roxana in the same series of events. Roxana develops as a realistic narrator exactly in proportion as she diminishes as an allegorist. The change is signaled most clearly in the different roles of narrator and character as the novel progresses. As *Roxana* opens, the character acts and the narrator, stepping back from the action, describes its meaning, function, and pattern. The young Roxana is never didactic, but simply caught up in her life. The older

Roxana slowly replaces the narrator as commentator. Thus, for example, when, near the end of the novel, Roxana maintains that she "reflected how sincerely, how affectionately this good-humour'd Gentleman embrac'd the most cursed Piece of Hypocrisie that ever came into the Arms of an honest man," the information does not come as the narrator's reflection on the action, but as a part of that action. The novel has moved, as Roxana has grown into a reflecting personality, from allegory to psychological novel. Where the narrator was necessary at the outset to provide the necessary allegorical ramifications of the plot, she is simply a psychological adjunct by the end. She represents Roxana's feeling that there is a "realer" person who exists somewhere judging her present self. The narrator testifies to Roxana's felt inauthenticity.

Roxana's growth from actor to judge corresponds to her full development as a realistic narrator. In fact, she comes to live her life as if she was creating herself and her experience as a fiction. Thus she begins to insist upon structure in her life as a novelist might, establishing a repetitive scenario to give her life meaning. She creates a fictional personality to present to the world as a novelist creates a character; she manipulates the audience in her world by her invented stories and personalities as an author affects his readers; she comes to lie, in her life, as a novelist lies in his fiction.

George A. Starr warns against an absolute equation of lies and fiction for Defoe, arguing that he discriminated between the two in terms of intent: "Defoe holds that so long as fiction is not designed to 'Deceive and Injure' the reader, but to delight and edify him, it cannot be branded lying: on the contrary, it can be defended as an 'honest cheat' " (*Defoe and Casuistry*). Roxana goes beyond mere lies. She creates a fictional life for herself by which to influence others, ensures a repetitive structure for that fictional self which slowly involves others in her fictions, and finally wrecks her life defending her creation. And in *Roxana*, Defoe seems to be investigating exactly those fictions which are designed to "deceive and injure" Roxana's audience in the novel. By analogy, the novel seems to suggest that Defoe shared some of his audience's misgivings about fiction itself. *Roxana* insists that its heroine's growth to the mature position where she can approximate the author involves a moral loss; that her immersion in realism is an overemphasis on worldly things. The novel, according to *Roxana*, is most naturally amoral; it involves an inherent preoccupation with realism which undercuts religious allegory. It seems clear that Defoe, like Roxana, could not move without guilt from a Puritan to a materialistic world.

While *Roxana*'s implicit condemnation of the amorality of fiction may help to explain why it is Defoe's last novel, it also suggests his insight into

the nature of his own fiction. All of his novels do what Roxana does as
"novelist": teeter uneasily on the knife edge between allegory and realism.
Roxana never gets beyond a self-doubting paralysis brought about by the
irreconcilable conflict between the double perspectives she has on her life.
But Defoe sees clearly Roxana's trap and the uses he can make of it. His
explicit claims for his novel involve the insistence that it taught impeccable
morality and that it was strictly true to life. But his final novel ultimately
subordinates both allegory and realism to psychology. The reader's interest
in the lessons—moral and prudential—Roxana preaches is directed toward
what they tell of her developing personality. Her didactic judgments of
herself and her life are not so absolutely reliable as to be directly applicable
to the reader's life and views, but they are crystal clear in their revelations
of her innermost self. Similarly, Roxana's version of "reality" comes less and
less to resemble the exterior world and more and more to resemble created
fictions; what she describes is only accurate in what it reveals of herself.
Roxana finally insists that fiction is the story of someone telling a story; that
the novel's action is shaped to reveal the personality of a fabricator. Roxana's
anguish comes because she cannot find a true self; Defoe's artistry comes
because he knows that the province of his fiction was to depict those whose
bedrock personality was their doubts of the truth of their selves. His fiction
explores those whose life is fictive and in so doing provides the first self-
conscious novel.

JOHN J. BURKE, JR.

Observing the Observer
in Historical Fictions by Defoe

Because Sir Walter Scott is customarily hailed as "the father" of the historical novel, Defoe's place in its development is often slighted when not ignored. Although Scott may well be responsible for its "classical form," as Lukács argues, he was not in fact the first important English writer to combine historical subject matter and fictional techniques—as Scott himself readily acknowledged. Scott's fondness for Defoe may be well known, but not perhaps his admiration for Defoe's historical fictions. He felt that Defoe "would have deserved immortality for the genius he has displayed in *A Journal of the Plague Year* as well as in the *Memoirs of a Cavalier*," even if he had not given the world *Robinson Crusoe*. My purpose in this essay will be to explore in those two major works what Scott called Defoe's "genius" at historical fiction. I hope to show that Defoe, though not responsible for the "classical form" of the historical novel, deserves credit for significantly advancing, if not establishing, one form of it.

Certain literary facts, it seems to me, dictate an approach to Defoe's major historical fictions. First of all, they, like his other major fictions, are cast in autobiographical forms. Events are reported by a literary character who is someone different from the historical Daniel Defoe. Secondly, these two fictions deal extensively and seriously with the public events of history in a way that Defoe's other major fictions do not. The key is in the relationship between the two. These historical fictions are not simply about their narrators. They are not simply about the history they report. They are about

From *Philological Quarterly* 61, no. 1 (Winter 1982). © 1982 by the University of Iowa.

how they report history, about their narrators' responses to history, and these responses are the center of interest. In evaluating them, it is important, as Maximillian Novak says of Defoe's other fictions, to separate the facts from the judgments of the narrators, or, in my own words, to observe the observer.

Although the *Memoirs of a Cavalier* (1720) followed closely upon Defoe's major success with *Robinson Crusoe* (1719), it presents something "new" in a sense quite different from its more illustrious predecessor. It is a fiction, but it takes as its subject matter some of the major historical events of the seventeenth century—the very events so curiously absent from the consciousness of Defoe's Crusoe. But the *Memoirs* has typically been ignored or slighted by students of Defoe, one reason surely being that it does so little to break from the conventions of the orthodox historiography of its time. Its characters are principally the characters of history, people of rank— political, military, and ecclesiastical leaders—and only incidentally, when at all, the people whom they lead. Consequently, interest can focus in the *Memoirs* on the appearance of Marie de Medicis, Gustavus Adolphus, King Charles I, Prince Rupert, and Sir Thomas Fairfax. Its events are the events of history, the spectacular, not the mundane. For history, at least to orthodox historians, is made, not by the dull, repetitive actions of everyday life, but by the extraordinary, often violent, actions that lead to dramatic changes. So historians focus more readily on war than on peace, and the *Memoirs* focuses—conventionally—first on the Thirty Years' War and later on the English Civil Wars—two of the more spectacular wars in Western European history, never mind the seventeenth century.

The autobiographical form of the *Memoirs* does, however, represent a departure because Defoe takes the form seriously. Its credibility is supposed to derive from the fact that the cavalier only reports those events to which he was an eyewitness. Defoe follows Lord Clarendon's dictum that the best history is composed by a man of action, a man actually participating in events, helping to make them happen, rather than the man of contemplation, the scholar poring over documents in his study. The cavalier will not, then, give us an overview of the Thirty Years' War or even of the Civil Wars in England. For that we are referred to other, more suitable works. This suggests again that the center of interest is not the history, but a man's response to it.

The exact character of Defoe's cavalier is, then, an important issue. First of all, he is suitably anonymous. Though by no means a representative of the "common man" in the modern sense of that term, he is most definitely a representative of the non-great. The only mention of him we might expect in conventional historiography would be as part of the battlefield statistics—battles being treated usually as duels between generals. He is representative because he is anonymous, as most people are as far as the history books are concerned.

Still, the cavalier is an individual, shaped, as he must be, by his location in time and place and by his social rank. He tells us he was born in 1608; so he is in his twenties when he fights in the Thirty Years' War, in his thirties during the English Civil Wars, and in his forties when, presumably, he starts to write his memoirs. The cavalier comes from Shropshire in the west of England, a region where Royalist sympathies were especially strong. So there is little surprise when he finally casts his lot with King Charles. It is even less surprising given his social rank. He is the second son of a wealthy member of the gentry. As a typical second son, he adopts the honorable profession of soldier to make his way in the world; he is not so typical in that he freely chooses to do so—his father offers him a handsome marriage settlement should he prefer to stay home. His rank will gain him access to Gustavus Adolphus and later permissive treatment from Sir Thomas Fairfax. His rank more than anything else determines his politics during England's Civil Wars:

> These proceedings [for the Exclusion and Militia Bills] began to alarm the Gentry and Nobility of England; for however willing we were to have Counsellors removed according to the happy Constitution of this Nation, and might ha' been forward enough to have owned the King had been misled, and imposed upon to do things which he had rather not been done; yet it did not follow, that all the Power and Prerogatives of the Crown should devolve upon the Parliament, and the King in a manner be deposed, or else sacrificed to the Fury of the Rabble.

If the monarchy were to be abolished, social hierarchy and the privileges of rank that follow from it might be deposed with it. The cavalier's motive for fighting on the side of the Royalists is primarily self-interest.

The cavalier's religion is more complicated. Though he fights in what are supposed to be religious wars, he tells us twice that he had "not much Religion" while fighting in those wars. Though presumably an Anglican and fighting in England for the prerogatives of the Established Church—at least theoretically—he is noticeably anti-clerical. He is, of course, duly anti-Catholic. And that is more significant than it might seem at first. The English had long associated papistry with treason, never more so than during the Civil Wars. As Clarendon points out, the greatest propaganda advantage for the Parliament had been the persistent suspicions among the English that King Charles and his chief supporters harbored secret papist sympathies. That Defoe's cavalier has no such sympathies helps to account for his doubts about the Royalist cause. He clearly does not want to fight for a Catholic England. Instead Defoe allows him good Protestant credentials, but his Protestantism is political and nationalistic, not religious, a blend of distrust for authoritarian government and a not so subtle North European contempt for his brothers to the South. The blood spilled during the Thirty Years' War is justified, he claims, because it would lead to the Peace of Westphalia, "the Foundation of Protestants Liberty" in northern Europe.

It is precisely the cavalier's lack of a strong religious commitment—his freedom from dogmatism, if you will—that accounts for his most striking characteristic, his spirit of moderation, almost tolerance. Despite his dislike for papistry, he warmly praises the charity of a Catholic priest in France. Though he idolizes Gustavus Adolphus, the valiant defender of Protestant liberties, he has generous words for his Imperialist archrival, "Brave old Tilly." He eulogizes King Charles tenderly, but also lavishes praise on the Parliamentary general Sir Thomas Fairfax. Fairfax—the man he admits was chiefly responsible for his beloved monarch's downfall—was, he tells us, the greatest leader (after Gustavus Adolphus) in seventeenth-century Europe, adding that he was a man of exceptionally "pleasant, calm, courteous, downright, honest Behaviour."

These traits serve to give the cavalier's personality substance, and they make him an appealing character. They are ways Defoe directs our attention away from events to a concern for the person involved in the events. The more engaged we become with the cavalier's generosity, with his warmth, with his vitality, but particularly with his befuddlement, his sense that somehow his private views do not quite fit into the public role he finds himself playing on the stage of history, the more concerned we become about him, the more interested we become in what effect events will have on him.

As the cavalier is educated in the ways of history, it becomes increasingly clear that events are slowly changing him. Moreover, Defoe drops an early hint about what to expect when he has his cavalier quote the proverb, *"Standers-by see more than the Gamesters."* The Cavalier at this point is a gamester himself and will continue to be for most of his narrative. Ultimately he does become a bystander, both because he must after giving his word to Fairfax and in the act of writing his memoirs. As a bystander, he tries to determine, not what happened, but why it happened.

At first, as an unreflecting gamester, the cavalier believes that men make history. Many of his observations reveal a conviction that the course of history can be altered by the actions of men, provided they have the necessary knowledge and will for seizing the "Opportunity." If they seize the opportunity and fail, it is either because they assessed their opportunity incorrectly or because they lacked the necessary will. Thus the cavalier portrays himself, along with Gustavus Horn, arguing before the battle of Nördlingen against committing the Protestant armies to fight the then superior forces of the Imperialists. Their advice is unfortunately rejected and the predicted disaster ensues. More often, though, his belief is communicated through contrary-to-fact conditions introduced by phrases such as "if only" or "had it not been for." Thus the cavalier believes that the Scottish armies to the north were the Achilles' heel in the Royalists' strategic position. The Scotch armies came to the assistance of the armies of the Parliament in 1642, and this "marked the general Turn in the Scale of War; for had it not been for this Scot's Army, the King had most certainly reduced the Parliament, at least to good terms of Peace, in two years time." The premise for such an observation is that history is undetermined. The Scots could have decided to remain neutral during England's Civil War, or they could have been neutralized by the military actions of Charles or of his generals. If either condition had been fulfilled, the outcome would have been different, no matter what other advantages the forces of Parliament might have enjoyed.

Gradually, however, the cavalier's views on history shift towards another pole, especially after he returns to England. English history presents a new problem for him. In Germany the value of his actions was vindicated by the successes of Gustavus Adolphus and ultimately by the Peace of Westphalia. If he was not making history by himself, at least he could feel that he was acting in tandem with it. But in England he is a member of the losing, though, presumably, better side. So he turns more and more towards some external explanation for why things turn out so badly. At times he sees a Providence directing events to predetermined ends, no matter what individual men might think or do. When King Charles, for example, decides to confront Essex at Edgehill rather than march immediately on a vulnerable London, the cavalier comments: the Londoners "expected us, and we expected to come, but Providence for our Ruine had otherwise determined it." At other times he falls back on the traditional distinction between a first cause that determines and the secondary causes through which it works—a distinction intended to leave some responsibility for events still in the hands of men. So when speaking of King Charles's decision to lay siege to Leicester rather than make a strategic retreat to the north, thereby allowing Fairfax and Cromwell the opportunity to crush his armies at Naseby in 1645, the cavalier comments: "Heaven, when the Ruine of a Person or Party is determined, always so infatuates their Counsels, as to make them instrumental to it themselves." With or without the distinction, the premise remains the same: the outcome of events is fixed beforehand, no matter what men might do. Such a theory of history, of course, has an understandable appeal to the newly defeated.

In the end the cavalier's search for a "deeper" explanation for the outcome of the Civil Wars leads him into superstition. In the final pages of his memoirs he tells us how "a Roman Catholick Gentleman of Lancashire," a suspect source, showed him how God dates his providences "so as to signify to us his Displeasure at particular Circumstances." So, for instance, King James I died on March 27, the same day on which he had published his book against Bellarmine; Queen Elizabeth died on March 24, the same day she made her decision to execute Mary Stuart. The Catholic gentleman, we learn, has interpreted such coincidences in date as unmistakable signs from God that England was being punished for her rebellion against the Pope.

Defoe's cavalier is understandably unenthusiastic about the Catholic gentleman's conclusion, but he is nevertheless intrigued by the method. He applies it to his recent experiences with English history, and he too finds curious coincidences in dates. King Charles, he notes, was beheaded on January 30, the same day the charges of high treason against the Earl of Strafford were read in the House of Lords. The Presbyterian Parliament restored young Charles Stuart to his father's throne on May 29, the same day the private cabal had concluded its secret league with the Scots twenty years earlier. The cavalier thus ends his memoirs by encouraging us to accept the inference that God "dated" his displeasure with the rebellion of the English against their monarch, that the events of history had actually been part of some Divine Plan of which we could, with hindsight, catch a few glimpses.

Such coincidences, however, would never convince the skeptical, and it is unlikely, in my view, that Defoe thought they would. If God had wanted to date his providences to indicate displeasure, why not more conclusive coincidences? Why not, for instance, have King Charles die on the same day that, against his conscience, he agreed to let the Earl of Strafford die rather than endanger his already tenuous hold on the throne? Or why not the day on which Strafford was actually executed? Wouldn't the message have been clearer if, say, Charles II had been restored on Cromwell's birthday, or on the day he assumed the title of Lord Protector, or, better, on the day the Long Parliament passed the Grand Remonstrance? A moment's reflection reminds us that the calendar year is by definition repetitious. A modicum of coincidence is inevitable and hardly evidence of anything at all, much less of a specific Divine Plan for human affairs.

In effect, the cavalier's attempt to make sense out of recent history is a failure, a failure that I believe Defoe expected the more alert to see. Nevertheless, his failure is not presented to leave us feeling comfortably superior. The failure to make sense out of history is not his failure alone. It is a human failure symbolizing the limitations of the human intellect. History is a problem, a problem that man by nature unceasingly tries to solve, but a problem that just as assuredly he cannot solve. That, after all, is part of what is means to be human. If Defoe allows for this judgment on his cavalier, he also appeals to our sense of fellow feeling, our sense of brotherhood.

Our feeling for the cavalier is further engaged because we see that he gains from his confrontation with history. At the end of his memoirs the cavalier describes a change in roles:

> I was now no more an Actor, but a melancholly Observator of
> the Misfortunes of the Times. I had given my Parole [to Sir
> Thomas Fairfax] not to take up Arms against the Parliament, and
> I saw nothing to invite me to engage on their Side.

This new role of observer actually epitomizes a process that has been slowly forming in him a freshly chastened view of the human condition.

If Defoe's cavalier will lose his confidence in the value of action in the end, in the beginning he merely takes it for granted. There he portrays himself as a restless, callow youth, hungry for romantic adventure. His experiences on the Continent begin to deromanticize history when the warmth of glory yields to the cold reality of smarting battle wounds. Yet, historical action still has the flavor of excitement. He has his part, however small, in the military successes of Gustavus Adolphus. He fraternizes with history's greats. When he leaves Germany for England in 1635, he is momentarily discouraged over the prospects for the Protestant cause, but he can still believe that he acts in harmony with history.

This confidence colors his behavior when he first arrives back in England. He responds to the new call to battle instinctively, not reflectively: "I confess, when I went into Arms at the Beginning of this War, I never troubled my self to examine Sides: I was glad to hear the Drums beat for Soldiers; as if I had been a meer *Swiss*, that had not car'd which Side went up or down, so I had my pay." But the cavalier soon finds his habitual responses are not adequate for the vastly different circumstances of civil war in England. During the Thirty Years' War he fought with a victorious army; during the English Civil Wars he fights with a losing one. Though the Thirty Years' War was in large part a civil war, the cavalier was a stranger in a strange land, insensitive to the painful irony that Germans were killing Germans; in England, however, the irony is unmistakable and painful.

It grieved me to the Heart, even in the Rout of our Enemies, to see the Slaughter of them; and even in the Fight, to hear a Man cry for a Quarter in *English*, moved me to a Compassion which I had never been used to; nay, sometimes it looked to me as if some of my own Men had been beaten; and when I heard a Soldier cry, *O God, I am shot*, I looked behind me to see which of my Own Troop was fallen. Here I saw myself at the cutting of the Throats of my Friends; and indeed some of my near Relations.

Under Gustavus Adolphus the cavalier could rationalize these same actions because he believed he was fighting for a cause, for Protestant Liberty against Papist Oppression; under Charles he finds himself fighting his fellow Protestants. When he begins to "examine Sides," his old rationalizations turn to ashes in his mouth.

The cavalier's character, in short, develops because he becomes a somewhat different man. He acquires through his historical experiences a new sensibility, "a Compassion" which he "had never been used to." He learns this, not by applying the lessons of the past to the present, the lessons of Germany to the situation in England, but by applying what he has learned in the present to the past, what he learns in England to his earlier experiences in Germany. With this emerges doubt, with this emerges reflectiveness. As he questions his role as a gamester in history, he assumes the role of a bystander, an observer, a process that is completed when he is finally removed from further historical action by his parole and then begins his memoirs. If the newly reflective cavalier does not see "thoroughly" or "comprehensively," he does see "more" than he did as a gamester. That is why, in the end, he is no longer sure that he acts in harmony with history.

The *Memoirs of a Cavalier* was not written to teach history, but to show one man's response to history. It does not provide new or usable information. It does not teach philosophy by example. It has no obvious polemical purpose; it does not show who was right and who was wrong. Its autobiographical form is the clue that Defoe constructed this fiction to allow his audience to become bystanders themselves. For the reader watches the cavalier as he learns to watch the game. Defoe gives us in the cavalier a moderately sensitive man, of ordinary intelligence, searching for the meaning of history. He shows us a man whose intelligence is overwhelmed and ultimately defeated by its stubborn anarchy. The reader does not see an answer the cavalier has missed; he sees only that his answers are not really answers and so shares his befuddlement. Defoe does not try to provide answers. He only shows the problem.

A *Journal of the Plague Year* (1722) follows but does not repeat the pattern of the *Memoirs of a Cavalier* (1720). Again, historical subject matter is incorporated into an autobiographical form; history is recounted from the point of view of a single eyewitness. Again, the focus is on a personal confrontation with history; interest centers on the narrator himself, how he observes, how he understands, what he gains. Again, Defoe's structure allows the reader to become a bystander watching the gamesters.

But there are important modifications. First and perhaps most obvious is the shift signaled by the change from "memoirs" to "journal." Though by no means completely distinct, the two terms clearly meant different things to Defoe. His Cavalier's memoirs account for a life over a relatively large block of time. More important yet, the emphasis is on memory, not how things happened, but how he remembers them happening from some point in the future looking back. The saddler's journal, by comparison, covers a relatively brief block of time, roughly a year of his life. More important, though, his journal implies (at least in its unpolished form) an immediate or near immediate recording of events and impressions when they happened—a safeguard against the slippery arts of memory. Such distinctions, however, should probably not be pressed too hard. Internal references to events that occurred after the plague tell us that H. F.'s original journal was polished into narrative form some twenty years or so after 1665, and a curious reference to the author's grave-site provides a teasing hint that we ought to consider the possibility of more hands yet in polishing this journal into final form.

Another important modification is the change in the nature of the historical data. This change becomes more significant when the London plague as a subject of interest is compared with the more usual subject matter of history. Though with the choice of the plague the emphasis is still on a cataclysmic event, on the historically dramatic, it is a subject matter that, like the great storm of 1703, would typically be slighted, when not ignored. The subject matter of the *Memoirs* is, by comparison, far more orthodox. Interest heightens during the cavalier's meetings with the greats of history such as Gustavus Adolphus and King Charles I. In the *Journal* the great are only of peripheral interest. We learn only that the court leaves for Oxford in June 1665 and returns to London after Christmas and that H. F. believes "their crying Vices" may have been instrumental "in bringing that terrible Judgment upon the whole Nation" in the first place. The nobility and gentry are also offstage. They flee from London even earlier than the court and return after them. The plague seriously threatens the middle and lower classes, wreaking its worst havoc among the poor. Public events that primarily affect the poor are of little interest to historians whose usual interests are the consultations of senates and the motions of armies. As an observation, that is by and large true of the *Memoirs of a Cavalier*, but it is not true of *A Journal of the Plague Year*.

Such a change in subject matter requires a different narrator, and Defoe seems to have chosen his new narrator with care. Defoe's practice in his fictions was to establish dramatic distance between himself and his narrators by assigning different external characters to them. H. F. is no exception. He, for instance, is a bachelor and an Anglican, whereas Defoe was married, with children, and a Presbyterian. But here the narrator is given something new—a historical coloring. References to the differences between now and then indicate Defoe's interest in creating an authentic Restoration atmosphere for the action. Defoe, we know, took care to recreate an accurate topography for the saddler's London. But there is more. H. F. mentions the lack of newspapers, that microscopes were not yet in use, and refers to the ongoing commercial wars with the Dutch. H. F. also speaks the concerns of a man of the 1660s, not those of man of the 1720s. He is dismayed at the corruption of the court, upset about the sectarian animosities between Anglicans and Dissenters, worried about the sudden growth in London's population following the Restoration, and keeps an eye on contemporary economic developments. Even his internal traits, such as his curiosity and his skepticism, can be seen as shaped by the spirit of the age, by the spirit of scientific inquiry symbolized and encouraged by the founding of the Royal Society in 1662.

H. F.'s character is also colored by the politics of the times. He is, like Defoe's cavalier, a moderate, but he clearly leans towards Whiggish views. He has harsh criticism for the court for its perfunctory response to the city's plight, but only warm words for the city officials who, he believes, responded admirably during the crisis. In other words, his views are the views of an early Restoration tradesman and citizen of London, the kind of man who might support Slingsby Bethel and vote to acquit Lord Shaftesbury more than a decade later. Still, H. F. is never simply a tradesman, never simply a Whig. He is notably sensitive to and compassionate about the special suffering inflicted on the poor by the plague. He translates his concern into civic duty when he accepts an appointment as one of the Examiners of Houses in his ward, despite his own worries about infection and his reservations about the wisdom of the policy of shutting up houses.

H. F. has other traits, and all mingle in a combination that individualizes him. By profession he is a saddler, a businessman prospering from trade with the English colonies in America. As such, he is a sober, intelligent type, efficient enough by habit to want to keep careful and orderly records. Being prosperous, he has the means to flee the plague, but he is single, without responsibilities to an immediate family, and just enough of a businessman to worry about leaving his shop and warehouses to the supervision of others. Moreover, he burns with a historian's itch, a curiosity that makes him want to stay in London and observe and record an extraordinary moment in history. He justifies his desire by allowing God to speak to him through verses 2 to 7 and 10 of the Ninety-first Psalm. They reassure him that he will be protected against infection should he choose to stay. A brief illness then seals the choice we feel he has already made.

H. F.'s lapse into bibliomancy may be sincere and important, but it is by no means typical. Temperamentally, he is free of the superstitious bent that would see mystic significance in the coincidences of calendar dates. He is, if anything, conspicuously skeptical about received opinions. Though the appearance of comets before the plague and the fire had convinced the populace that they were divine portents, H. F. insists that their appearance could easily be explained by "natural Causes." Nor is he any more easily awed by official-sounding statistics. The government reports that 68,590 Londoners died from the plague, but he explains for us why a figure of about 100,000 is probably more accurate. He repeats, with methodic doubt, the rumors and anecdotes he has picked up through hearsay. Though he acknowledges that they sometimes contain a kernel of truth, he is quick to discredit them in their popular form.

The cast of H. F.'s intelligence is further revealed in his taste for historical ironies. He informs us that the poor were later made "full amends" for the double calamity of plague and fire. Because so much that was lost had to be replaced and because demand had been abnormally suppressed, "there never was known such a Trade all over *England* for the Time, as was in the first seven Years after the Plague, and after the fire of *London*." He also reports how the apparent blessing of an unusually abundant harvest during the plague year yields "a most excessive Plenty of all Sorts of Fruit, such as Apples, Pears, Plumbs, Cherries, Grapes." But this blessing turns into a curse because abundance leads to lower prices, leading the poor to "eat them to excess, and this brought them into Fluxes, griping of the Guts, Surfeits, and the like, which often precipitated them into the Plague. Despite, however, such evidence of keen intelligence, of a sharp ironic edge on his mind, H. F. does not go on to examine the implications of what he observes.

The fact that he does not is, I believe, the crux of this fiction by Defoe. For H. F. is a believer. Unlike Defoe's cavalier, his saddler is portrayed as a sincerely religious man, a devoted Anglican, but pious rather than doctrinaire. He preaches toleration, accommodation, and brotherly love, and the acrimonious disputes between sects clearly upset him. His Christian faith is a crucial ingredient in his personality, and it is this faith more than anything else that is challenged by his confrontation with history in the plague.

The ravages of the London plague confront H. F. personally with the classical problem of theodicy. As an orthodox Christian, he believes in an omnipotent, omniscient, and wholly benevolent Deity, and this is difficult to reconcile with the palpable existence of evil and suffering in the world. According to H. F., God has merely permitted the plague to strike London as a sign of his judgment on the sins of the English. Its ultimate purpose, he argues, is beneficent: "a visible Summons" to turn from the matters of the flesh to the things of the spirit. But if the plague is a divine judgment, then a benevolent, loving God is also guilty of patent cruelty. It would also seem that, if the plague was indeed God's will, it would be sinful to act against it. Londoners should simply accept the plague and its consequences as merited punishment for their sins, collective and individual.

But, for H. F., such conclusions are untenable. He stoutly rejects "the *Turkish* Predestinarianism" that would leave men passive and helpless in the movement of history. Insofar as the circumstances conducive to contracting the plague can be determined, men have an obligation to avoid them. In other words, the actions of men are undetermined because they have free choice; they are capable of and responsible for appropriate actions during the time of plague. Therefore, "*the best Physick against the Plague is to run away from it.*"

In order to reconcile these apparent contradictions for us, H. F. falls back on the customary philosophical distinction between first and second causes, a logical maneuver designed to preserve the omnipotence of the Deity at the same time that it grants men free will and full responsibility. God is the first or supernatural cause of all operations in the universe, but he characteristically prefers to work his will through secondary or natural causes. Hence, according to H. F., the plague is "a Distemper arising from natural Causes" and "propagated by natural Means," there being no need to put it "upon Supernaturals and Miracle." God, then, did not directly will an evil, he only permitted it, and is therefore only responsible indirectly, if at all. All this might be well and good if it were not for a glaring inconsistency in H. F.'s views. Though he refuses to put the start and the spread of the plague "upon Supernaturals and Miracle," he does exactly that when it comes to explaining how the plague came to an end. Since he cannot find a "natural explanation" for its mysterious end, it "was evidently from the secret invisible Hand of him, that had at first sent this Disease as a Judgment upon us."

Though doubters may scoff, those "who had the least Share of Religion in them, were oblig'd to acknowledge that it was all supernatural."

What becomes increasingly evident to the more alert is that the saddler's intelligence, like that of the cavalier, is overwhelmed by history. There is no convincing reason why the outbreak of the plague should be "a Distemper arising from natural Causes" while its cessation is assigned to "Supernaturals and Miracle" except that such a Janus-faced explanation best fits the saddler's own a priori assumptions about the workings of history: good results from the benevolence of the Deity, but evil comes from the wickedness of men. However tortured the logic, H. F. is unmistakably and uncharacteristically inflexible on this point. He strongly implies that he would not accept "Reasons in Nature to account for it," even if any should be found.

Nor is this the only instance when H. F.'s explanations conflict with his observations. He may feel that the poor were made "full amends" when the plague and the fire trigger a boom in the English economy, but it is doubtful that those of the poor who suffered and died from the plague and in the fire would share his sentiments. He himself points to the vices of the court as the main reason why God's judgment in the plague was brought to bear on England in the first place. Yet, as he himself notes, the court rides out the plague in comfort at Oxford while the poor suffer terribly. If the plague was supposed to be a judgment on the vices of the nation, why were so many of the innocent punished—again, as he notes—while so many of the guilty were not? His explanations are simply not satisfactory.

Nor is H. F. himself entirely unaware that this might be the case. He notices, for instance, that the empirical evidence does not validate his theory of the plague:

> I can go no further here, I should be counted censorious, and perhaps unjust, if I should enter into the unpleasant Work of reflecting, whatever Cause there was for it, upon the Unthankfulness and return of all manner of Wickedness among us, which I was so much an Eye-witness of my self.

After all, if God had intended to win back the hearts of the English to his ways, his plan would have to be judged a failure. "I wish I cou'd say, that as the City had a new Face, so the manners of the People had a new Appearance," "but except what of [Devotion] was to be found in particular Families, and Faces, it must be acknowledg'd that very little Difference was to be seen." Whatever H. F.'s optimism at the end, its basis cannot be what he has seen with his own eyes.

The source of his final optimism clearly resides in his Christian faith, not his reason. That makes the *Journal* a spiritual autobiography, even if its emphasis is not on conversion, but on reaffirmation. For if it is about anything, it is about the severe test to which the saddler's faith is put by the unaccountable evil of the plague. His reaffirmation of the beneficence of the Deity is a triumph of his faith over his experience. If that is to be the larger message of the journal, as some will say it is, it is a message for only part of Defoe's audience. H. F.'s final response may convince the already convinced, but it surely is not one to convince the skeptical, much less "the Atheistic part of Mankind"—nor is it likely Defoe ever thought it would.

An alert reader, observing the observer in *A Journal of the Plague Year*, looking at the facts and evaluating H. F.'s judgments about them, cannot help but notice the unresolved discrepancies. The meaning of history remains elusive, a problem even to the good-hearted and the pious. Though H. F. says little to indicate that he is fully aware of the contradictions his own observations have generated, he speaks a few words near the end that seem to indicate that Defoe does not intend us to see him as completely unaware of what has happened.

> If I should say, that this is a visible Summons to us all to Thankfulness, especially we that were under the Terror of [the Plague's] Increase, perhaps it may be thought by some, after the sense of the thing was over, an officious canting of religious things, preaching a Sermon instead of writing a History, making myself a Teacher instead of giving my Observations of things; and this restrains me very much from going on here, as I might otherwise do.

Of course, H. F. does not restrain himself very much. He still insists on his point. But he does show some awareness that he has been better at "writing a History," better at giving his "Observations of things" than at "preaching a Sermon" or making himself "a Teacher."

To say that we as observers may find the saddler's sermonizing inadequate is not to say that Defoe only appeals to our judgment. That would make Defoe a satirist in the vein of Swift and Pope. Defoe is clearly not that, at least not here. He creates in H. F. a complex literary character who succeeds in engaging, once again, our fellow-feeling. A response that would merely condemn his befuddlement would clearly be insufficient. For H. F. engages us, even if we are intellectually skeptical, because as observers we have seen him grow. His cannot be the same dramatic change we see occurring in Defoe's cavalier because here we are limited to the year's time of the plague, and that is a small part of a man's life. But still there is a change, a development in his character. In the case of Defoe's saddler it is a change of heart, or, better, a stretching or broadening of his heart—the effect of the plague, of history, on him. Presumably, before the plague struck London, he was much the same man we observe in his journal—pious, good-hearted, public-spirited, but nevertheless a man whose horizons were largely restricted to his family, his relations, his friends, and, of course, to nurturing his prospering business. The plague forces him out of that narrow circle to a concern for all the people of his city, especially the poor—and that is seemingly a new and different experience for him. The tears he sheds for Robert the waterman and his family are meant to be moving and emblematic of the more compassionate man he becomes. When it becomes obvious later that the plague eludes his ability to make sense out of it, we are not inclined to judge him harshly. If he cannot make sense out of it, neither can we. History remains an enigma for all, pious and not so pious alike. Thus, our final response to H. F. is made up of several elements, and as such it is complex, equivocal, and a bit uncertain, as most of our responses to life truly are.

Defoe, in my view, has a serious claim as an early historical novelist, as Scott recognized. If he did not establish the classical form of the historical novel, he certainly advanced one form of it by combining autobiographical forms and historical subject matter, by mixing fact and fiction. Though he is often praised for his accuracy and general reliability in presenting historical material—even to the point where it was once argued that his *Journal* is truly history, not fiction—his principal interest was rather the responses to history of individual human beings who, though always individual, become representative. His two major historical fictions show signs of being structured to invite complex responses to his narrators, of being dramatically structured to allow for a variety of responses, no single, unequivocal response being demanded. That perhaps is why readers of widely differing ideological and religious convictions can still find these fictions richly satisfying, even if unsettling, experiences. That, however, could not have occurred by chance. That must be a tribute to Defoe's art.

MARY E. BUTLER

The Effect of the Narrator's Rhetorical Uncertainty on the Fiction of Robinson Crusoe

Because the text of *Robinson Crusoe* is a representation of itself in the process of being created, its successfully completed form depends upon its own promotion of the illusion that it is hopelessly *in*complete. Defoe's essential technique in accomplishing this fictive incompletion is to use a narrator who includes his own endless self-corrections in the final version of his story. Thus, while Crusoe's constant rhetorical refinements may at first be seen only as fussy interruptions of what we assume to be his primary purpose (getting the story told), they are actually the source of Defoe's fiction. While the narrator's perpetual self-criticism within the text achieves one obvious fictional effect, that of making the narrator seem real because of his admitted fallibility, it has a second rather more subliminal effect: that of making the narrative itself seem to claim possession of qualities that we associate with concrete matter rather than with fiction, or the abstract effect in our minds of a certain arrangement of words.

A fiction in prose is an indeterminate abstraction generated by the abstract medium, language. But despite Locke's dictum about the inherent abstraction of language, and despite the somehow obvious truth that no fiction, however perfectly wrought, can ever become reality, Daniel Defoe seems rather defiantly to try to endow the fiction of *Robinson Crusoe* with a nearly organic existence, just as he asks us to believe in the actuality (not the potential actuality) of his narrator. As any organism must, by definition, have both substance and vitality, so the text of *Robinson Crusoe*, precisely

From *Studies in the Novel* 15, no. 2 (Summer 1983). © 1983 by North Texas State University.

185

because of Crusoe's habit of self-correction, seems to insist upon trying to acquire both concretion and autonomous intellectual energy. Because it is subject to its narrator's endless qualifying statements, the text gives the illusion of improving itself even as we read, and thus makes its claim to perpetual self-creation independent of its narrator and of its author. A correlative effect of the narrator's self-correction is the physical presence within the text of thousands of words that are not essential to a simple relation of the action. Because we are so often given a choice between two words, or a near reduplication of others, the text acquires an unusual density, as if its abstract existence in our apprehension might consequently tend, if ever so slightly, toward substantiation. This is ridiculous, of course: no number of words, however intricately related, can possibly transform made-up experience into experience that a real person really had. But Defoe does seem to wish that the fiction created by his language could approximate reality, as that his invented character could approximate a man. Perhaps because he is writing in a relatively new and thus uncertainly defined genre, he seems to opt for the noble failure inherent in such an attempted approximation rather than for the somewhat impotent success of mere imitation.

As Crusoe seems to be persuaded that a large enough collection of concrete particulars associated with civilization (chairs, pots, dwelling places) approaches the actuality of civilization, so Defoe operates on the principle that a large enough collection of references to concrete particulars will persuade the reader of the actuality of Crusoe and his experiences. I wish to argue further that Defoe applies this theory even within his medium, language, by using certain rhetorical structures that represent and therefore claim the actuality of the narrator's mental processes. It is, as I have suggested, by means of Crusoe's rhetorical idiosyncrasies that Defoe seems to try to push his fiction into the realm of real creation. Considering the impact that the character Robinson Crusoe has had on Western civilization in the last 250 years, his creator has in a sense not fallen too far short of his impossible goal. The irony is that he should be faulted for creating a fiction that seems so capable of intruding upon our real experience.

Crusoe's rhetorical uncertainties can be divided most generally into two types: those which reveal his concern about the inherent clarity of his writing, and those which reveal his concern about the reader's ability to understand the writing. Very briefly, because I will be concerned here exclusively with the rhetorical constructions that directly or indirectly seem to question Crusoe's narrative abilities, I will say that the second category is made up of what we might call signposts for the reader, such expressions as "viz.," "as it were," "as I just said." I will concentrate here, however, on the rhetorical uncertainties that are more clearly, though in varying degrees of directness, aimed at the text itself. These may be seen to have one of several purposes: to claim (directly or indirectly) that a subject is ineffable, to confess that the narrator cannot identify the things he speaks of, to avoid detailing a given object or event, or to confess in various ways his uncertainty about the translation of what he sees into what we read.

When his subject matter simply seems ineffable, Crusoe's responses run a gamut from absolutely direct confrontation to very obviously attempted circumvention of the problem. On the one hand, he says that certain things are simply "inexpressible," or "indescribable," without taking any responsibility for the insufficiencies of his language; on the other, he uses rhetorical formulas that allow him to avoid the rigors of specific detail. In passages that conform to the former principles, Crusoe makes a point of calling our attention to his difficulties, but deflects it from himself: language, not his use of it, is shown to be the problem. He speaks of being "inexpressibly sick," and of "an inexpressible joy," "inexpressible labour," "inexpressible hacking and hewing," and "inexpressible impressions of joy." He also avoids liability for any linguistic incompetence by using expletive constructions: he says that "it is impossible to express" "the astonishment," "the terror," and "the comfort." On some occasions, he says that his subject is "indescribable" rather than "inexpressible" (or he uses them both for good measure): "it is impossible to describe the horrible noises"; "Nothing can describe the confusion of thought which I felt"; and "his countenance was most inexpressibly dreadful, impossible for words to describe." And, of course, of his discovery of the footprint, he says, "nor is it possible to describe how many various shapes affrighted imagination represented things to me in."

It is worth noting that the most concrete of these ineffable subjects is the noun "countenance," which is more likely to refer abstractly to a transitory facial response than to the face itself. The other nouns (or gerunds) referring to the things he could not describe are even more abstract: "joy," "labour," "hacking and hewing," "impressions," "astonishment," "terror," "comfort," "noises," "confusion," and "shapes." In short, a lot of what he despairs of verbalizing is indeed rather intractable material. The larger point, though, is that if Crusoe satisfies his usual perfectionism by confessing the difficulties of writing, Defoe is able, by means of his narrator's confessions, to draw our attention as much to the convincing perplexity of his narrator as to the objects of his narrator's description. Crusoe's characteristic attempts at exactness serve Defoe's ulterior motives for the fiction.

Defoe also makes his narrator admit that he, rather than the language itself, is responsible for possible narrative inaccuracies. Sometimes, Crusoe admits that he simply does not know exactly what the facts under consideration are. The adventures he has with Xury include an encounter with two "creatures," of which he says, "nor could I at that distance know what [they were]," and "we could not tell" their genders, or their sport from their rage. He later writes, "what they [some other creatures] were I knew not" and "whether it was a boat or not, I do not know"; of some seafowl he says, "[their] names I know not," and of some "savages' " meat, "How they had cooked it, that I knew not, or what it was." He also says that the "savages" were "dancing in I know not how many barbarous gestures and figures." Whether or not Crusoe is able to be precise in these descriptions has little bearing on the progress of the story, but his insistence on the imprecision of his narrative is that upon which Defoe's fiction lives or dies. If these far-fetched events are related by someone whose compulsive honesty is apparent to the most casual reader, then they have a chance of seeming plausible. These two types of admission of the difficulties of writing, one of which places responsibility on the shortcomings of language, and one of which places responsibility on the writer for any narrative weaknesses, will almost certainly get our attention, and perhaps our credulity, even if all the more subtle hemming and hawing fail to do so.

Despite his boldness in making these confessions, however, Crusoe does sometimes seem to wish to avoid admitting that he has failed to verbalize his experience accurately. But a cover-up, once it is exposed, may serve to highlight that which it claims to obscure. Thus, when Crusoe uses rhetorical formulas to veil his failure to provide us with unique descriptions, the veil may well get more attention than does the plain shortcoming it seems to hide, and Crusoe's stylistic habits may be seen once again as serving Defoe's larger purpose. When Crusoe wants to indicate an unspecified plurality of events or objects, he says that they happened "a thousand times," or that there were "a thousand" of them ("a thousand pieces," "a thousand gestures and motions," "a thousand questions"). A second formulaic modifier that he uses is "perfectly," which appears at least ten times before adjectives, at least seven times before past participles, at least twice before prepositional phrases, and at least once each before a present participle and the simple past tense of a verb. By using these monochromatic qualifiers, Crusoe implies that the details were for one reason or another actually unspecifiable at the time of writing (he might not have observed them accurately to begin with, or he might have forgotten them) or that they are simply not significant enough to warrant more exact documentation. But the larger implication, useful to Defoe, is that the narrator does have realistic limitations—a real person might be expected to fail in determining and recalling every detail.

Crusoe also uses a much more complex formula (which admits variables in its particular grammatical slots) that describes events or objects in super-lative terms. The most prevalent of such constructions follow the pattern "the most [adjective] [noun] that ever [verb in the past tense with appropriate subject]" (for example, "the most miserable wretch that was ever born"). An alternate construction is "the [adjective in superlative form] [noun] that ever [verb in past tense and appropriate subject]" (for example, "the unhappiest voyage that ever man made"). Also formulaically, Crusoe makes the expe-rience or event he describes seem unique by claiming that "never" did a comparable thing occur in equal magnitude. He writes, "never was such a glorious sight seen," "never man or horse ran like him," "never was a more furious charge." He also ascribes uniqueness to certain events by using a construction whose language is, considering its claims to particularity, ex-traordinarily general; he speaks of "the greatest haste imaginable," "the great-est openness imaginable," "the greatest diversion imaginable," "the most lively manner imaginable," "all the signs . . . imaginable," "as brave as could be imagined." Though Defoe may sacrifice some color in making his narrator use formulaic language, Crusoe's failures, whether he acknowledges them or not, are Defoe's fictive gain.

In the examples of his rhetorical uncertainty that we have examined so far, Crusoe is either saying directly that a subject is ineffable or that he cannot absolutely identify it, or he is seeming to confess by indirection that he is incapable of managing the details. In all of these constructions, his attention seems to be seriously divided between what he is trying to narrate and his difficulties with the process of narration. A similar blurring of focus occurs when Crusoe uses the modifier "a kind of." This usage allows him to identify the object in question clearly enough for the reader to have an idea of what the subject is, but tentatively enough so that he (the narrator) cannot be accused of making a mistake. Hence, we read about "a kind of" "miracle," "wild pigeons," "ecstasy of joy," "rum," "trapdoor," and "hand-barrow," and "letter of naturalization," "hawk," "hut," [with "an"] "anchor," "frog," and "full stop."

Crusoe's unwillingness to commit himself completely as to the identity of the thing he is talking about or as to the accuracy of his words is also apparent in two of his uses of the word "like" in the sense of "similar to." When he writes "a thing like a hod" or "a thing like an anchor," he is both questioning the degree of precision with which he has reproduced one of his "things" that represent civilization and complaining about the limitations of language. Just where he needs one particular noun to cover the contingency of his less than perfect hod or anchor, he is forced to collapse into the near-babble of "thing."

In addition to all his anxiety about the inherent describability of his material, or about the accuracy of his identification of it, Crusoe undergoes a great deal of uncertainty about his actual choice of words. He seems to catch and then correct himself in countless acts of unclarity, but, instead of expunging the original imperfections from the manuscript, he purposely leaves us the record of his dissatisfaction with his own writing. The book is almost a palimpsest—the roughness of a first draft is incorporated into the final version, without even an apology. In fact, a lot of his changes of mind are clearly flagged for us by his use of qualifying phrases. He introduces an intensification with "even" or "indeed," or with a contradictory "nor" or "nay." He begins qualifications of various types with the phrase "at least," and works into alternate phrasings with "or rather." These last two phrases have such complex rhetorical implications that his use of them is worth examining in detail.

Of the eighteen occurrences that I count in *Robinson Crusoe* of a construction involving "at least," ten also contain a negative; of these, in turn, three have a common form: the initial statement is a flat denial of a given possibility, which is followed immediately by a qualification. Thus, we read, "it [the grain] never came up at all, at least not as it would have done [had he sown it in the proper season]"; "[I] was no more sad, at least not on that occasion"; and "[Friday] would never care for salt with his meat, or in his broth; at least, not a great while, and then but very little." In the second two instances, Crusoe seems to catch himself in the act of exaggerating, or of representing the truth more as he perceived it at the time of the action than as he did at the time of writing, when his perspective includes facts that temper the original absolute negative. By putting both sets of perspectives into the text, Defoe shows Crusoe's reluctance to allow his artistic distance as narrator to override his original experience of the event in question.

This is clearly illustrated by the first instance I listed of this self-correcting construction ("it [the grain] never came up at all, at least not as it would have done"), whose major implication is that Crusoe rather petulantly believed that the grain's not coming up perfectly was tantamount to its not coming up "at all." A rigorous explication of these two clauses yields precise information about their writer's apparent processes of thought during his writing of them. The first clause, "it never came up at all" is an emphatic denial that the grain sprouted, ever. Of course, just the first negative, "never," is sufficient to establish the fact of the grain's failure, but Crusoe emphatically adds "at all." And indeed, for as long as Crusoe, while he was on the island, saw that the grain was not sprouting, for so long this statement was true. That is, the fact that the grain had failed was true—for a while. As narrator,

Crusoe is perfectly aware that the grain eventually flourished, but to say so right off would deny him the opportunity of conveying to the reader his real (if only temporary) disappointment. As he finally writes about the experience—"it never came up at all, at least not as it would have done"—he manages to be faithful to both versions of it, and his self-qualifying mode is that which enables him to do it. If, as narrator, he eventually corrected himself, he knew that he had been inaccurate; if he knew that he had been inaccurate, he could have cut out the faulty clause. He obviously chose not to do so. Within the nooks and crannies of his own narration, he keeps his former self as close to life as possible.

Crusoe is equally purposeful in his use of the qualifying phrase "or rather." Of the twelve instances I count, eleven are, at first glance, very similar in structure and in intention. Usually, what he does is to use a verb that he almost immediately finds unsatisfactory, and which, in order to improve, he follows with "or rather" and his new choice of verbs. Of these eleven constructions, only one is exceptional in the degree to which its writer's mind has changed between the occurrences of the two verbs. When Crusoe writes, "It would make the reader pity me, or rather laugh at me, to tell [about his difficulties in making jars,]" his subject matter, the putative reaction to his narrative of a putative anonymous reader, is not naturally the most predictable; and we may assume that the conscientious narrator made this change in order to cover as many contingencies as possible.

The other ten "or rather's" intend more specifically just to refine the first verb, to provide a more exact picture of the same facts. If in these cases Crusoe had omitted the first choice of verbs and the qualifying phrase, he would have been able to give us the "better" version right away, which is all we really need in order to comprehend the action, but he persists in letting the first draft permeate the final one. Eight of these ten constructions are very straightforward: "After we had rowed, or rather driven"; "that wave having driven me, or rather carried me"; "the sea . . . landed me, or rather dashed me"; "I proposed to myself to grind, or rather pound"; "I set to work a-tailoring, or rather indeed a-botching"; "I would build, or rather make"; "After we had dined, or rather supped"; "six or seven [wolves] fell, or rather jumped." The remaining examples are worth commenting on individually.

When Crusoe writes, "It would take [too long] to set down all the contrivances I hatched, or rather brooded upon in my thoughts," he does some polishing. He wants here to make the point that none of these "contrivances" (his plans to prevent the savages from landing on the island) ever succeeded—as he writes a few clauses later, "all was abortive." Thus, while "hatched" is appropriate in a general sense to the birth metaphor that Crusoe is developing, its denotation is misleading because his plans never come to life. "Brooded," however, is appropriate, both metaphorically and denotatively—it does not claim any fruitful results. What is especially relevant here to our discussion of Defoe's wish to give substance to his narrative is that Crusoe's rhetorical self-correction is almost emblematic of his thought processes. His "brooding" upon his choice of words represents (or even recreates) in language the cognitive process he is writing about (his brooding upon his plans).

Ironically, the last of the refining constructions in this particular pattern ("[verb] or rather [verb]") that we will look at gets Crusoe into syntactical difficulties even as he attempts to make his language more accurate. He writes, "the Spaniard and the old savage . . . went away in one of the canoes which they might be said to come in, or rather were brought in." Here, Crusoe gets involved with two qualifying phrases at once: "might be said" and "or rather." Certainly, the reason for his use of the latter phrase is not difficult to discern: the infinitive "to come" suggests that the Spaniard and the old savage had chosen to visit the island, while they had actually made the journey in captivity. So Crusoe's substitution of a passive verb for an active infinitive is very reasonable—"to come" wrongfully imputes at least some volition to its subjects. The complications arise because Crusoe is so worried in advance about using the word "come" that he precedes it with a different qualifier, "might be said." One result of this excessive hesitancy is his curiously divided focus; the clause "which they might be said to come in" is grammatically so constructed that the process of narration is made to seem more important than the event it narrates. The verb referring to the action (the savage's and the Spaniard's arrival) is in the infinitive ("to come") while the verbs referring to the narrator's choice of words ("might be said") are the main verbs in the clause. Thus, we see that Crusoe appears to be attending more carefully to documenting the process of his writing than to leaving us with a definitive statement of the facts. Defoe's interest in portraying the process of Crusoe's narrative muffles the narrative itself.

As we have been seeing, when Crusoe uses "or rather" between any two verbs, the order of words on the page corresponds (supposedly) to the step-by-step progression of thought through time. (This is not necessarily the normal mode of thought, but it is the form we see thought taking as it is expressed in the English language.) We imagine him writing down the first verb, reconsidering, and then trying out the second. But some of his uses of "or rather" (as does his use of "they might be said" in the clause we have just examined) indicate that he has both alternatives in mind coincidentally, or even that the less satisfactory alternative is an afterthought. He writes: "it was rather a pale than a hedge"; "After he had slumbered, rather than slept"; and "we could not say [that they were] eating of him, but picking of his bones rather." In the first example, the position of "rather" predicts the upcoming alternative "hedge"; in the second example, the first choice of verbs, "slumbered," is the one Crusoe is committed to—he has no need to override a previous choice, and yet he includes the less satisfactory "slept"; in the third example, "we could not say" indicates Crusoe's anticipation of his own dissatisfaction with "eating," so that we know he could have gone straight for the word he did like. I think we must conclude that Defoe occasionally errs in an excess of artistry. He puts the cart before the horse (or both before and after, as in the case of his using "might be said" and "or rather"), sentencing Crusoe to change his mind about a word, and then penning in a correction which anticipates even the poor narrator's original choice.

Robinson Crusoe sometimes seems to be not so much a book as an artifact from an archaeological excavation. In order to discover the definitive version, we must patiently brush off the accretions of second and third rhetorical choices. It is not a good analogy, though, because Defoe himself has made the pot indistinguishable from the shards. There is a final text—the one we have before us—and yet there is not. Its necessarily imperfect form precludes its own consummation. But I have suggested that Defoe is more intent on re-creating (if not somehow creating) actual experience than he is on imitating it, and he is surely aware that completeness is only a very temporary attribute of physical process. Uncertainty and imprecision are always with us, however, and Defoe's rendition of uncertainty and imprecision in Crusoe's language goes a long way toward validating the narrator's experience.

I would like to look at one more large category of Crusoe's rhetorical uncertainties. Here, he does not express his nervousness by heralding an intended change with an egregious qualifying phrase. Instead, we see his hesitation expressed in his unwillingness to commit himself to choosing one word over another for a particular grammatical slot. I will discuss four different recurring arrangements of words: "[noun] or [noun]"; "[verb] or [verb]"; words of like grammatical function joined by "and"; and unnecessary reduplication of words (near redundancies). The most prevalent of these self-corrections are the ones in which Crusoe offers us one noun, and then a very close substitute, apparently leaving it up to the reader either to make the final choice, or to go along with Crusoe's own indetermination. Within the 126 of these constructions that I count, we can distinguish various classifications.

In twelve of the pairs of nouns, both nouns are abstract; in two more, one is abstract; in three cases, the second noun translates the first ("Bay de Todos los Santos, or All Saints' Bay," "*assientos*, or permission"; "*proviedore*, or steward"; in four cases, the second noun is noticeably more general than the first ("spear or weapon," "verdure, or flourish of spring," "pestle or beater," "footsteps, or signals"; in four cases, the second noun is more specific, and/or more accurate in its context than the first ("noise or report of the gun," "writings, or covenants," "means or door of our deliverance," "side, or gunnel, of the canoe." The quality and/or the degree of the difference between all the other words in pairs is less obviously definable, though probably each set of alternatives would, under close analysis, yield an interesting point or two. However, I will remark only on those pairings that seem especially noteworthy on their own, and on those whose terms appear throughout the list.

Crusoe's most persistent concern over which of two possible words to use appears in his four distinct references to "tortoise or turtle" (or "turtle or tortoise") (here, the second word is in the plural). [Elsewhere,] though he does not immediately offer a choice, he seems to tergiversate a little: "the last day, which was the 26th, [I] found a very large tortoise, which was a treat to me, and my food was regulated thus: I ate a bunch of raisins for my breakfast, a piece of the goat's flesh, or of the turtle, for my dinner." It is possible to give this concern about naming the local fauna a very nice allegorical interpretation. If we compare Crusoe's self-imposed responsibility for the identification of animals on his island (and he is very cautious about it) to Adam's parallel responsibility in Eden, it is indeed a serious matter, one that might even be thought of as divinely ordained. Or, at the very least, we might speculate that his obsessive desire to avoid doing a stumpy little chelonian an injustice by naming it incorrectly reveals an admirable amount of tenderness for such minutiae. The bathetic fact is that Crusoe does not care two cents for the turtle/tortoise unless they are gracing his dinner table. But Defoe cares about demonstrating Crusoe's self-critical habit of mind. Unfortunately, it seems a little unrealistic in this case: very simple inferences tell us either that Crusoe can never determine whether the creatures in question are aquatic (turtles) or terrestrial (tortoises), or that he can identify their respective habitats, but never learns which name fits which type. The first explanation is slightly more reasonable (as narrator, so many years later, anyone as compulsive as Crusoe would have gotten help with the merely verbal confusion), though it is hard to imagine that in the course of twenty-eight years on the island, he can never satisfy himself about where the creatures live. This particular provision of alternatives, then, is really rather specious—Defoe's usually successful technique is again misapplied.

Another pair of words that seem to get under Crusoe's skin is "canoe or piragua," or "piragua, or canoe," as do "shovel or spade," "spade or shovel," and "savannas, or meadows," "meadow land, or savanna." He also uses certain words in combination with a variety of alternatives, as though nothing really suitable could be found. He writes, "tide or eddy," "current or eddy," and "counterstream or eddy"; "fence or fortress," "fence or wall," "outer wall, or fence"; and "cave or way into," "room or cave," "cave or vault," "apartments, or caves," "vault, or cave." On at least three occasions, Crusoe is so uncertain as to offer us three options: "a work, wall, or fortification," "a bag or sack, or what I could make," and "(a quandary, as we call it), a doubt or hesitation."

If sheer numbers are an accurate indication, Crusoe has less trouble choosing verbs than he does nouns. Only on twenty different occasions does his lack of commitment express itself as two verbs separated by "or," and on one as a choice among three ("injure, fight with, or attack"—he seems to intend these to represent three different contingencies, but they do in fact overlap). Once, the most significant difference between the verbs is the transformation of the active voice into the passive ("[the boat] either sank or was driven off to sea"; once, Crusoe very awkwardly tries to put a transitive and an intransitive verb into parallel construction: "having nothing to shelter us, or retreat to." However, only one pair of verbs seems to trouble him anywhere near as much as the tortoise/turtle dichotomy: the nemeses here are "row" and "paddle." The first two times he gets stuck with them, he is so bothered that he adds a qualifier also: "rowing, or paddling, as it is called," "I saw them all take boat, and row (or paddle, as we call it)," "rowing or paddling," "rowed or paddled."

Crusoe shows a related uncertainty in his habit of coordinating, or linking by means of an "and," two words that are all but redundant. Actually, we can justify such pairings as "I am singled out and separated . . . from all the world." "I spent my days now in great perplexity and anxiety of mind," or "laborious and tedious"; the words in question have distinct denotations, though we still wonder whether just one of them in each case could not have conveyed the necessary information. Just these three examples, however, would hardly catch our attention, it if were not for the other thirty-three such pairings (at my count), among which are some words very badly coordinated indeed. His favorite redundancy of this sort is "eaten and devoured," or "devouring and eating"—"devouring" says everything that "eating" does, only more intensely. Similarly, the second word subsumes the first when he writes that he was "cast down and disconsolate," as the first subsumes the second when he writes of some grapes that their being transported had "broken them and bruised them." Even reversing the two words in question in the latter example, and thereby speaking of an ascending degree of damage, would have made more sense. When he speaks of trying to "cure and dry" the grapes, the "and" belies the actual relationship of drying and curing: "to cure by drying" or "to dry and thus to cure" would be a more accurate description of the process. In a similarly odd coordination, Crusoe says, of the Spaniard he rescues and his shipmates, "their councils always ended in tears and despair"; here, he speaks of an emotional state ("despair"), and a typical physical reaction to that emotional state ("tears") as if they had essential qualitative parity. This is complicated further because we must assume that the tears are figurative, specifically, metonymical, standing in this case for—well, for something very much like "despair." So Crusoe has coordinated here the physical symbol of an emotional state, and the emotional state the symbol represents; the construction is redundant and then some. But many others are more straightforwardly repetitive: "confounded and amazed," "ruin and destroy," "teaching and instructing," "astonished and amazed."

If, when he offers us so many pairs of words separated by "or" Crusoe is admitting his inability to decide which word is better, when he uses so many poor coordinates, he seems simply to be ignoring his critical responsibilities. But to exclude either term of the many sets of alternatives would be to suppress some of the process of his verbal rendition of that experience. What Crusoe's rigorous correction of his own prose, and his concomitant reluctance to obliterate the traces of that correction, finally reveal is Daniel Defoe's fascination with his ability to create fiction. That is, in the interest of representing the process of his creativity, Defoe settles for a product that is apparently less than perfect. But if, as I have suggested, both the particular vitality and the particular density of the narrative depend exactly upon Crusoe's self-correction, and if Crusoe's believability depends upon the same thing, then much of the success of the whole fiction does likewise. We may conclude, then, that with a few exceptions, what appear to be stylistic interruptions are the basis for artistic triumph.

The subject of *Robinson Crusoe* is the process of making: Crusoe making civilization out of tables and chairs, which he makes out of next to nothing; Crusoe making a book out of his life's experiences; and Defoe making a fiction out of words. "Fiction" itself is a word in process, a verb turned noun, a being thing. And what it names is also a complete interdependence, a symbiosis, of process and substance. The bits and pieces of fiction—the objects it mentions—do refer to kinds of things we are familiar with as parts of the real world, but except for these tokens of reality, it is the process of a fictional narrative that entirely creates the fictive substance. It was perhaps incredulity over this miraculous transformation, through the medium of the reader's mind, of words into imaginary things, that led Defoe to animate his narrative so strongly, and to stuff it with apparently extraneous words. Because of its author's anxiety, the fiction *Robinson Crusoe* seems to be always on the verge of becoming creation.

JAMES H. MADDOX

On Defoe's Roxana

A crucial moment for the Defoe protagonist arises when he becomes aware of his status as victim or slave and resolves to master the force that has dominion over him. When Moll Flanders emerges from her first love entanglement and her resultant marriage to Robin, she comes to the conclusion that "I had been trick'd once by *that Cheat call'd* LOVE, but the Game was over; I was resolv'd now to be Married, or Nothing, and to be well Married, or not at all." Moll is never again a naive lover; henceforth, she is always aware of the instrumentality, the usefulness, of love as an emotion she can call up in men. She objectifies the emotion which once victimized her, and she makes of it a tool of conquest. The same sort of process is at work in those obsessive pages of *Robinson Crusoe* where Crusoe, terrified by the cannibals who appear on his island, seeks to redirect all his inchoate emotion and transform it from helpless terror to powerful, dominant revenge. In Moll's subsequent exploitation of men and in Crusoe's subsequent massacre of the cannibals, moreover, the antagonist, the other, has become an image of the protagonist's own earlier, weaker self. Mastery of the other in Defoe is an external emblem of self-mastery.

We can isolate two stages in this dialectic of victimhood and mastery, and an understanding of them will help us to see why the search for mastery brings about such absolute disaster for Defoe's final novelistic protagonist, Roxana. First, the Defoe protagonist at a crucial stage learns to divide himself in two, and a mastering self comes to assert control over a victimized self. Second, the self-dividing, self-mastering protagonist works toward a re-

From *ELH* 51, no. 4 (Winter 1984). © 1984 by the Johns Hopkins University Press.

creation of some earlier traumatic event, but in this recreation the protagonist
has the power, and some other is now the victim. Such, in brief, is the path
toward triumph and control followed by Crusoe, Moll, and Colonel Jack.
The triumph, to be sure, often seems precarious, especially as the character
tries to face down his own earlier weaknesses and self-doubts through a
simple display of wealth or power. But Defoe allows the character the
triumph—until, that is, he arrives at the case of Roxana. In Defoe's last
novel, Roxana attempts to follow the same formula of success as the other
protagonists, and it blows up in her face. In what follows, I want to show
how Defoe's subtler understanding of the self-dividing, self-mastering character leads inexorably to tragedy in *Roxana*; then in closing, I will look briefly
at the way Roxana's story serves to explode the more complacent myths of
the earlier protagonists.

Roxana's first crucial moment of self-consciousness comes, rather like
Moll's first such moment, when she discovers how victimized she is in her
first marriage. In her reflections upon that marriage, we can already hear
her characteristic voice:

> Never, Ladies, marry a Fool; any Husband rather than a Fool;
> with some other Husbands you may be unhappy, but with a Fool
> you will be miserable; with another Husband you *may*, I say, be
> unhappy, but with a Fool you *must*; nay, if he wou'd, he cannot
> make you easie, every thing he does is so awkward, every thing
> he says is so empty, a Woman of any Sence cannot but be sur-
> feited, and sick of him twenty times a-Day: What is more shock-
> ing, than for a Woman to bring a handsome, comely Fellow of
> a Husband, into Company, and then be oblig'd to Blush for him
> every time she hears him speak? To hear other Gentlemen talk
> Sence, and he able to say nothing? And so look like a Fool, or,
> which is worse, hear him talk Nonsense, and be laugh'd at for a
> Fool?

There is an awful astringency in this passage, a cold beam of contempt
directed at the husband. In particular, Roxana registers an almost intolerable
exasperation at that particularly galling rub of the marital bond, the husband's
constant humiliation of her before company. This sensitivity to humiliation,
one of the very hallmarks of Roxana's character, finely distinguishes her from
Moll. Moll fully succeeds in objectifying men—in looking upon them as
objects and, eventually, as instruments. Even when she is not completely
independent of them, her dependence is the dependence of the exploiter;

she is whole without them. Roxana, on the other hand, never fully achieves Moll's freedom. In Roxana's eyes, her men directly reflect something about herself, and she is therefore much more intensely dependent upon them than is Moll. Fleeing from the experience of shame and humiliation with her first husband, Roxana seeks out men who are glorious and prestigious enough to heighten her self-esteem. Thus during her years as a courtesan she remains existentially dependent upon her prestigious men, to bolster her sense of her own worth. Only after having experienced the most prestigious man of all, the king, does Roxana begin to free herself from this sort of dependence. And exactly then she redirects her attention toward that other source of possible esteem and possible shame, the long-abandoned children.

Roxana's intense susceptibility to shame goes far toward explaining the nature of her fascinating relationship with Amy. Amy, as many readers have noticed, is the most developed example of a character who frequently appears alongside the Defoe protagonist—Moll's "governess," for example, or the Quaker William in *Captain Singleton*. They are the helpers, the agents of the protagonist. But far more than the others, Amy is of psychological interest in her own right, as she acts out of powerful compulsions of her own. She is strongly, indeed obsessively devoted to Roxana— "faithful to me," says Roxana, "as the Skin to my Back." Amy's most accomplished skill is to propose as her own ideas those shameful acts that Roxana cannot quite acknowledge as arising in her own consciousness. It is Amy who manages the jettisoning of the children, Amy who counsels Roxana to become the mistress of the landlord, and Amy who finally murders the wretched Susan. Amy thus offers herself up as a ready-made doppelgänger, responsible both for the shameful thought and often for its execution. And, in Amy's scenario, she herself doesn't really incur any guilt either, since she does everything for Roxana's sake; Amy's obsessive love for Roxana is so great that Amy seems to feel no personal responsibility for the immoralities she commits to protect her mistress. In Amy's mind, she and Roxana are two hands washing each other, and all the dirt is left behind in the basin.

Roxana's problem is that she perceives the real nature of Amy's offices even as she accepts and profits from them. Amy tries to help Roxana disburden herself of moral responsibility, but Roxana actually works to keep alive her secret sense of her own sin. In the important episode of Roxana's sleeping with the landlord, for example, Amy puts forward a powerful argument that Roxana in fact has no choice. As for the landlord, he has no sense of wrongdoing; but Roxana cannot escape thinking of herself as a whore. She is uncomfortable, and she seeks to rid herself of the discomfort in the famous scene in which she strips Amy, "thrusts" her into bed with the landlord-lover, and then stands by to watch their fornication. She thus explains her behavior:

> I need say no more; this is enough to convince anybody that I did not think him my Husband, and that I had cast off all Principle, and all Modesty, and had effectually stifled Conscience. . . .
>
> Had I look'd upon myself as a Wife, you cannot suppose I would have been willing to have let my Husband lye with my Maid, much less, before my Face, for I stood-by all the while; but as I thought myself a Whore, I cannot say but that it was something design'd in my Thoughts, that my Maid should be a Whore too, and should not reproach me with it.

Embedded in these words is the inextricable ambivalence of self-assertion and self-accusation that characterizes Roxana. On one hand, Roxana is doing something very shrewd and self-profiting. Earlier, Amy took Roxana's own unvoiced motives, articulated them and made them her own, and encouraged Roxana to regard them as external to herself. The only price that Roxana might be said to pay is the damaging knowledge of the truth she can read in Amy's eyes. Now she once again makes of Amy an objectification of her own condition: she places Amy in her own, earlier vulnerable position and gazes down at her. There would seem to be no clearer instance of that tendency Defoe's characters have to make the other an image of their own vulnerability and thereby gain a dual victory over both self and world. And yet, on the other hand, this scene has the effect of burning even more deeply into Roxana's conscience the image of herself, precisely, as whore. By forcing Amy into nominal whoredom and her lover into promiscuity, Roxana effectually ridicules the sexual constancy and sexual affection she shares with her lover, and she thereby brings back to mind the original, essentially financial foundation of the relationship. Certainly, then, the scene does not at all prove, as Roxana says it does, that she "had effectually stifled Conscience." To the contrary, the scene shows the workings of a powerful masochistic conscience, which operates entirely as a mechanism of self-punishment, insisting, among all the trappings of happiness and prosperity, that the real self is the hidden, abject, shame-ridden whore, and that the trappings are *only* trappings.

Roxana alternates between the strenuous effort to improve her self-esteem and a countervailing retirement into self-contempt. A harrowing dialectic thus develops: each worldly success only compounds Roxana's sense of shame, because she keeps vivid in her mind the price she has had to pay for it; to still that sense of shame she seeks more worldly success; and so forth. The self-division of the Defoe character in *Roxana* is not so much an instrument of self-overcoming as it is a terrible machine of self-torture. This dialectic becomes permanently fixed within Roxana while she is the prince's mistress, for during that time her growing consciousness of her beauty comes to reinforce her already well-developed attention to the observing eyes of others. Roxana, acutely sensitive to the possible scorn in others' eyes, longs to see admiration beaming from the eyes of one so prestigious as the prince and so she becomes victim to that other-directedness which is the occupational hazard of the very beautiful. As she says, once the prince has begun to court her, "I was now become the vainest Creature upon Earth, and particularly, of my Beauty; which, as other People admir'd, so I became every Day more foolishly in Love with myself, than before."

Exactly because she both fears and reveres the eyes of others, Roxana labors to present herself as a polished, two-dimensional, depthless surface; she wishes to be looked at, but never seen into. The strategy of this self-presentation is especially clear in her account of the three years she spent living in absolute seclusion in Paris, as the prince's mistress. Except for the brief period of a lying-in in the country, she does not set foot outside the house during these years, and she describes as an especially cherished time a fortnight when her prince also stayed completely inside their love nest. One of course would expect that these years would be presented (or referred to in passing) as a time of intense privacy and intimacy, spent in an emotional and amatory hothouse. But the fascinating glimpses that Roxana gives of those years reveal instead an intensely public world, in which the prince is spectator at Roxana's formal self-displays. Each of the lovers, after all, exists for the other as a polished porcelain surface: Roxana is in love with the prince's rank, while the prince is in love with Roxana's great beauty. There is in Roxana's descriptions of these scenes nothing like our idea of a "private self"; instead, their three years are spent in a constant display of their different forms of prestige.

The paradox of Roxana's behavior with the prince is that, as they retire more completely into their private world, she presents herself more and more completely as a dazzling surface. Thus on one occasion the prince gives her "three Suits of Cloaths, such as the Queen of *France* would not have disdain'd to have worn at that time; yet I went out no-where." Instead of "going out," she dresses in their apartments and parades before the prince, to his speechless admiration. In such a scene as this, Defoe has with great finesse caught and presented Roxana's problems of self-definition. Like other eighteenth-century figures such as Clarissa or even James Boswell, Roxana is intensely preoccupied with the display of a public self; but there is none of that sense in Roxana that there is in Clarissa or Boswell of a private self with an activity and life of its own. In part, we are dealing here with a malaise at the center of Defoe's characterization in virtually all his writings, an odd poverty of inner life. But we are dealing with that problem in a very particular form in Roxana, for she exists as a personality with an appalling missing center: her "public self" is her beautiful and graceful "person"; her "private self" is what she at one point calls the "secret Hell within," that underlying pit of self-contempt from which her public self is her only refuge. This totally binary feeling of her own identity becomes especially clear just after that memorable scene when Roxana, in order to prove to the prince that her complexion is real and not painted, has him vigorously rub her cheek with a handkerchief and then herself washes her face in his presence. Roxana then proceeds to reflect on the folly of men who are baited by such superficial beauty:

> I, that knew what this Carcass of mine had been but a few Years before; how overwhelm'd with Grief, drown'd in Tears, frighted with the Prospect of Beggery, and surrounded with Rags, and Fatherless Children; that was pawning and selling the Rags that cover'd me, for a Dinner, and sat on the Ground, despairing of Help, and expecting to be starv'd, till my Children were snatch'd from me, to be kept by the Parish; I, that was after this, a Whore for Bread, and abandoning Conscience and Virtue, liv'd with another Woman's Husband; I, that was despis'd by all my Relations, and my Husband's too; I, that was left so entirely desolate, friendless, and helpless, that I knew not how to get the least Help to keep me from starving; that I should be caress'd by a Prince, for the Honour of having the scandalous Use of my Prostituted Body, common before to his Inferiours; and perhaps wou'd not have denied one of his Footmen but a little while before, if I cou'd have got my Bread by it.
>
> I say, I cou'd not but reflect upon the Brutallity and Blindness of Mankind; that because Nature had given me a good Skin, and some agreeable Features, should suffer that Beauty to be such a Bait to Appetite, as to do such sordid, unaccountable things, to obtain the Possession of it.

Here, Roxana's already abundant self-contempt is compounded by her memory of her former poverty. She believes that she is really a whore rather than a lovable lady, really a carcass rather than a beautiful body. And the feeling here is deeply existential: she also believes that she is really that "desolate, friendless, and helpless" woman left abandoned rather than a wealthy and pampered lady living in Paris. Like a Dickens character miraculously granted a sudden rise in social prestige, she recurrently finds the "real" to be the old poverty and the old disgrace.

Roxana thus repeatedly stamps upon her memory the very idea of herself she seems to be fleeing; she thereby keeps that idea alive, constantly in mind, with the result that each effort she makes to cut a new "figure" in the world only works to reinforce the secret hell within. The hidden logic of her identity is that she actually depends upon this masochistic self-division as the definition of who she is. She does not really seek to resolve the division; she is constantly at work to perpetuate it. And nothing perpetuates the division better than the status of the courtesan. Exactly because the courtesan lives with the constant possibility of the disappearance of her present way of life, she is always aware of keeping up a role which is tenuous, having no legal or moral sanction. Roxana genuinely prefers this state of affairs, because all of her psychological energy goes into self-creation, and is diverted from prolonged reflection. Or, to put the matter another way, the dynamics of her character make Roxana strikingly similar to Hawthorne's Dimmesdale, and undoubtedly the similarity between the two can be traced back to the self-dividing activities of the Puritan autobiographer. Both characters think they long for a unitary, unambiguous sense of themselves, but both Roxana and Dimmesdale come to depend upon self-torment as self-definition. We can thus detect in Roxana a dread of resolution, a dread of stasis. When her relationship with the landlord is on the point of stabilizing, she puts Amy to bed with him. When, later in her narrative, her career as a courtesan begins to wane and a future of domestic respectability stares her in the face, she will bring back alive that first source of her guilt, her abandonment of her children, and the whole fragile structure of her life will come crashing down upon her.

Roxana's self-division infects not only her character within the story, but also her narrative. As narrator, Roxana intensifies that sense of the precariousness of her many adopted identities as she uses again and again an ominous kind of anticipatory phrasing which is the very hallmark of her style in the novel. These phrases—"as you shall hear," "of which hereafter," "but of that in its place," and the like—constitute something like a nervous tic in Roxana's writing. Their cumulative effect is at once to anticipate and postpone a narrative future, often a narrative future charged with great dread. They function stylistically very much as Roxana's many roles and costumes function thematically: they create an extraordinary air of contingency and precariousness. Roxana's anxious consciousness of a shameful truth under-lying and negating whatever prosperity and happiness she experiences is thus built into the narrative itself.

These narrative anticipations of an ominous future point ultimately to the harrowing events that close out Roxana's story: Susan's frenetic search for her mother and Amy's murder of Susan. These sombre events cast their shadow back over the earlier narrative and coerce the very form of Roxana's story into a shape expressive of the tensions it portrays. This narrative wrenching begins about two-thirds of the way through the novel, when Roxana pauses momentously:

> I must go back here, after telling openly the wicked things I did, to mention something, which however, had the Face of doing good; I remember'd, that when I went from *England*, which was fifteen Years before, I had left five little Children, turn'd out, as it were, to the wide World.

The earliest, most abiding cause of Roxana's shame—the abandonment of the children—begins to emerge, like an earlier text showing through on a palimpsest. From this point forward, Roxana shuttles back and forth re-peatedly between two narratives: first, the story of her courtship by the Dutchman, his purchase of titles, and their prosperous life in England and Holland; second, the story of her finding her surviving children, Susan's countersearch for her, and Amy's murder of Susan. Roxana's procedure is to carry forward the story of her life with the Dutchman, and then to retreat and bring up to date the second story, the story of the children, which cancels out the triumphs of the story of her life with the Dutchman. The second narrative constantly explodes the first.

Roxana's faltering attempt to help her children is an effort at redeeming the past and reversing the spiral of self-contempt she has been caught up in ever since the original fateful act. The characteristic—and pathetic—way in which she tries to work out this redemption is clear as she explains why she went to such lengths to remain the unknown benefactor of one of her sons, whom she sets up as a merchant in Messina:

> I cou'd not find in my Heart to let my Son know what a Mother he had, and what a Life she liv'd; when at the same time that he must think himself infinitely oblig'd to me, he must be oblig'd, if he was a Man of Virtue, to hate his Mother, and abhor the Way of Living, by which all the Bounty he enjoy'd, was rais'd.

> This is the Reason of mentioning this Part of my Son's Story,
> which is otherwise no ways concern'd in my History, but as it
> put me upon thinking how to put an End to that wicked Course
> I was in, that my own Child, when he shou'd afterwards come
> to *England* in a good Figure, and with the Appearance of a Mer-
> chant, shou'd not be asham'd to own me.

Roxana finds unbearable the prospect of an unmediated meeting with one
of the children, and so she devises an elaborate manipulation of roles and
appearances which she thinks will be the solution to her dilemma. The son
is to be sent away, long enough to acquire "a good Figure" and "the Appearance of a Merchant"; while he is gone—so Roxana's scenario seems to
run—she will refashion herself. She will cease to be Roxana and become a
demure lady who can make use of all the paraphernalia of respectability to
welcome the returning son and the other surviving children once they have
been similarly revolutionized.

We need to be careful in unraveling motive here, for we are very close
to an explanation of the subsequent Susan-tragedy. Roxana's dealing with
the son is of course a postponement, a way of putting off a discovery scene
and thereby maintaining the status quo, even as Roxana claims to be moving
toward change and revelation. Moreover, the whole scheme is immensely
pathetic in its foredoomed effort to arrive at tenderness and love through a
complicated shifting-about of masks. The only way in which Roxana can
even conceive of herself as a good and loving mother is to transform the
children into the social roles to which a caring—and very wealthy—mother
would have assisted them, and then to transform herself into her idea of the
mother who would have done such a thing. Her touchingly naive expectation
seems to be that the children, once they have been magically transformed,
will come back to her, look upon her as a loving mother, and presto, that is
what she will be—just as the prince once transformed her into an object of
virtù by his admiring gaze. Roxana's efforts to redeem the past thus only
perpetuate that absolute fissure within her, as she rushes from her intolerably
shameful idea of herself toward some imagined construct into which she
seeks to fit herself.

But all of Roxana's plans are thrown into disarray by Susan's demands
for recognition. Roxana's anxiety and terror at Susan's discovery are entirely
convincing; the writing in these pages is strong and compelling. But we
should ask: just why *is* Roxana so terrified? Roxana herself actually offers a
superfluity of reasons. She does not believe Susan's promise to keep their
relationship a secret; instead, she says she fears that Susan would expose

her, either before the first husband's relatives or before her husband the Dutchman. She fears as well exposure before her children, who would now see their mother as a heartless whore. Her stated reasons for fear are many, diffuse, and free-floating. The one constant underlying everything else is fear of exposure itself. Like Clarissa, that very different heroine a quarter of a century later, Roxana is extraordinarily sensitive to the eyes of others. She is avid in her desire for admiration and terrified to the point of frenzy at the idea of exposure to eyes that are critical, knowing, and thereby awesomely dominant. Roxana's greatest fear is of being seen in this way—being exposed to what Clarissa calls "glare." That glare, rather than any of the various actual consequences that might flow from it, is the deepest source of her terror.

Roxana evidently believes that her exposure to Susan would plunge her back into that despised, vulnerable position of helplessness which was her condition when her first husband left her. And so, heavily, ominously, her story begins to repeat itself. Here, indeed, is where Roxana's story inverts the pattern of the earlier novels. Like the earlier protagonists, Roxana seems to be on the verge of redeeming the past by returning to it and gaining control over it; but her attempt to redeem the past devolves into a tragic and darker repetition of her original sin, as she tries once more to abandon the children. Once again Roxana is irresolute, while Amy knows just what to do. Before, Amy could advise: abandon the children; sleep with the landlord. Now she says simply: kill the girl. Roxana's response to Amy's clear intent is perhaps the finest instance in all of Defoe's writings of that quality that George A. Starr calls the "casuistry" of Defoe's prose. Here, for example, Roxana describes Amy's fury at Susan's attempts to find her mother:

> This put *Amy* into such a Hurry, that she cry'd; she rav'd; she swore and curs'd like a Mad-thing; then she upbraided me, that I wou'd not let her kill the Girl when she wou'd have done it; and that it was all my own doing, *and the like:* Well however, I was not for killing the Girl yet, I cou'd not bear the Thoughts of that neither.

In all their crises, Amy is active, while Roxana remains paralyzed in what she calls at one point "a silent sullen kind of Grief" and awaits the outcome of events. Nevertheless, there can be a purpose in Roxana's very passivity. Roxana is very explicit in forbidding Amy to murder Susan; at the same time, Roxana is quite aware of Amy's impetuousness, and she does in truth want the girl dead. Defoe's rendering of this divided consciousness is very fine indeed; the phrase in the passage quoted above—"I was not for killing the Girl yet"—is one of the very few hints Roxana drops of her actual desire for the murder itself. Such hints, coupled with Roxana's later feelings of guilt and complicity, eloquently suggest that all of Roxana's protestations conceal a desire that she does not fully articulate, even to herself.

As Roxana approaches the central horror, the actual murder of Susan, her narrative becomes more and more violently disrupted. It becomes extremely circumlocutory and elliptical—and we realize that Roxana cannot bring herself to narrate the murder. She anticipates it, she hints at it, she alludes to the murder as something "which however, *Amy* found Means to bring to pass afterwards; *as I may in time relate more particularly*," but she never does relate more particularly. Roxana does with her readers what she does with her son the merchant: she proposes a full revelation, but she postpones it indefinitely. Thus, as the novel approaches its end, Roxana's narrative becomes predicated upon certain unspeakable events about which she simply will not tell us.

Once again, Roxana's narrative form is a replica of her agonized consciousness. Her tendency toward narrative reticence and secrecy has, after all, been growing since the beginnings of her liaison with the prince. Before that liaison, Roxana is even disarmingly open in recounting the events of her life: the famous bed scene is but the most extreme version of her candor early in the novel. But when her trysts with the prince begin, a new tone creeps into her writing, as is evident in her description of the first night they pass together:

> You are perfectly obliging, *says he*, and sitting on the Bed-side, *says he*, Now you shall be a Princess, and know what it is to oblige the gratefullest Man alive; and with that, he took me in his Arms,—I can go no farther in the Particulars of what pass'd at that time; but it ended in this, that, in short, I lay with him all Night.

The slightly coy suggestion and avoidance here arise in part from the sexual nature of the subject matter, but also from the fact that this is a prince: he is a public person, and his intimate affairs are not to be revealed in any detail. That intense division between public and private, which we have already noticed as developing in Roxana herself so markedly during the affair with the prince thus also begins to affect the narrative at this point, as Roxana lets us know that there are some matters she is leaving shrouded in obscurity. And what is true of a prince is of course even truer of a king. When Roxana (apparently) later becomes mistress to Charles II, decorum forbids her to tell more than this:

> There is a Scene which came in here, which I must cover from
> humane Eyes or Ears; for three Years and about a Month, *Roxana*
> liv'd retir'd, having been oblig'd to make an Excursion, in a Man-
> ner, and with a Person, which Duty, and private Vows, obliges
> her not to reveal, at least, not yet.

Thus Roxana's narrative moves away from its initial confessional mode
and comes to embody the same radical division that characterizes its narrator.
In the affairs with the prince and the king, the motive is a respect for the
privacy of public persons. Later, the motive is terror and dread, when Roxana
approaches and avoids the murder of Susan. And then, at the very end of
the book, there is one final event for which Roxana again deploys this strategy
of avoidance in its extremest form—the great catastrophe that befalls her
after her removal to Holland, the exact nature of which we never learn. The
final two paragraphs of the book, in which Roxana alludes obscurely to those
events, deserve our closest attention.

Roxana has first told her story of the Dutchman, ending in their prosperous marriage; then she has told the story of Susan, which completely
explodes the happy ending of the Dutchman story. Now, that explosion
having been accomplished, Roxana comes again to the period of her arrival
in Holland. Here is the penultimate paragraph of the novel:

> I can say no more now, but that, *as above*, being arriv'd in *Holland*,
> with my Spouse and his Son, *formerly mention'd*, I appear'd there
> with all the Splendor and Equipage suitable to our new Prospect,
> *as I have already observ'd.*

This little sentence, an intense concentration of the *Roxana*-style, is an extraordinary attempt to repress what the narrative has just recounted. "I can
say no more now," the sentence begins, with that effect of peremptoriness
and of time-saving haste which is one of Roxana's efforts at avoidance and
closure in the novel's final pages. The "*as above*," the "*formerly mention'd*,"
the "*as I have already observ'd*"—these three backward-looking phrases concentrated in one sentence reflect the sentence's strenuous effort to overleap
the Susan memory and to serve as capstone to the longed-for story of prosperous success. The whole sentence has the strategy of conquering the truth
through appearances. Roxana shows herself arriving "with my Spouse and
his Son," thereby placing herself, for the first time since the original abandonment of the children, in a domestic, familial vignette, as if the image
would negate the memory of herself as child-murderer. And finally the
phrasing: "appear'd . . . Splendor . . . Equipage": the old strategy of facing

down shame through a splendid, dazzling blaze of surfaces is still present in that sentence.

But that sentence is Roxana's final stand. It is followed by the abrupt, enigmatic, haunting final paragraph.

> Here, after some few Years of flourishing, and outwardly happy Circumstances, I fell into a dreadful Course of Calamities, and *Amy* also; the very Reverse of our former Good Days; the Blast of Heaven seem'd to follow the Injury done the poor Girl, by us both; and I was brought so low again, that my Repentance seem'd to be only the Consequence of my Misery, as my Misery was of my Crime.

Something terrible happens, but its nature remains completely obscure. Roxana's voice in the novel was generated out of the anxious disparity between the proud self she presented to the world and the shameful self she secretly felt herself to be. As soon as Roxana is exposed and "brought low," the disparity collapses, and the voice ceases. It ceases on a note of absolute self-damnation, for Roxana is unable to believe in the sincerity of her own repentance, which seems to her simply "the Consequence of my Misery" and not true contrition. It is probably theologically true to say that Roxana is damned, either by her hardheartedness or by her despair. Those states are *real* in the book because Defoe has so thoroughly imagined their attendant psychology. Roxana has lived so long with the secret conviction that her pretenses to worthiness were pure sham that she can now give no credit at all to her last effort at worthiness, her attempt at repentance. She accepts the knowledge of her own damnation because that knowledge exactly corresponds to what she has throughout the novel tried to deny and to what throughout the novel she has secretly believed herself to be. Like Dimmesdale again, she exposes the truth about herself and ceases to be—Dimmesdale by dying, Roxana by falling into abrupt silence—as if existence itself were predicated upon the tension between a comely surface and a shameful secret.

II

When Roxana lapses into that final, terrible silence, so does her creator, at least in his role as novelist. And *Roxana* can appropriately be looked upon as a final statement, a reflection upon the career, for it recapitulates the themes of the earlier novels and ends by exploding their myths. Earlier novels such as *Captain Singleton*, *Moll Flanders*, and *Colonel Jack* give a series of colorful adventures, often morally equivocal at best, which reach their end point in the protagonist's resolve to turn religious and prudent and to retire on a substantial income, the questionable sources of which are conveniently forgotten. *Roxana* obviously subverts this plot, especially as it addresses the guilt and anxiety that the earlier protagonists are so skilled at leaving behind them. *Mutatis mutandis, Roxana* looks back upon the earlier novels as *Great Expectations* looks back upon *Oliver Twist* or *David Copperfield*.

This process of self-undermining is itself symptomatic of a procedure apparently central to Defoe's imagination. Daniel Defoe seems to have been a conservative and conventional man with a powerfully subversive imagination. He was a man of strong moral views who yet could project himself with complete imaginative sympathy into the views of his opponents and into the skins of the rascal protagonists of his novels. Examples of his great powers of impersonation are well known—especially his role as journalistic double agent as a writer for Nathaniel Mist's *Weekly Journal* and, most famously, his self-defeating ventriloqual performance in *The Shortest Way with the Dissenters.* My point is not simply that Defoe was capable of imaginative expansion and self-multiplication when he wrote, but more centrally that his imagination led him to a systematic testing of and attack upon his own ideas.

Twice in his novelistic career Defoe engaged in this form of self-subversion by presenting a myth of the self in one book and exploding the myth in a second. In the first pairing, Defoe created a strong myth in *Robinson Crusoe* and then subverted that myth in *The Farther Adventures of Robinson Crusoe.* As I have argued elsewhere, *The Farther Adventures* surprises because, far from being simply an extension and repetition of the earlier novel—a *Robinson Crusoe II*—it in fact undermines the earlier book's confident myth of mastery and self-sufficiency. The second pairing consists of Defoe's two novels about women, *Moll Flanders* and *Roxana*, and again the second is an undermining of the first. In both of these pairings, Defoe first writes a celebration of the self-fashioning protagonist and then writes an aggressively opposed novel whose major preoccupation is the destruction of an identity. Here, I wish to suggest very briefly how Roxana's narrative, which subverts itself, is also a radical critique of Moll's way of mastering the world.

We can see the nature of the one novel's myth and the other's countermyth by examining the highly charged, traumatic subject of child-murder, a covert activity in *Moll Flanders* which the juxtaposition with the more explicit *Roxana* helps to elicit. These two female novels of aggressive self-assertion have child-murder as their central, terrible image, just as the two Crusoe novels have cannibalism as theirs; in both cases, the central image is the nightmarish emblem of the self's living at the expense of the other.

One of the boldest of Moll's many accomplishments is her smuggling into her narrative her own indirect involvement in child-murder. She does not, of course, even tell what happens to most of her children. They are somehow simply forgotten; they disappear behind the smokescreen of benign tolerance Moll can generate for herself when she is in need. She does, it is true, at least begin the story of what happens to one of them. In a tone of self-congratulation for her motherly solicitude, she tells of farming an infant out to a poor woman; only some time later does she add that she was soon forced to discontinue the annual payments—thus abandoning the child to its unstated fate. Roxana on the other hand exposes exactly the details that Moll glides over. Roxana professes with an acerbic candor her own distaste for children; she says of one of them who dies soon after birth, "nor, after the first Touches of Affection (which are usual, I believe, to all Mothers) were over, was I sorry the Child did not live, the necessary Difficulties attending it in our travelling, being consider'd"; later she frankly avows that she wished the child of her Dutch merchant had died. And Roxana is devastatingly clear-eyed when she describes a wet nurse, such as the one Moll farms her child out to, as one of "those She-Butchers, who take Children off of [unwed mothers'] Hands, as 'tis call'd; that is to say, starve 'em, and, in a Word, murther 'em." Both mothers try to abandon their offspring as so much detritus; but Moll can to an amazing extent simply repress the memory of their existence, while Roxana burns into her memory the fact of her own callousness and thereby reminds herself yet once again of the original child abandonment. Moll, we might say, has a form of consciousness—and conscience—perfectly adapted to picaresque experience; her consciousness, like her life, is intensely episodic. Roxana has a more "novelistic" consciousness which perdures, in which the buried events of the past continue to coerce the present.

On two other important occasions, Moll verges upon the subject of child-murder. First, there is the famous account of one of her first exploits as a thief, her theft of the necklace from the little girl:

> the Child had a little Necklace on of Gold Beads, and I had my Eye upon that, and in the dark of the Alley I stoop'd, pretending to mend the Child's Clog that was loose, and took off her Necklace and the Child never felt it, and so led the Child on again: Here, I say, the Devil put me upon killing the Child in the dark Alley, that it might not Cry; but the very thought frighted me so that I was ready to drop down, but I turn'd the Child about and bad it go back again, for that was not its way home.

This glimpse of Moll's momentary terrible temptation reveals an unexpected, underlying connection between her two professions, whoring and thieving, both of which are haunted by the possibility of child-murder. Moll's "governess," of course, who instructs her in both trades, does a wholesale business in putting unwanted children out of sight. The whore, after all, remains independent through the practice of infanticide. For the thief, too, the child is the ideal prey, the ultimately helpless victim, and underneath all her rationalizings, Moll frequently has deep antagonism and contempt for her victims; the quick flare-up of the desire to murder is appropriate to Moll's personality. If this seems too harsh a judgment, it seems so only because Moll is so successful a sentimental narrator: she is very adept indeed at convincing us and herself that she pities, even feels strong affection for, the very victims she has just robbed blind. Here, as a classic instance, is a part of that wonderful passage in which she lays to rest the memory of the little girl with the necklace—and here is the whole difference between her and Roxana:

> THIS String of Beads was worth about Twelve or Fourteen Pounds, I suppose it might have been formerly the Mother's, for it was too big for the Child's wear, but that, perhaps, the Vanity of the Mother to have her Child look Fine at the Dancing School, had made her let the Child wear it, and no doubt the Child had a Maid sent to take care of it, but she, like a careless Jade, was taken up perhaps with some Fellow that had met her by the way, and so the poor Baby wandred till it fell into my Hands.

The way in which Moll scarifies the vain mother and the careless jade of a (hypothetical) maid and actually arrogates to herself maternal solicitude for the child, "poor Baby," is of course masterful; she disarms by the sheer bravado of her chutzpah. But then this is frequently the way Moll rolls from adventure to adventure: when one of the escapades leaves some residue of unpleasant feeling, she is the most adept of any of Defoe's protagonists at finding some scapegoat to bear that ill feeling away.

Such a discovery of a surrogate victim is clear in a second episode verging upon child-murder, when Moll is almost detected in the act of lifting a lady's watch. Moll reacts by raising a cry herself and claiming she has felt someone tugging at *her* watch:

> AT that very instant, a little farther in the Crowd, and very Luckily too, they cried out *a Pick-pocket* again, and really seiz'd a young Fellow in the very Fact. This, tho' unhappy for the

Wretch was very opportunely for my Case, tho' I had carried it off handsomely enough before, but now it was out of Doubt, and all the loose part of the Crowd run that way, and the poor Boy was deliver'd up to the Rage of the Street, which is a Cruelty I need not describe, and which however they are always glad of, rather than to be sent to *Newgate*, where they lie often a long time, till they are almost perish'd, and sometimes they are hang'd, and the best they can look for, if they are Convicted, is to be Transported.

The scene is an almost uncannily perfect paradigm of the submerged theme of child-murder in *Moll Flanders*: Moll escapes scot-free, and the young boy is killed, seemingly in her stead. The boy's function as surrogate, moreover, is only emphasized by Moll's arguing that he, "poor Boy," is actually happier being brutally murdered by a mob than he would be if he were sent to Newgate to be threatened with hanging and perhaps eventually transported. This latter fate is of course Moll's own, and Moll discovers that being transported to America is in fact considerably more pleasant, thank you very much, than being trampled to death in the London streets.

I have dwelt upon only a few select episodes in *Moll Flanders*, and I should perhaps say at this point that Moll is not constantly on the verge of child-murder. Nevertheless, the juxtaposition with *Roxana* helps to make clear how child-murder is tucked away, quite comfortably and untraumatically, without repercussions, in Moll's novel. Moll absorbs those events because she, like Roxana, operates by a sharp self-division, but Moll's is the self-division not of the self-tormentor but of the thoroughgoing sentimentalist. Her feelings of pity for her victims are clear instances of sentimental effusions, self-flattering emotions divorced from, very often opposed to, her actions. A sentimentalist of this description will find repentance after a life of crime a surprisingly easy thing; the sentimentalist is indeed he who would enjoy without incurring the immense debtorship for the thing done. Roxana's self-torment constantly brands the consciousness of her guilt deeper into her brain; Moll's sentimentality constantly diffuses her sense of her own responsibility.

The narratives of both Moll and Roxana come to their conclusions when the mother discovers her long-lost child, the symbol of the most shameful event in the mother's past—and the great difference between the two books is illustrated in the contrast between Moll's almost operatic embrace of her son and Roxana's mediated murder of her daughter.

Moll's son, one might think, would be a reminder of the incest that has

twice haunted Moll's life, first when she married Robin and "committed
Adultery and Incest with [the elder brother] every Day in my Desires" and
again when she unwittingly married her own brother and subsequently gave
birth to this very child; but Moll's meeting with her son is totally unanxious,
untraumatic. Moll can be so carefree in great part because she once again
has someone handy to conduct away all her negative feeling: for, skulking
on the periphery of the mother-son reunion is the shadowy figure of the
brother-husband, half-blind, an incestuous Oedipus. He serves her as a
surrogate, much as the young pick-pocket did back in London. And there
are other, more immediately obvious reasons for Moll's complaisance in the
reunion. Her son, after all, is a handsome young man rather than one of
those troublesome, dependent infants Moll has so quietly disposed of earlier
in the narrative; indeed, in a reversal of Defoe's favorite biblical story, the
parable of the Prodigal Son, the son showers wealth upon the returned
mother.

Most interestingly, Moll even experiences a moment of something like
mental infidelity to her Jemy when she reflects upon her handsome son:

> and thus I was as if I had been in a new World, and began secretly
> now to wish that I had not brought my *Lancashire* Husband from
> *England* at all.
>
> HOWEVER, that wish was not hearty neither, for I lov'd my
> *Lancashire* Husband entirely, as indeed I had ever done from the
> beginning; and he merited from me as much as it was possible
> for a Man to do, but that by the way.

Now we have seen Moll undergo moments of vacillation such as this before,
have we not? She early on learned to weigh on an inner scale the man she
had safely in hand against the more attractive and profitable prospect before
her; she in fact made exactly that sort of computation in deciding between
her banker-lover and this very Lancashire Jemy. This moment with the son,
then, is wonderfully funny and wonderfully Moll-like. Far from looking
upon the son as the terrible emblem of incest, Moll finds herself thinking of
him in terms of the strategies she has earlier deployed to ensnare sexual
partners; her hasty recantation of the thought is the sign of a buried recognition of that eerily familiar way of thinking of men. Moll's fugitive thought
is a brilliant instance of just how fully she gains power over the old evils
that once controlled her. She now uses to her own advantage those troubling
familial bonds that once were her nightmare.

Moll returns to her family and finds that she can revolutionize the
relationships of power within it. Roxana returns and finds the old traumas

even more deeply etched than before. Moll, protean and shape-shifting, can spend much of her life engaged in a species of child-murder and still close her narrative with a sentimental picture of herself as a loving mother. Roxana returns and actually attempts to redeem her role as mother, only to find the old crime repeating itself, this time even more terribly.

Moll is foremost among Defoe's characters in expressing a kind of freedom that was to entrance many eighteenth-century writers—a freedom that begins as liberation from class bonds and from family, and that ends as liberation from strict definitions of identity, so that the self is involved in a constant process of transformation. In Moll are the beginnings of Lovelace, that fictional character named James Boswell, the Shandys when they succeed in losing themselves in hobby-horsicality, and Jane Austen's charming, fraudulent young gentlemen, epitomized in Frank Churchill; here is Laclos's Valmont, and here, in the most extreme form, is Diderot's nephew of Rameau. But all these characters, and in particular the English characters on the list, are profoundly anxious—even including the robust Moll. For all of them self-transformation is also a form of self-evasion; for all of them constant movement betrays the self's wish to avoid knowing itself and to escape into all-absorbing activity or the delights of impersonation and theatricality. Roxana too attempts that flight into impersonation, but she is never deeply convinced of its legitimacy. Her novel offers the century's most hellish vision of the effort to escape into a newly fabricated identity.

Chronology

1660	Daniel Foe born in London to a fairly prosperous tallow chandler, James Foe, and his wife, Alice.
1662	Family follows their pastor, Dr. Samuel Annesley, out of the Church of England because of the Act of Uniformity; they are now Presbyterians.
ca. 1668	Mother dies.
ca. 1671–79	Studies at the Reverend James Fisher's school at Dorking, Surrey, then, Oxford and Cambridge being closed to Dissenters, attends the Reverend Charles Morton's School at Newington Green. Foe's education, although preparing him for the ministry, includes science and is broader than studies at the universities.
1683	Merchant in the import/export business in Freeman's Yard, Cornhill (London). Publishes first political tract; no copy is known.
1684	Marries Mary Tuffley, daughter of a prosperous Dissenting wine-cooper. She bears him eight children, six of whom survive.
1685–92	Prospers in business: trades in hosiery, imports wine and tobacco, insures ships. Travels in England and on the Continent for business. Publishes political tracts.
1685	Joins the Protestant Duke of Monmouth's rebellion against Catholic James II; manages to escape after the disastrous Battle of Sedgemoor.
1688–1702	Supports William III, serving him in various offices.

1688   Admitted to the Butcher's Company, a guild. Publishes his first extant political tract against James II. Rides to Henley to join the advancing forces of William of Orange.

1690–91   Contributes to the *Athenian Mercury*; belongs to the Athenian Society.

1692   Declares bankruptcy, a result of rash speculations and losses in his ship insurance caused by the war with France. Within ten years, pays back all but £5,000, but is never again quite clear of debt.

1695   When manager-trustee of the royal lotteries, changes his name to "De Foe."

1697   Publishes *An Essay upon Projects*, which attracts politicians' attention.

1701   Publishes *The True-Born Englishman: A Satyr*, a poetic defense of William III's Dutch ancestry. Youngest child, Sophia, baptized.

1702   William III dies; Anne's accession ends Defoe's hopes of preferment. The rise of the Tories increases pressure on the Dissenters. Defoe writes *The Shortest Way with the Dissenters: Or Proposals For The Establishment of The Church*, an ironic attack on the intolerance of the High Church.

1703   Accused of seditious libel, Defoe is arrested for writing *The Shortest Way*. Fined, sent to Newgate, and sentenced to stand in the pillory. Writes *Hymn to the Pillory*. Second bankruptcy. Appeals to Harley, who secures his release and employs him. Publishes an authorized edition of his collected works.

1703–14   Pamphleteer and intelligence agent for Harley.

1704–13   Writes and edits *The Review* (a weekly, later triweekly), the main government organ (moderate Tory), in which Defoe discusses current affairs, politics, religion, trade, and manners and morals. The paper influences both later essay periodicals and the newspaper press.

1706–10   As government secret agent, travels frequently in Scotland to promote the Act of Union.

1708	Moves to Stoke Newington, a suburb north of London, where he lives the rest of his life.
1713–14	Repeatedly arrested by Harley's political enemies, once for publishing ironical tracts in support of the Hanoverian succession.
1715	Publishes *The Family Instructor*, a conduct manual, his most popular didactic work.
1715–30	Undertakes propaganda and intelligence work for successive Whig ministries after Harley's fall.
1718	Publishes the second volume of *The Family Instructor*.
1719	*The Life and Strange Surprising Adventures of Robinson Crusoe of York, Mariner* and *The Farther Adventures of Robinson Crusoe*.
1720	*Memoirs of a Cavalier; The Life, Adventures, and Pyracies of the Famous Captain Singleton*.
1722	*The Fortunes and Misfortunes of the Famous Moll Flanders, A Journal of the Plague Year*, and *The History and Remarkable Life of the Truly Honourable Colonel Jacque, Commonly Call'd Colonel Jack*.
1724	*The Fortunate Mistress: Or . . . Roxana*.
1724–26	*A Tour thro' the Whole Island of Great Britain* (three volumes).
1725	*The Complete English Tradesman* and pirate and criminal "lives."
1726	*The Political History of the Devil*.
1727	*Conjugal Lewdness (A Treatise Concerning the Use and Abuse of the Marriage Bed), An Essay on the History and Reality of Apparitions, A New Family Instructor*, and a second volume of *The Complete English Tradesman*.
1728	"Augusta Triumphans: Or, The Way To Make London The most flourishing City in the Universe" and *A Plan of the English Commerce*.
1731	Dies of a "lethargy" in Ropemaker's Alley (London), hiding from creditors. Buried in Bunhill Fields along with John Bunyan and other Puritans.

Contributors

HAROLD BLOOM, Sterling Professor of the Humanities at Yale University, is the author of *The Anxiety of Influence, Poetry and Repression*, and many other volumes of literary criticism. His forthcoming study, *Freud: Transference and Authority*, attempts a full-scale reading of all of Freud's major writings. A MacArthur Prize Fellow, he is general editor of five series of literary criticism published by Chelsea House. During 1987–88, he was appointed Charles Eliot Norton Professor of Poetry at Harvard University.

E. M. W. TILLYARD was Master of Jesus College, Cambridge. His books include *The English Epic and Its Background* and *The Elizabethan World Picture*.

MARTIN PRICE is Sterling Professor of English at Yale University. His books include *Swift's Rhetorical Art: A Study in Structure and Meaning, To the Palace of Wisdom: Studies in Order and Energy from Dryden to Blake*, and a number of edited volumes on literature of the seventeenth, eighteenth, and nineteenth centuries.

JAMES SUTHERLAND is the author of several books on English literature and editor of the works of Defoe, of Nicholas Rowe, and of *The Dunciad*. He has edited *The Oxford Book of English Talk* and *The Oxford Book of Literary Anecdotes*.

MANUEL SCHONHORN is Professor of English at Southern Illinois University. His research interests are Defoe, Pope, eighteenth-century history of ideas, and literature and politics.

HOMER O. BROWN is Professor of English at the University of California, Irvine. He has written articles on, among others, Defoe, Lawrence, and Joyce; he is the author of *James Joyce's Early Fiction: The Biography of a Form*.

H. DANIEL PECK teaches in the Department of English at Vassar College.

LEO BRAUDY, Professor of English at The Johns Hopkins University, has written extensively on film. His books and articles on eighteenth-century literature include *Narrative Form in History and Fiction: Hume, Fielding and Gibbon*.

GEORGE STARR is Professor of English at the University of California, Berkeley. Among his works are *Defoe and Spiritual Autobiography* and essays on Defoe.

ARNOLD WEINSTEIN is Professor of French Studies and Comparative Literature at Brown University. He is the author of *Fictions of the Self: 1550–1800*.

DAVID DURANT teaches in the Department of English at the University of Kentucky. He has written extensively on eighteenth-century literature.

JOHN J. BURKE, JR., is Associate Professor of English at the University of Alabama. He has published anthologies of Chaucer and Samuel Johnson, as well as articles on Defoe and Fielding.

MARY E. BUTLER teaches English at Agnes Scott College, Decatur, Georgia.

JAMES H. MADDOX, is with the Department of English at The George Washington University. He is the author of numerous articles on eighteenth-century English literature and of *Joyce's* Ulysses *and the Assault upon Character*.

Bibliography

Alkon, Paul K. "Defoe's Argument in *The Shortest Way with the Dissenters*." *Modern Philology* 73 (1976): S12–S23.

Allen, Walter. *The English Novel: A Short Critical History*. London: Phoenix House, 1954.

Alter, Robert. *Rogue's Progress: Studies in the Picaresque Novel*. Cambridge: Harvard University Press, 1964.

Anderson, Hans H. "The Paradox of Trade and Morality in Defoe." *Modern Philology* 39 (1941): 23–46.

Boardman, Michael M. *Defoe and the Uses of Narrative*. New Brunswick, N.J.: Rutgers University Press, 1983.

Castle, Terry. " 'Any, Who Knew My Disease': A Psychosexual Pattern in Defoe's *Roxana*." *ELH* 46 (1979): 81–96.

Damrosch, Leopold, Jr. "Defoe as Ambiguous Impersonator." *Modern Philology* 71 (1973): 153–59.

———. *God's Plot and Man's Stories*. Chicago: University of Chicago Press, 1985.

Durant, David. "Roxana's Fictions." *Studies in the Novel* 13 (1981): 225–36.

Flanders, W. Austin. "Defoe's *Journal of the Plague Year* and the Modern Urban Experience." *The Centennial Review* 16 (1972): 328–48.

Hunter, J. Paul. *The Reluctant Pilgrim: Defoe's Emblematic Method and Quest for Form in Robinson Crusoe*. Baltimore: Johns Hopkins University Press, 1966.

James, E. Anthony. *Daniel Defoe's Many Voices: A Rhetorical Study of Prose Style and Literary Method*. Amsterdam: Rodopi N.V., 1972.

Joyce, James. "Daniel Defoe." *Buffalo Studies* 1, no. 1 (1964): 7–25.

Koonce, Howard L. "Moll's Muddle: Defoe's Use of Irony in *Moll Flanders*." *ELH* 30 (1963): 377–94.

Lannert, Gustav. "An Investigation of the Language of *Robinson Crusoe*." Uppsala, Sweden: Almqvist & Winsells, 1910.

McNeil, David. "*A Journal of the Plague Year*: Defoe and Claustrophobia." *Southern Review* 16 (1983): 374–85.

Maddox, James H., Jr. "Interpreter Crusoe." *ELH* 51 (1984): 33–52.

———. "On Defoe's *Roxana*." *ELH* 51 (1984): 669–91.

Mason, Shirlene. *Daniel Defoe and the Status of Women*. St. Alban's, Vt.: Eden Press Women's Publications, 1978.

Novak, Maximillian. "Defoe and the Disordered City." *PMLA* 92 (1977): 241–52.

————. *Defoe and the Nature of Man*. New York and London: Oxford University Press, 1963.

————. *The Economics and the Fiction of Daniel Defoe*. Berkeley: University of California Press Publications in English Studies, 1962.

Richetti, John J. *Defoe's Narratives: Situations and Strategies*. Oxford: Clarendon, 1975.

Rogers, Pat. "Literary Art in Defoe's *Tour*: The Rhetoric of Growth and Decay." *Eighteenth-Century Studies* 6 (1972–73): 153–85.

————. *Robinson Crusoe*. London: Allen & Unwin, 1979.

Spacks, Patricia. "The Soul's Imaginings: Daniel Defoe, William Cowper." *PMLA* 91 (1976): 420–35.

Starr, George A. *Defoe and Casuistry*. Princeton: Princeton University Press, 1971.

————. *Defoe and Spiritual Autobiography*. Princeton: Princeton University Press, 1965.

Sutherland, James R. *Daniel Defoe: A Critical Study*. New York: Houghton Mifflin, 1971.

Swados, Harvey. "*Robinson Crusoe*: The Man Alone." In *Twelve Original Essays on Great English Novels*, edited by Charles Shapiro. Detroit: Wayne State University Press, 1960.

Tillyard, E. M. W. *The Epic Strain in the English Novel*. Fair Lawn, N.J.: Essential Books, 1958.

Watt, Ian. *The Rise of the Novel: Studies in Defoe, Richardson, and Fielding*. Berkeley: University of California Press, 1957.

Weinstein, Arnold. *The Fictions of the Self: 1500–1800*. Princeton: Princeton University Press, 1981.

Zimmerman, Everett. *Defoe and the Novel*. Berkeley: University of California Press, 1975.

Acknowledgments

"Defoe" by E. M. W. Tillyard from *The Epic Strain in the English Novel* by E. M. W. Tillyard, © 1958 by E. M. W. Tillyard. Reprinted by permission of the estate of the author and Chatto & Windus Ltd.

"The Divided Heart: Defoe's Novels" by Martin Price from *To the Palace of Wisdom: Studies in Order and Energy from Dryden to Blake* by Martin Price, © 1964 by Martin Price. Reprinted by permission.

"The Relation of Defoe's Fiction to His Nonfictional Writings" by James Sutherland from *Imagined Worlds: Essays on Some English Novels and Novelists*, edited by Maynard Mack and Ian Gregor, © 1968 by James Sutherland. Reprinted by permission.

"Defoe's *Journal of the Plague Year:* Topography and Intention" by Manuel Schonhorn from *The Review of English Studies* 19, no. 76 (November 1968), © 1968 by Oxford University Press. Reprinted by permission of Oxford University Press.

"The Displaced Self in the Novels of Daniel Defoe" by Homer O. Brown from *ELH* 38, no. 4 (December 1971), © 1971 by the Johns Hopkins University Press. Reprinted by permission of the Johns Hopkins University Press, Baltimore/ London.

"*Robinson Crusoe:* The Moral Geography of Limitation" by H. Daniel Peck from *The Journal of Narrative Technique* 3, no. 1 (January 1973), © 1973 by the Eastern Michigan University Press. Reprinted by permission.

"Daniel Defoe and the Anxieties of Autobiography" by Leo Braudy from *Genre* 6, no. 1 (March 1973), © 1973 by Donald E. Billiar, Edward F. Heuston, and Robert L. Vales. Reprinted by permission.

"Defoe's Prose Style: The Language of Interpretation" by George Starr from *Modern Philology* 71, no. 3 (February 1974), © 1974 by the University of Chicago. Reprinted by permission of the University of Chicago Press.

"The Self-Made Woman: *Moll Flanders*" (originally entitled "Orphans: The Self-Made Woman, I: *Moll Flanders*") by Arnold Weinstein from *Fictions of the Self: 1550–1800* by Arnold Weinstein, © 1981 by Princeton University Press. Reprinted by permission of Princeton University Press.

"Roxana's Fictions" by David Durant from *Studies in the Novel* 13, no. 3 (Fall 1981), © 1981 by North Texas State University. Reprinted by permission.

"Observing the Observer in Historical Fictions by Defoe" by John J. Burke, Jr., from *Philological Quarterly* 61, no. 1 (Winter 1982), © 1982 by the University of Iowa. Reprinted by permission.

"The Effect of the Narrator's Rhetorical Uncertainty on the Fiction of *Robinson Crusoe*" by Mary E. Butler from *Studies in the Novel* 15, no. 2 (Summer 1983), © 1983 by North Texas State University. Reprinted by permission.

"On Defoe's *Roxana*" by James H. Maddox from *ELH* 51, no. 4 (Winter 1984), © 1984 by the Johns Hopkins University Press. Reprinted by permission of the Johns Hopkins University Press, Baltimore/London.

Index

229